D0776937

THE
10%
SOLUTION
FOR A
HEALTHY LIFE

Also by Raymond Kurzweil

The Age of Intelligent Machines

THE
10%
SOLUTION
FOR A
HEALTHY LIFE

HOW TO ELIMINATE VIRTUALLY ALL RISK
OF HEART DISEASE AND CANCER

RAYMOND KURZWEIL

**with Steven R. Flier, M.D., Robert Bauer, M.D.,
Peter Kurzweil, M.D., medical advisers**

FOREWORD BY STEVEN R. FLIER, M.D.

CROWN PUBLISHERS, INC. NEW YORK

Copyright © 1993 by Raymond Kurzweil

All rights reserved. No part of this book may be reproduced or transmitted in any form or by any means, electronic or mechanical, including photocopying, recording, or by any information storage and retrieval system, without permission in writing from the publisher.

Published by Crown Publishers, Inc., 201 East 50th Street, New York, New York 10022.
Member of the Crown Publishing Group.

Random House, Inc. New York, Toronto, London, Sydney, Auckland

CROWN is a trademark of Crown Publishers, Inc.

Manufactured in the United States of America

Book design by June Bennett-Tantillo

Library of Congress Cataloging-in-Publication Data
Kurzweil, Ray
The 10% solution for a healthy life : how to eliminate virtually all risk of heart disease and cancer / Raymond Kurzweil, with Steven R. Flier, Robert Bauer, Peter Kurzweil, medical advisers; with a foreword by Steven R. Flier.—1st ed.
p. cm.
Includes index.
1. Low-fat diet. 2. Heart—Diseases—Prevention. 3. Heart—Diseases—Nutritional aspects. 4. Nutritionally induced diseases—Prevention. I. Title. II. Title: The ten percent solution for a healthy life.
RM237.7.K87 1993
613.2—dc20
92-19993
CIP

ISBN 0-517-59106-5

10 9 8 7 6 5 4 3 2 1

First Edition

To my doctor, Steven Flier,
and our mutual explorations
of health and well-being

Contents

■

PART TWO: THE 10% SOLUTION

Acknowledgments

■

I would like to express my gratitude to many people, among them:

- My wife, Sonya, for having lovingly explored a new way of life with me, not to mention having participated in many enjoyable collaborations on the recipes in this book
- My son, Ethan, and my daughter, Amy, for their patience through hundreds of dinnertime conversations on nutrition and for putting up with some of the less-than-successful culinary experiments
- My mother, Hannah, and my sister, Enid, for many pleasurable conversations on nutrition and life-style
- Alison Roberts for her wonderfully proficient and exhaustive research and irreplaceable assistance with many aspects of this project
- My medical advisory team—Steven Flier, Robert Bauer, and Peter Kurzweil—for generously contributing their time and expertise, discussing extensively relevant issues, and supplying highly detailed commentaries to review the medical and scientific accuracy of this work
- My editor, Erica Marcus, and the team at Crown: Kim Hertlein, June Bennett-Tantillo, Bill Peabody, Etya Pinker, and Ken Sansone
- Nancy Mulford for her expert assistance with the research, glossary, and food charts
- Warren Stewart for his culinary insights and enhancement of the recipes with flavorful spices and herbs
- Jill Jacobs for her valuable administrative support and ideas
- Don Gonson for his ideas, support, and encouragement
- Aaron Kleiner for hundreds of discussions on nutrition and health
- My readers—Loretta Barrett, Harry George, George Gilder, Don Gonson, Jill Jacobs, George King, M.D., Aaron Kleiner, Ethan Kurzweil, Hannah Kurzweil, Sonya Kurzweil, Erica Marcus, Nancy Mulford, Steve Rabinowitz, Mitch Rabkin, M.D., Alison Roberts, Martin Schneider, Enid Kurzweil Sterling, Warren Stewart, and Laura Viola—for their many valuable comments and criticisms
- And, finally, all of my friends and associates and the many engaging discussions we have had that have helped to shape my perspective on health and well-being versus the "civilized" diet.

Author's Note

■

Medical research has shown that the nutrition, exercise, and other life-style principles described in this book can help control weight and diseases, including heart disease, stroke, cancer, hypertension, and type II diabetes, and reduce the risk factors associated with these diseases.

However, neither the author nor the medical advisers for this book make any representation or warranty of any kind whatsoever regarding the effectiveness or appropriateness of this program, principles, or information for any individual.

- No person should engage in this or any other dietary, exercise, or health program without advice from his or her physician.

- In particular, persons who have or believe they may have a disease, including but not limited to heart disease, cardiovascular disease (such as stroke), hypertension, diabetes, or cancer, or who are taking medication for such conditions, should take particular care to be monitored by a doctor when undertaking this or any other nutritional, life-style, or health program.

Introduction

■

Shortly after World War II, the idea that cigarette usage may be damaging to one's health was controversial. Yet when my father's doctor suggested that there may be some benefit to cutting down on smoking, my father stopped immediately and never thought about it again. In 1961, he had his first heart attack. It was suggested that he cut down on salt to reduce the strain on his heart, so he simply cut out salt from his diet. In 1970, at the age of 58, he died of heart disease. I was 22, ten years older than my father was when his father died of the same cause.

I carried two feelings that stemmed from my father's experience. One was the sense of a cloud in my future. The trend, indicated by the only two data points I had, suggested that I might only live to see my own son reach the age of 32. On the other hand, I also had a vague sense of confidence that somehow I would figure out a way to overcome this problem. That latter feeling was typical of my optimistic orientation, but it was nonetheless a strongly held conviction. As it turned out, I had some help along the way.

Thus began my interest in heart disease. I am not a doctor, although I do consider myself to be a scientist, and consequently I began to approach this issue from the perspective of the available scientific literature. I tried to engage my doctor in a discussion of the issues, with only limited success. While he talked to me about it to some extent, he clearly had only limited interest in doing so, and, admittedly, I was unusually demanding. Finally, exasperated with my persistent questions, he said, "Look, I just don't have time for this, I have patients who are dying that I have to attend to." Not one to be easily put off by attempts to appeal to my sense of guilt, I couldn't help but wonder whether any of these patients now dying might possibly have benefited from earlier explorations of ways to prevent disease. I decided to change doctors and find one who had an interest in preventive medicine. It also wouldn't hurt if he had some time on his hands.

As it turns out, I heard about a new doctor who was just setting up a practice. He had a reputation for a brilliant mind, an engaging curiosity in new medical frontiers, and, most important, the willingness to struggle with issues of prevention with his patients. I became Steven Flier's patient in 1982. It turned out to be a good decision. Just recently, *Boston Magazine* recognized him as one of the leading physicians in the city.

Most significant, he had the time and the patience to engage in my extensive interrogations on medical issues. One of his early discoveries was that I had a glucose intolerance, an early form of type II diabetes (a major risk factor for heart disease). This only intensified my interest in understanding what was known about heart disease and its prevention.

We decided I should lose about 25 to 40 pounds, so there followed a number of years of largely futile efforts in this direction. I tried numerous diets of various kinds (low-calorie, low-carbohydrate, and others) and while some worked temporarily, I kept gravitating back to the same weight. I began to despair that I didn't have the willpower to take this vital first step.

In late 1987, on Dr. Flier's advice, I decided to adopt the recommendations of the American Heart Association and reduce fat intake to 30 percent of calories and cholesterol intake to no more than 300 milligrams per day. This had a modest positive effect. My cholesterol went down from 234 to 193. According to the Framingham Study—a massive longitudinal (long-term) study of more than 5,000 Americans with a view toward understanding the factors underlying heart disease—one can obtain an estimate of one's risk of heart disease by considering the ratio of total serum (blood) cholesterol to high-density lipoprotein (HDL) cholesterol, the so-called good cholesterol. The lower the ratio, the lower one's risk. My ratio fell from 8.7 to 6.9, which, according to the Framingham Study, means that my risk fell from 175 percent of "normal" risk to 143 percent of "normal."[1] That's a shift in the right direction, but not entirely comforting when you consider that "normal" (i.e., average) risk for Americans is a 75 percent chance of a heart attack in one's lifetime![2]

In 1988, I ran across the writings of Nathan Pritikin. I had heard of his approach before but had always dismissed it as too radical and too Spartan. Pritikin maintained that by adopting a diet that was very low in fat and cholesterol (specifically 10 percent of calories from fat and 100 milligrams of cholesterol per day), one can obtain dramatic reductions in the risk of heart disease and other diseases. With my heightened interest in preventing heart disease, I decided to take a closer look.

Nathan Pritikin's own story is interesting.[3] In 1957, at the age of 40, he was diagnosed as having coronary insufficiency caused by advanced atherosclerosis. He was prescribed a variety of drugs and told to restrict his mobility. Distressed with these recommendations, he decided instead to examine the scientific literature and discovered extensive evidence that atherosclerosis could be reversed in animals if they were given diets very low in fat and cholesterol. With this and other clues, Pritikin went on to pioneer an approach to treating heart disease using diet and exercise. Using himself as his first test subject, all of his symptoms of heart disease disappeared.

Paradoxically, Pritikin also made a profound mistake in 1957. His doctor had prescribed a series of X-ray treatments to destroy a fungus infection that was causing anal itching. Pritikin was very concerned that the X rays would hit parts of his body that would be damaged by this radiation, but his doctor assured him that it was a safe procedure. Today, we would recognize the procedure as irresponsible, but Pritikin reluctantly went along with the recommendation and underwent the treatment, which involved receiving 220 rads of unfiltered X rays. Two days later, a blood test revealed a seriously elevated white blood cell count, which was subsequently diagnosed as monoclonal macroglobulinemia, a blood disorder caused by excessive radiation and an early stage of leukemia. Twenty-eight years later, Nathan Pritikin died of leukemia. An autopsy revealed that he had the heart and arteries of a young man, completely clear of any signs of heart disease or atherosclerosis.[4]

I examined Pritikin's evidence and became impressed with the extensive documentation establishing a link between nutrition and disease. Despite the medical profession's early resistance to Pritikin's advocacy of nutrition and other life-style modifications as a treatment for heart disease, there has been increasing interest in this approach in the medical community since Pritikin's death. Some of the best evidence has been fairly recent, including the first concrete evidence of atherosclerotic reversal in humans brought about entirely by life-style modification.

I discussed what I had read with Dr. Flier and he thought that it made sense. I was still concerned about my ability to undergo such an apparently radical change in my eating habits, given my rather dismal efforts through more than five years of attempted weight loss. Nonetheless, in October of 1988, I decided to give it a try. Since I had found much more moderate changes to be difficult to sustain, I braced myself for a significant discipline. The results were rather surprising.

It turned out to be a lot easier than I had expected. In fact, it felt rather natural. I discovered a new world of foods that were very tasty, diverse, and satisfying. I never felt deprived and, unlike my experiences with other "diets" I had been on, *I never felt hungry.* Gradually my tastes and orientation to food changed and my desire for the higher-fat foods I had been used to went away.

Within 3 months, I had lost 25 pounds. More surprising were the results of my cholesterol test. "I'm stunned" was Dr. Flier's response, to which he added that he was going to start the diet himself the next day. My total serum cholesterol was now 110. My HDL had also gone up (primarily from increased exercise), so my ratio (of total cholesterol to HDL) was now 2.5. According to the Framingham Study statistics, my risk of heart disease was now only 5 percent of normal (down from an original 175 percent of normal). Altogether, that represented a 97 percent reduction in my risk. Extensive testing also indicated that my glucose intolerance had vanished as well. I went on to lose another 15 pounds to put me at my ideal weight. I felt that the cloud had disappeared.

A BRIEF MEDICAL HISTORY

	JUNE 1987	OCTOBER 1988	JANUARY 1989
Diet: percent of calories from fat	40	30	10
Exercise (in calories per week)	800	1,200	2,000*
Weight	185	185	160
Serum cholesterol (total)	234	193	110
LDL ("bad" cholesterol)	not computed	94	57
HDL ("good" cholesterol)	27	28	44
Triglycerides	616	354	43
Ratio (of total cholesterol to HDL)	8.7	6.9	2.5
Percentage of normal risk (from Framingham Study)	175	143	5
Glucose intolerance	yes	yes	no

*Walking approximately 20 miles per week.

Further extensive research of the literature during this period revealed a rich tapestry of scientific and medical evidence, including extensive animal studies and human intervention and population studies, that revealed nutrition and other life-style factors as much more significant influences on health than I had previously realized. The common wisdom was that "taking care of yourself" (i.e., moderating fat and cholesterol intake, exercise, etc.) was worth doing, but that your genetic heritage was a bigger factor. The respective influences of these two factors were often estimated at a ratio of 70 to 30 in favor of genetics over life-style. It became clear to me, however, that this was only true if one restricted oneself to the compromised nutritional recommendations that still comprise the official position of American health agencies.

Indeed, my own experience bore this out. By following the recommendations of the American Heart Association, I had reduced my heart risk by about 20 percent. But by going down further, to the level of fat and cholesterol characteristic of societies in which heart disease is virtually unheard of, I reduced my risk by 97 percent. Extensive human population studies show the same pattern. Those societies that eat 30 percent of calories from fat have heart disease rates about 30 percent lower than those that eat 40 percent of calories from fat. But societies that eat diets characterized by whole grains, vegetables, and fruits with, about 10 percent of calories coming from fat, have heart disease rates that are at least 90 percent lower than the societies that eat about 40 percent calories from fat. The primary reason put forth by the medical community for putting out the highly compromised recommendation of 30 percent calories from fat is that people will resist bigger changes, that these are too difficult for an American palate wedded to a high-fat diet. Ironically, the more complete change is, I believe, easier to make and maintain. For a variety of reasons that I detail in the rest of the book, following the nutritional recommendations that I call the 10% solution eliminates food urges and is self-sustaining in ways that other, more limited, approaches are not.

There were a number of bonuses that I had not expected. The pattern that exists for heart disease exists also for the most common cancers. Cancer of the breast, ovaries, colon, prostate, and even of the lung are very rare in societies that eat very little fat. Also, if you follow a low-salt dietary plan, you can virtually eliminate hypertension and stroke. We can greatly ameliorate many other conditions, including osteoporosis and most forms of arthritis. Indeed, there are a wide range of these "diseases of affluence" that are caused by our "civilized" diet (in particular, the *Western* civilized diet). But perhaps of greater significance was the way I felt, in terms of increased energy, improved ability to sleep and relax, and a deeper sense of well-being.

I then encountered two unexpected conflicts. If you see someone standing precariously on a ledge oblivious to the fact that they are in danger of a great fall, you feel a sense of obligation to inform them of their unrealized plight. If the person is someone you care about, then the urgency is even greater. I did not have to look very far to find others that were desperately in need of this knowledge I had gained. Typical were adult male friends with elevated cholesterol, strong family histories of heart disease, and perhaps a few extra inches around the middle. Others included adult female friends with family histories of breast cancer. There were many variations of concern.

So invariably I got drawn into extended conversations on the topic of preserving health and well-being through nutrition and life-style. These turned out to be longer conversations than I had expected. To make the case, I felt compelled to go through a lot of the evidence. Then there were more subtle issues. *Why aren't the American Heart Association recommendations good enough? This is mostly genetics anyway, isn't it? What happened to moderation?*

If I made it through these issues, there was always the big one of palatability. *Sure, you'll live a long time, but who wants to live that way? If you eat this way, maybe it just seems like a long time!* That this could be an enjoyable, even liberating way to eat and live took a bit of explanation.

Then if someone was still interested, there was the core issue of the recommendations of the 10% solution. And scores of follow-up questions: *How do I shop? Can I convert my recipes? Is walking better than jogging? What about restaurants? How about parties, functions, airplanes, traveling?*

Things were getting out of hand. I had developed a reputation for having accumulated knowledge on this subject, so I was getting calls from many friends and colleagues. I needed a more efficient way to share this knowledge. None of the books available on the subject was quite right. Nathan Pritikin's books, while having made a major contribution in their time, did not include enough of the scientific evidence to make an optimally persuasive case for the audience I had in mind. Besides, some of the best evidence had become available since his death. Other books, such as *The Eight-Day Cholesterol Cure*, put too much evidence on such over-the-counter drugs as niacin and did not represent an optimal diet. Many others stuck to the compromised

30-percent-calories-from-fat recommendation and were definitely not satisfactory.

I decided to write my own essay and put down my thoughts, accumulated research, evidence, and experience so that I could share this material in an effective way with what was apparently a growing audience. The essay also got out of hand and turned into a book. In this, I again had the guidance of Dr. Flier and several other devoted and insightful physicians.

The second conflict had to do with proselytizing. Being a scientist and a trained skeptic, I was always turned off by people with strong singular agendas. People out to save my soul or even just my health and well-being were strongly suspect. I felt very uncomfortable, therefore, in this role myself, telling other people how they should eat or live. Recognizing my own resistance to these types of messages, I also realized what I was up against in terms of getting people to take ideas such as these seriously.

After some lively internal debate, I finally decided that I had a responsibility to share my knowledge on this issue, but that I should strive for a certain loving detachment when it came to people choosing their own eating and living styles. This is not an easy balance to achieve. It is hard not to feel some pride if someone accepts my ideas and then shares with me their excitement at 30 lost pounds or 50 lost cholesterol points. If nothing else, such experiences demonstrate that I was successful in communicating my thoughts.

I have come to consider my responsibility to be that of effectively communicating a set of messages—empowering people to set their own priorities and to make their own compromises. That is what I object to in the public-health recommendations. They come precompromised, as if the American people were incapable of making their own decisions on these matters.

Having written a book on the subject makes this objective of objectivity easier for me to achieve. I can deliver someone a complete message, and people can consider it on their own terms and on their own time. Any follow-up is up to the reader.

Even this limited goal of effective communication is a challenging one. If you wanted to deliver a message to a king, it would probably not be fully effective to scribble down a note on a piece of paper and throw it onto the royal lawn. Any self-respecting king will have many layers of obstacles to prevent stray messages from penetrating the royal solitude. Similarly, we have all erected formidable barriers to messages.

We have little choice. We could hardly survive if we allowed all of the thousands of messages that bombard us daily to get through. Penetrating the subtle, yet common, misconceptions, fears, and folklore that underlie the public understanding of nutrition is particularly difficult. Eating is an activity to which people devote a large portion of their time and effort. Food and its images are deeply interwoven in our myths, our rituals, our fantasies, and our relationships. While most people profess ignorance of nutrition, virtually everyone nonetheless maintains strongly held views on the subject and its relationship to the rest of our lives. Getting people's attention, let alone truly broadening someone's perspective, is not an easy task. But that is the challenge of any writer.

I have now influenced hundreds of people to adopt this approach to health. Consistently, people report back to me that once they made a commitment to it, they found that adopting it was "no big deal." People will say that they anticipated having to employ significant discipline, that it would be a formidable undertaking, only to discover that it was surprisingly easy. Sure, they cut out butter, mayonnaise, and other fats, cut down significantly on meat, and so on, but they also discovered that when they were done cutting things out, there was a great deal left that they enjoyed, and many substitutions that made the process much easier today than ever before. The physical and medical results that my friends, relatives, associates, and many others have achieved have been very gratifying for me. People have expressed gratitude for enormous improvements in cholesterol levels, weight, blood pressure, and their general sense of well-being. Many have thanked me for saving their lives.

As for myself, I have happily kept up the "diet" and the benefits. I really will have to find a better word here, because "diet" is associated with being onerous and temporary and my new eating habits are neither.

It is too bad that I cannot go back and share this knowledge with my father. Unlike many people, he accepted health and nutritional advice readily and easily. Six simple words—*eat 10 percent calories from fat*—could have saved his life. He could be alive today.

Foreword

■

A doctor's activities center on diagnosis (finding and defining conditions or problems that exist), prognosis (what one can expect for the future), and treatment of those that are treatable. These were the steps I went through when I first met Ray Kurzweil many years ago. I am his doctor. I practice internal medicine in Boston, and I am an instructor at the Harvard Medical School.

Making the diagnosis was easy: a simple blood test, a routine examination. And the diagnosis was clear—high cholesterol and a glucose intolerance, an early stage of adult-onset (type II) diabetes. A cholesterol level in the mid-200s, a triglyceride level of more than 600, and an abnormal glucose tolerance test were readily defined by routine laboratory tests. The prognosis was also easy. These were chronic conditions—not amenable to cure, only to *management*, the term doctors often use to describe the regular testing and follow-up of medical conditions. We manage diabetes with insulin or oral medications, we treat high cholesterol with diets and medications, but we never cure them. Ray would be a "patient" for life—always on some sort of therapy for these conditions. Of this I was sure.

I reviewed his family history: Ray's father died of coronary artery disease at the age of 58. I went through the list of other risk factors, and Ray had a host of them, including excess weight, high levels of stress, and only occasional exercise. Thank goodness he wasn't a smoker. When added to his high cholesterol and diabetes, these risk factors placed his likelihood of future coronary artery disease at a very high level. Even at high levels of risk, however, prognostication is imprecise. Would he have a myocardial infarction (heart attack), and if so, when? Anything less than 100 percent is not certainty. Most of us feel uncomfortable with uncertainty. It is especially difficult for doctor and patient. Our inability to predict who among those at risk will, in fact, develop specific diseases—which smoker gets lung cancer, for instance—is frustrating. It also enables some people to continue with unhealthy behaviors. People often believe that a serious disease won't happen to them, and they take some comfort in the fact that they might be right. How silly to have wasted all that energy on diet, or

exercise, or medications for that matter, when it might not be needed
after all. For greater certainty about disease we turn to published studies. The medical literature contains case reports, reviews, and controlled clinical trials designed to help define the natural history of
disease. Unfortunately, the complexities of individual cases (specifics
of their history) often differ from published reports of combined data.
It is hard to infer one specific individual's risk from combined population studies. But despite these imprecisions, weighing all the known
factors, it was clear that Ray had a higher than normal risk of future
coronary artery disease, which would most likely strike him at an
early age.

Next was the issue of treatment. There are uncertainties with medications, too. *Risk benefit ratio* is the term we apply to the quantification
of these questions: How likely is a good therapeutic benefit, compared
to the likelihood of a side effect or a complication? With these questions (as with prognosis) we turn to published studies. As physicians
and as scientists, we are taught that controlled studies, those where
test conditions are carefully designed to eliminate the effects of
chance, placebo, and bias, are the only ones to value. Testimonials
and anecdotal reports are of limited interest, since their scientific validity is doubtful. It is impossible to infer cause and effect from what
could be chance occurrences. Faith healers and charlatans throughout
history have pointed to cases where they claim success. The trouble is
that the ideal medical investigation—a randomized, controlled clinical
trial—is costly, time consuming, and difficult to do, and often misses
the exact circumstances of a particular patient problem. Neverthe-
less, decisions need to be made and treatments prescribed. With Ray's
conditions, two types of treatments were available: life-style changes in
diet, exercise, and weight; and medications, such as insulin, oral antidi-
abetic medications, and cholesterol-lowering medications. It was not
necessarily an either-or decision. Both could be tried.

The sad truth is that most doctors are terrible at teaching people
about changing their life-styles, mostly because it takes time and it is
frustrating. A prescription can be written out in seconds, but teaching
and explaining require time, often more than a busy doctor can spare.
The frustration comes from repeated failure. Despite the best advice,
people rarely change. Of every twenty smokers intensively counseled
by their doctor on how to quit and why, nineteen of them will still be
smokers a year later. From a doctor's point of view, this is a major failure. It feels as though the benefit is not worth the effort. It is hard for

doctors to acquire the skills needed to help their patients. Medical schools have no courses in behavior modification or patient education. Nutrition is a largely ignored subject. Therefore, most often, doctors relegate education and motivation for life-style change to others—dietitians, commercial weight-loss programs, smoke cessation programs, and psychotherapists. But even here, it is usually a piecemeal effort, without the full force and impact of a well-defined and clearly thought-out program. It is also hard to find the facts, since scientifically sound studies centered on life-style modification have been few and far between. Last, doctors have the same failings as their patients. They, too, can be seduced into the seemingly easy path of high-fat diets, high-stress lives, and inadequate exercise and the quick fixes of fad diets and fast-acting medications.

I am grateful that these failings did not deter Raymond Kurzweil. He forced me, through the power of his intellect and his dogged enthusiasm for life and knowledge, to reach deeper than I had before. I, too, was overweight. I, too, had little time or inclination for exercise. My cholesterol, though not as high as Ray's, was more than 200. I, too, had been doing nothing about it. Ray asked questions that I could not answer, and he proposed alternatives that I had not considered. Ray took the approach of an engineer and a scientist, the approach of a problem solver and a creator. He looked deep into the medical literature. He amassed scientific, medical, demographic, sociological, anthropological, and historical data and synthesized a coherent plan for changing his life. The scientific foundations were there, and to Ray the uncertainties were not sufficient to deter him from change. He did change. In doing so he proved to himself and to me the profound physical and emotional benefits of gaining control over one's life. I saw his cholesterol plummet, his weight melt, and his glucose intolerance disappear. Though his case was not a randomized, controlled clinical trial, it proved to me what can be done by a motivated and intelligent person who values life and health. It proved to me that compromises based upon ease and convenience are not adequate, and that knowledge is power for patients and physicians.

I began to incorporate the changes of a low-fat near-vegetarian diet into my life. I began to exercise on a daily basis, and I saw my weight fall from 244 pounds to its current level of 185. I saw my cholesterol fall from 210 to 150. I experienced the thrill of self-discovery and self-control, the improvement in my sense of well-being and level of energy, and I found this in a context not of self-deprivation or restriction, but rather of expansion and self-awareness. I found that my changes were inspirational and motivational for my patients as well. Seeing me change my ways proved to them that they could change their ways and experience the same benefits.

I am happy to report that my prognostications for Ray were wrong. Despite my certainty that Ray would be a "patient" for life, he is not. He is no longer diabetic, he is no longer overweight, and he is no longer at risk for coronary artery disease. He has gone from being a patient whose illness is "managed" to being a person with mastery over his fate. He has also become a colleague and a teacher, instructing me in the value of curiosity, an open mind, and intellectual honesty. Ray and his family have already benefited from the synthesis of these issues you are about to read—so have I and so have scores of my patients. My hope is that the millions of Americans who need this information learn from it, too.

Steven R. Flier, M.D.,
Associate in Medicine, Boston's Beth Israel Hospital;
Clinical Instructor in Medicine, Harvard Medical School,
Boston, Massachusetts

Knowledge has an important property.
When you give it away, you don't lose it.

—Raj Reddy

PART ONE

■

HEALTH AND WELL-BEING VERSUS THE "CIVILIZED" DIET

1

Aside from That, Mrs. Lincoln, How Did You Enjoy the Play?

Atherosclerosis

From this printout, all of your tests appear to be normal. Your levels of serum cholesterol, triglycerides, and other lipids are normal. Other blood tests, such as thyroid function, are all normal.

That's great. I do try to take care of myself, but it's always good to hear that I'm in good health.

Yes, except for your fatal illness, you're just fine.

Excuse me??

Oh, didn't I mention that to you?

Mention what??

I'm talking about *atherosclerosis.* It's almost certain that you have it. But aside from that one fatal disease, your health appears fine.

Fatal disease? How much time do I have?

Well, it won't kill you right away. It is a fairly slow fatal disease with no symptoms for many years, kind of like AIDS, at least in that one regard.

Oh my God, I had no idea. I have to sit down. How does one catch this?

Actually, you don't catch it. It's a direct result of your life-style.

Now wait a minute. There's nothing wrong with my life-style. I'm not all that overweight. I exercise fairly frequently. I watch what I eat, don't go overboard on desserts, and all that.

Yes, by American standards, your life-style—that is, your eating habits and exercise—are perfectly normal, probably better than normal.

What do you mean by American standards? You're American, aren't you?

Yes, I am. But American eating habits—and this is true of much of the civilized world, particularly the Western civilized world—are a disaster. They are so far afield from what we were evolved to eat that most of the diseases we see are linked to what people eat and other aspects of their life-style.

So just what's wrong with what I eat?

Well, the fat level, for one thing.

I hardly eat any fat at all. I'm very careful to cut the fat off my steaks. I can't remember the last time I ate any fat.

That's a good idea, to cut the fat off of your meat. Because the fat on meat is indeed 100 percent fat. But the "lean" meat of a typical steak can be 40 to 50 percent fat—that is, more than 40 percent of the calories are from fat.

You mean there's actually fat in the steak itself?

Yes. Fat is one of the basic constituents of food. The calories from food are made up principally of fat, protein, and simple and complex carbohydrates. Meat gets its calories from its protein and fat content. Vegetables and fruits are primarily carbohydrates, although they also contain protein and even a little fat. The calories in an apple are 6 percent fat.

Is that a lot?

No, not at all. You need some level of fat in your diet. You couldn't live without obtaining certain essential fatty acids that the body is unable to produce itself. But if you are getting a sufficient level of calories, then it is almost impossible to have an insufficient level of fat, at least for adults. The problem is with the excessively high level of fat in the diet. The typical American diet gets 35 to 40 percent of its calories from fat. Beyond the fat that is naturally in foods, we add more. The American food rule is, "drench everything in fat": vegetables, add a butter sauce; fruit, top them with whipped cream; salad, add an oil-based dressing; bread, cover it with butter or margarine. Even milk is about 50 percent fat.

Oh, I use that 2 percent low-fat milk.

That's about 37 percent of calories from fat.

Wait a minute, it says 98 percent fat-free—how can it be 37 percent fat?

Most of it is water, which has no caloric content. It's 98 percent fat-free by *weight*, but 37 percent of its calories are fat calories (5 grams of fat per cup, which is equivalent to 45 calories from fat out of a total of 120 calories).

I see, so fat is pretty pervasive.

Yes, in our society it certainly is.

But what's so bad about fat? I'm not very overweight.

Fat certainly contributes to the obesity problem we have in this society. Each fat gram has more than twice the calories of a gram of protein or carbohydrates.[1] Beyond that, studies have shown that even calorie for calorie, fat contributes to weight gain more than the other components of food.[2] But that's not the worst aspect of fat. Diets high in fat and cholesterol produce high levels of blood cholesterol.[3]

Oh, I avoid cholesterol as much as I can. I eat a lot of foods that are "low in cholesterol" or even "no cholesterol."

The fact that you eat some foods low in cholesterol doesn't mean that your diet is low in cholesterol overall. A single egg has more than 200 milligrams of cholesterol, which is more than you should have in two days. But perhaps more important, the amount of cholesterol you eat is only one factor affecting the level of cholesterol in your blood, and not the most important one at that.

I thought the cholesterol in my blood came from the cholesterol I ate.

That's one of the big misconceptions. Some of the cholesterol in your blood (called serum cholesterol) does come directly from the cholesterol in your food (known as dietary cholesterol), and it is, therefore, important to avoid cholesterol in food. But the majority of the serum cholesterol in your blood is produced in your body, with most of that manufactured by your liver. You could eat no cholesterol at all and still have a very high serum cholesterol level if you eat a diet high in fat.[4]

Well, then, what's the point of avoiding cholesterol in my food?

If you eat an excessive amount of dietary cholesterol, it will contribute significantly to an unhealthy cholesterol level in your blood. But the most important factor is the amount of fat you eat.[5] Eating a diet high in fat causes a lipid (i.e., fat) metabolism that affects the liver's production and distribution of cholesterol. The more fat you eat, the more cholesterol is produced by the liver (specifically two factions of cholesterol, called low-density lipoprotein, or LDL, and very low density lipoprotein, or VLDL).[6] The cholesterol produced, particularly the LDL, travels in the bloodstream and is the primary cause of atherosclerosis.[7]

But what makes you think that I have atherosclerosis?

It's a reasonable assumption, since 90 percent of all Americans do.[8] Given that your lipid levels (blood levels of cholesterol) are "normal" (i.e., average), the probability that you have atherosclerosis is extremely high. Your levels need to be dramatically better than the American average not to have atherosclerosis.

Well, that puts a different light on things. How serious can it be?

Serious enough to cause a million and a half heart attacks a year and to kill about half a million Americans each year, which is about a third of all deaths. In addition, atherosclerosis is the primary factor in another 400,000 deaths per year from other cardiovascular diseases, such as stroke. It was a national tragedy when we lost 60,000 American lives in the Vietnam War over a 10-year period. We lose that many from heart and cardiovascular disease in just four weeks.

So what is atherosclerosis?

It is a progressive disease of the arteries, a gradual buildup of a rigid, plaquelike material in the walls of the arteries that over time narrows the passageways. It also weakens the walls of the arteries, which become increasingly hard, eventually becoming calcified and bonelike. The arteries, themselves, become diseased and are ultimately distorted by the plaque. This makes the arteries brittle and inflexible. But more important, the vessels have less and less room for blood to flow. We call this type of blockage an occlusion. Once the occlusion reaches about 70 percent of the diameter of an artery, there is great danger of a blood clot forming on or getting stuck in the damaged surface of an artery, leading to complete blockage by the atherosclerotic plaque, thus stopping blood flow altogether. If this happens in one of the coronary arteries, which are pencil-thin arteries feeding oxygenated blood to the heart itself, we call this a coronary thrombosis, or heart attack. Being deprived of oxygen, portions of the heart muscle die. Note that we are not talking about the large arteries, such as the aorta, that supply blood to the body, but rather the small coronary arteries that feed the heart itself. About a third of all heart attacks are fatal within a few minutes or hours. Most heart attacks cause permanent damage to the heart muscle and weaken heart function.

If a blood clot forms around the atherosclerotic plaque in one of the arteries feeding the brain, we call that a thrombotic stroke. If a circulating blood clot gets stuck in the atherosclerotic plaque in a cerebral artery, we call that an embolic stroke. These are the most common forms of stroke in the United States and typically cause massive death of brain cells, paralysis, and possibly death. There are many other conditions caused by atherosclerosis. In men, blockage of one of the arteries feeding the penis can cause impotence.[9] Blockage of one of the arteries feeding the legs can cause claudication, a painful and dangerous condition in which blood does not reach the muscles and tissues of the legs.[10] Plaque damage of the aorta can result in a potentially fatal aneurysm.

Where does the word atherosclerosis *come from?*

"Athero" in Greek means "grease" or "fat," and "sclerosis" means "hardening," so the word "atherosclerosis" literally means a fatty invasion and hardening of the arteries. But it is important to note that an analogy of atherosclerosis to built-up grease in a pipe is not entirely accurate. The grease in a pipe, while somewhat hard, is a lot softer than the pipe, so a strong cleaning agent and scouring device can scoop it out without damaging the pipe. In atherosclerosis, the plaque is very hard, while the pipe or vessel wall is soft. And it is not simply a matter of the plaque being embedded in an otherwise healthy vessel. The vessel is diseased as well.

It is not possible to simply clean out the accumulated plaque. There are medical procedures which attempt to widen the narrowed passage caused by the plaque. One procedure called balloon angioplasty involves inserting an inflatable device into the artery through a catheter (a long tube) and then inflating the device to compact the plaque and widen the passageway. While these procedures may have some medical merit, they do not cure or even slow down the underlying atherosclerosis process. They also involve significant risk. Even the popular bypass surgery does nothing to alleviate the underlying plaque-formation process, and it is very common for "successful" bypass surgery patients to have their newly grafted coronary arteries clog up rather quickly after surgery.[11]

While bypass surgery can relieve angina pain, studies have failed to prove that they actually extend the patient's life. For example, the Coronary Artery Surgery Study presented at the 1990 annual scientific meeting of the American Heart Association followed 780 people who had chest pain caused by angina and severely clogged arteries diagnosed 10 years earlier. Half of the group was randomly assigned to receive bypass surgery and the other half received dietary and drug treatment. The study found no improvement in survival rates for the bypass group as compared to the nonsurgery group after 5 years, or after 10 years.[12]

It seems that one should do something about this disease before you get to that 70 percent level of artery blockage at which a heart attack is possible.

Unfortunately, the disease of atherosclerosis is symptom-free. For many individuals, the first symptom is sudden death. Sixty percent of all people who die from a sudden heart attack have never had angina pain, although they may have had, in retrospect, some poorly identified distress that may have been heart related.[13]

I thought you said that my heart was fine.

Fat and Cholesterol

It is. The disease underlying the vast majority of heart disease is not a condition of the heart structure at all, but a disease of its arteries. By the time the heart muscle is affected, it is often too late to take remedial action. Since this disease, atherosclerosis, is primarily related to the excessive level of cholesterol handled by the liver, you might actually consider the underlying condition to be a dysfunction of the liver. And to the extent that the liver is being influenced by your eating patterns, the underlying condition is really an eating disorder.

So you mean that eating all this hidden fat in food is tricking my liver into producing an excessive level of cholesterol, which in turn is clogging up my arteries.

That's a reasonable way of putting it.

I thought you said the level of my cholesterol was normal.

Yes, it is. Your total serum cholesterol level is 190, a perfectly "normal" level. Also, your level of what we call high-density lipoprotein, or HDL, which is the "good" cholesterol, is also a "normal" 42.

Good cholesterol? I thought cholesterol was bad.

Actually circulating cholesterol is a fat-soluble, waxy substance (specifically the crystalline steroid alcohol $C_{27}H_{45}OH$) made up of primarily three factions: LDL, VLDL, and HDL. The cholesterol in these different factions is actually identical. The lipoproteins, which act as vessels carrying the cholesterol in the bloodstream, differ from one another in terms of what they do with the cholesterol they carry. LDL, which transports cholesterol from the liver to the body's tissues, has been strongly implicated as a primary agent for the buildup of atherosclerotic plaque by transporting cholesterol to the body's cells. VLDL is also involved, although its role appears to be less direct. VLDL level is closely linked to the level of triglycerides, which is the level of free-floating fat in the bloodstream. A study in the January 1992 issue of *Circulation*, published by the American Heart Association, has identified elevated triglyceride levels as another risk factor for heart disease, particularly in combination with elevated cholesterol levels.[14]

HDL apparently plays a constructive role, carrying cholesterol away from the arteries and back to the liver to be discarded.[15] Major studies have shown that the total level of cholesterol, as well as the ratio of cholesterol to HDL, are primary risk factors for the development of heart disease.[16] Your total serum cholesterol is a "normal" 190 and your cholesterol-to-HDL ratio is a "normal" 4.5.

So why, then, do you say I have atherosclerosis?

Because it is *normal* for Americans to have atherosclerosis. The "normal" ratio of 4.5 translates into a 75 percent chance of having a heart attack in your lifetime.[17] Most of the 25 percent who will not have a heart attack still have atherosclerosis. It's just that something else will get them before they have a heart attack—something like cancer, which is also strongly linked to high levels of fat consumption. A "normal" ratio of 4.5 means, therefore, that the probability of atherosclerosis is well in excess of 90 percent. So "normal" in this instance does not equate with healthy.

I see, I think.

The medical community's standards with regard to what is a healthy level of serum cholesterol have been progressively changing for the past 20 years. Originally 300 was the threshold for concern. Ten years ago, a cholesterol level of 260 was considered okay. Then it became 240, then 220, and now it's 200. But 200 is generally not healthy. Most people with a level of 200 have atherosclerosis. If their HDL is below 45, then it can add up to be a rather high rate of atherosclerosis. And the rate of atherosclerosis is important. The faster the rate, the faster your arteries get clogged, and the sooner you will develop conditions like a heart attack, stroke, claudication, aneurysm, angina, and many other dangerous, painful, and potentially fatal complications. The higher your cholesterol level, the more likely it is that you have a high rate of atherosclerosis. There are other risk factors that also affect the rate at which your arteries will clog up: smoking cigarettes, having high blood pressure, being overweight, having diabetes, and leading a sedentary life-style, to name a few.[18]

One further note on the role of HDL is in order. HDL appears to have some protective role if total serum cholesterol is elevated. However, if your total cholesterol is low enough—150 milligrams per deciliter (mg/dl) or less—then it does not seem to matter what the level of HDL is. For example, the Tarahumaras (Indians who live in the Sierra Madre region of northwestern Mexico) have an average serum cholesterol level of 125 mg/dl but a very low average HDL level of 25 mg/dl. Despite their very low HDL and very high total-cholesterol-to-HDL ratio (over 5), they have virtually no heart disease or atherosclerosis.[19] Other studies have also found that nonindustrial societies consuming a low-fat diet have low rates of coronary heart disease despite low-HDL levels, suggesting that low HDL is most notably a risk factor only for populations with high-fat diets.[20]

So how much can I really do about this? I mean, aren't my genes the primary controlling factor here?

Yes and no. One's genetic inheritance is certainly very important. It is particularly important if you eat a high level of fat and cholesterol. And since that accounts for virtually all Americans, it would be reasonable to say that it is a crucial factor. In other words, if you eat a high-fat and -cholesterol diet, some people will develop artery disease quickly, others more slowly, and some—a relative few actually—not at all. It is also important to note that the level of fat in our diet is so high, that even people who think that their diet is reasonably low in fat are in most cases still eating an excessive level of fat. But virtually everyone, regardless of their genes, can dramatically reduce the likelihood of heart disease through the right life-style, primarily by focusing on diet and exercise. In other words, with the right diet and exercise, almost everyone can stop the process of atherosclerosis. So genetics is a critical factor only if you are eating a high-fat diet, which almost everyone in the United States does.

There is now convincing evidence that in many cases, atherosclerosis can actually be reversed through controlling these life-style factors. Reversal of disease was, until recently, a controversial proposition. We have known for a long time that atherosclerosis could be reversed in animals such as rhesus monkeys and swine, but for some reason people were skeptical that this could be achieved in humans.[21]

How much healthier are the people in countries that eat low-fat diets compared to Americans?

If we look at societies that eat a very low fat diet—and low fat generally implies low cholesterol—we indeed find extremely low rates of heart disease. For example, an autopsy study of 22-year-old American soldiers from the Korean War, published in the *Journal of the American Medical Association,* found that 77 percent of the Americans had significant levels of atherosclerosis. The researchers contrasted this with the virtually nonexistent level of atherosclerosis in Asian males of the same age.[22]

In China, the diet consists primarily of vegetables and grains. Most Chinese are not wealthy enough to afford the luxury of our high-fat foods. Cholesterol levels are typically 100 to 150, with an average level around 127. A level of 180, which we consider low, is considered very high in China. And heart disease is very rare.[23]

The same results have been noted for many populations eating low-fat diets, including the Bantus of Africa and the indigenous peoples of Brazil and New Guinea.[24] For New Guinea natives, cholesterol levels, which tend to run about 100, do not vary with age.[25] Interestingly, blood pressure is also constant, and low to normal, throughout their lives.[26] Studies of 25 other societies eating low-fat, low-cholesterol, and low-sodium diets have shown the same results.[27]

In those nonindustrialized countries where the fat level in the diet is very low, serum cholesterol tends to be low, generally under 150, and there is a virtual absence of coronary heart disease.[28] Even in the United States, the more than 40-year-long Framingham Study (an extensive research project that has been tracing approximately 5,000 individuals since 1948 to determine the risk factors for coronary heart disease) found that people who ate a very low fat diet tended to have serum cholesterol levels below 160 mg/dl. It also found essentially no deaths from heart disease when serum cholesterol levels were below 160. According to Dr. William Castelli, director of the Framingham Study, researchers have not seen a single heart attack in subjects whose cholesterol level was below 150 in the 40 years that the study has been in effect.[29] The study found that, in general, the higher the serum cholesterol level, the higher the incidence of heart disease. For example, in the 30-to-39-year-old age group, persons with a cholesterol level of 260 or above had four times the number of cardiovascular events as those with a level below 200.[30]

Heart disease is epidemic only in those countries where the typical diet is high in fat and cholesterol. In these same countries, serum cholesterol typically exceeds 200 mg/dl. Only a handful of countries have higher rates of heart disease than the United States. These northern European countries have diets that are even higher than ours in animal and dairy fat as well as cholesterol, and they also have correspondingly higher serum cholesterol levels (see chapter 15, "Ranking the Killers: How to Save a Million American Lives a Year").

A major study called the International Atherosclerosis Project, completed in 1965, involved more than twenty-two thousand autopsies in fourteen countries over a five-year period. All were conducted by the same group of pathologists. The findings were that the artery surface area damaged by plaque and the overall plaque damage was directly proportional to both the serum cholesterol level and the dietary intake of fat and cholesterol. Race, vocation, climate, and nationality did not affect the results.[31]

How do we know that this apparent link of fat in the diet to heart disease isn't a coincidence? How do we know it isn't just genetic?

Good question. Consider this. Japanese men and women who eat a traditional low-fat Japanese diet have very low rates of heart disease. Yet when these same Japanese people come to the United States and adopt an American diet, they also end up adopting American levels of serum cholesterol and American rates of heart disease. A major study of Japanese who migrated to Hawaii and California documented a threefold increase in coronary heart disease rates within a generation for those who migrated to the West Coast and a twofold increase in Japanese who migrated to Hawaii.[32] So Japanese genes don't protect Japanese people from the American diet.

In Hawaii, the level of fat in the diet is about 30 percent, which is between the 10 percent level of the traditional—pre–World War II— Japanese diet and the 40 percent level of the "traditional" American diet. Interestingly, those Japanese who move to Hawaii increase their rate of heart disease exactly to the Hawaiian level, which, not surprisingly, is between that of Japan and the continental United States.[33] In parts of Japan, such as Tokyo, the diets have been affected by Western influences and are gradually becoming higher in meat, high-fat dairy products, and the like, and heart disease rates have been increasing since World War II.[34]

Fat consumption in Japan (now 20 to 25 percent of calories) is still only about half of that in the United States, and their rate of death from heart disease is about a third of the American rate. Forty years ago, when Japanese fat consumption was closer to 10 percent of calories, heart disease was almost nonexistent.

Isn't stress a big factor?

Stress is an important issue and can accelerate an existing condition. We'll talk more about that in chapter 8, "The Mind-Body Connection." To obtain some insight into the relative importance of diet and stress, it's worthwhile to examine the experience of European countries (England, Finland, Sweden, Holland, Norway, and others) under food rationing during World War II. Despite the enormous stress of those years, the death rate from heart disease in countries where rationing was imposed dropped dramatically to about one-fourth of prewar levels. In countries without food rationing, such as the United States, there was no drop in heart disease rates. And when the war was over and rationing ended, the heart disease rates in the rationing countries rose quickly again to "normal" levels. So the "hardships" of rationing—being forced to do without butter, cheese, eggs, and milk; substantially reducing the intake of meat and subsisting instead on such staples as potatoes and rice—resulted in a dramatic and relatively quick drop in heart disease. This drop occurred despite the fact that these people had been eating high-fat diets all their lives up to the period of rationing. The rationing, notably, was not completely meat-free, but was simply a reduction in high-fat foods.[35]

An even more dramatic finding from World War II had to do with the survivors of the concentration camps. Those who had been in the camps for the full four years, many of whom had been diagnosed earlier with heart disease, were found to be completely free of this disease after their release from the camps. The dietary restrictions in these camps were more severe than the rationing found in many European countries, but the diet was nonetheless sufficient for these individuals to survive. Their atherosclerosis had stopped and, in fact, had reversed. Interestingly, they were also found to be free of hypertension and, in most cases, diabetes.

Similar results were found in autopsy studies in central Europe during the post–World War I period. Actual regression of atherosclerosis was noted during this period, in which the most notable characteristic of the people's diet was a severe shortage of eggs, milk, butter, and meat.[36]

The case for a diet very low in fat and cholesterol does not rest on any single study or even a single type of study, but rather a rich mosaic of evidence, drawing together many human population studies (i.e., studies comparing different populations), human longitudinal studies (studies conducted on a population over a long period of time), human intervention studies (studies of the effect on a group of persons of prescribed changes in diet, life-style, or medication), and animal intervention studies.

The point is that if you eat an unhealthy diet, you had better hope that you have benevolent genes. You may survive an unhealthy diet, but you are playing a particularly deadly form of Russian roulette. On the other hand, the vast majority of the population can overcome atherosclerosis through a very low fat, low cholesterol diet. In the parts of Japan where people eat the traditional low-fat Japanese diet, as well as in the regions of China and other societies of Asia where people eat this way, heart disease is virtually unheard of. This simply cannot be

IS THERE A SIMILARITY HERE?

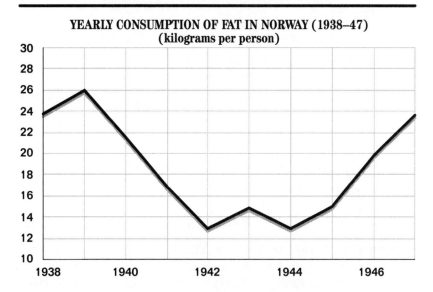

YEARLY CONSUMPTION OF FAT IN NORWAY (1938–47)
(kilograms per person)

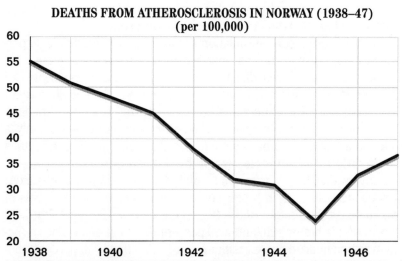

DEATHS FROM ATHEROSCLEROSIS IN NORWAY (1938–47)
(per 100,000)

The reduction in consumption of high-fat foods during World War II in Norway produced an immediate corresponding reduction in deaths from atherosclerosis. Similar results occurred in other European nations that reduced the intake of high-fat foods during World War II as a result of rationing or lack of availability.

Data from: H. Malmros, "The Relation of Nutrition to Health," Acta Medica Scandinavia, suppl. 246, 1950.

attributed to good genes, because when these same people move to Western societies and adopt our eating habits, they develop our high rates of this disease.

So I have to adopt a concentration camp diet to avoid heart disease?

No, not at all. What a healthy diet and a concentration camp diet have in common is that they are both low in fat, cholesterol, and sodium. However, concentration camp victims were not given a sufficient number of calories and that caused malnutrition in many cases, which can be immediately health threatening. But your healthy diet can be satisfying, diverse, and appealing.

Okay, so how low in fat do I need to go? If I cut out some of my more fattening desserts, is that enough?

The Public-Health Recommendations

I'm afraid that's not going to do it. The dietary changes you need to make to make a real difference are significant. The diet can be very interesting and enjoyable, but it requires a major change in eating patterns. Dropping a few high-fat items, adding a high-fiber cereal, and other little changes won't make much of a difference.

The American Heart Association recommends a diet that is 30 percent of calories from fat, as opposed to the usual 40 percent.[37] In advanced cases of heart disease, they recommend 20 percent. But these recommendations do not go nearly far enough. The 30 percent recommendation in particular is, in my view, the moral (and health) equivalent of telling a two-pack-a-day smoker to cut down to only a pack and a half a day. That's a change in the right direction and does make a difference, but is clearly not the right answer.

Many studies have shown that a diet of 30 percent of calories from fat does indeed result in better cholesterol levels and lower levels of heart disease than a diet of 35–40 percent calories from fat, but a 20 percent diet is better still, and a 10 percent diet best of all. The reduction in risk of heart disease resulting from a diet that is 10 percent calories from fat is dramatically greater than the reduction resulting from a diet that is 30 percent calories from fat. At 10 percent, which is the level of a traditional Japanese or Asian low-fat diet, atherosclerosis and the resulting heart disease virtually do not exist.

Are there studies that show the plaque from atherosclerosis actually being reduced?

A particularly interesting study that showed regression of athero-sclerotic plaque was reported at the 1988, 1989, and 1990 annual meetings of the American Heart Association by Dr. Dean Ornish, a professor of medicine at the University of California at San Francisco.[38] He compared two groups of patients who had been randomly assigned from a pool of subjects, all of whom had experienced angina pain caused by proven partial blockage of the coronary arteries. The control group followed the standard medical recommendations of cutting down to 30 percent calories from fat and ceasing cigarette smoking. They also received standard advice for hypertension and performed aerobic exercise approximately one and a half hours per week. The experimental group followed a program very similar to the 10% solution described in this book, including a diet of less than 10 percent calories from fat, exercise of at least three hours per week, and stress management. After a year, the average total cholesterol for the control group decreased from 251 to 230 mg/dl, a still very dangerous level despite their having followed all of the standard public-health recommendations for high serum cholesterol levels and heart disease. More significantly, the average blockage of their coronary arteries, as measured by an advanced technique called quantitative coronary angiography (a computer analysis of angiogram X rays), got worse!

In contrast, the total cholesterol of the experimental group fell to 135 mg/dl, a very healthy level. Only one subject (out of 22) in the experimental group did not follow the advice, and his arteries got worse. The other subjects in the experimental group followed the program and none of them had an increase in blockage of their coro-nary arteries. Eighty-five percent had a *decrease* in blockage. Encour-agingly, the greatest decreases in blockage were found in the arteries with the greatest blockage. Ornish also measured their actual coro-nary flow reserve, a measure of the flow of blood to the heart, using a sophisticated imaging technology called positron emission tomo-graphy. Here again, the coronary flow got worse for those following the standard medical recommendations, including 30 percent calo-ries from fat, but improved for the group following the recommen-dations of 10-percent-calories-from-fat diet, exercise, and stress management. Other studies have shown similar regression of athero-sclerotic plaque, given sufficient reduction of serum cholesterol levels, confirming many years of animal studies and human popu-lation studies.

With regard to population studies, most of the studies you've mentioned compare populations that differ in diet but also differ genetically.

Perhaps the most exciting population study of a genetically homogeneous population is a vast and comprehensive study of 6,500 Chinese, comprised of 100 people from 65 Chinese counties, conducted by a team of Chinese and American researchers and published in 1990.[39] The study, which has been called the Grand Prix of epidemiology, tracked in considerable detail the eating habits and health of each of these individuals.[40] The study was conducted in China for several reasons. First of all, the Chinese represent a very large population that generally eats a diet that is very low in fat and cholesterol. Most important, the population is genetically similar, so the difference in habits that do exist between counties can be examined without the confounding factor of genetic differences. Third, the very low cost of labor in China allowed the collection of a vast set of data that would be virtually impossible in American society.

The overall difference between Chinese eating habits and health patterns and those of Americans is dramatic. The average percentage of calories from fat in the Chinese population is less than 15 percent, compared with about 39 percent for Americans. Their average cholesterol level is 127, compared with 212 for Americans. And there is virtually no heart disease, colon cancer, breast cancer, prostate cancer, and ovarian cancer among the Chinese, compared with very high rates of these diseases in American society. What little heart disease and cancer that do exist in Chinese society are seen in those counties that eat the highest levels of fat and cholesterol. The rate of heart disease, for example, in the rural counties of China is 26 per 100,000 adults, compared with 4,036 per 100,000 adults in the United States. In other words, the American rate of heart disease is 155 times higher than the rate in rural China. According to Dr. T. Colin Campbell, nutritional biochemist at Cornell University and one of the study's researchers, the Chinese data provides a very clear picture in a genetically similar population that eating 10 to 15 percent calories from fat provides a very high level of protection from heart disease and cancer, whereas the level of 30 percent, recommended by public-health authorities in the United States, is completely inadequate to provide optimal protection from these diseases.[41]

So what do the Chinese die of?

In those few regions that are affluent and therefore eat relatively high levels of fat and cholesterol, the primary causes of death are similar to those in American society: heart disease, cancer, and diabetes. In those regions that are poor and therefore cannot afford animal sources of protein, these diseases virtually do not exist. Because of limited refrigeration and health care, infectious diseases are the leading causes of death in these regions. In some counties, a high level of salt is used to preserve food, and this combined with a high level of sodium in the food itself causes a high rate of hypertension and stroke caused by hypertension, similar to Japanese society. In those counties that eat low levels of fat as well as low levels of salt, there are low levels of blood pressure and correspondingly little stroke.

This extensive study has provided other intriguing results. Despite the fact that the Chinese eat only half of the calcium of Americans, there is virtually no osteoporosis. Adjusted for height, the Chinese actually eat 20 percent more calories than Americans, yet Americans are 25 percent fatter.

The overall message of the study is this: While eating 30 percent calories from fat is a bit better in terms of health and weight than eating 40 percent calories from fat, going down to about 10 percent calories from fat is necessary to virtually eliminate the risk of heart disease and most cancers and to readily control weight. Given the wealth of American society, we have the opportunity to avoid the diseases of poverty (i.e., infectious diseases) as well as the diseases of affluence (heart disease, cancer, and the other degenerative diseases).

So why the recommendation of 30 percent?

That is a very good question and the source of some considerable and complex controversy. I have talked with doctors involved in setting these guidelines. Many of these doctors are aware that the recommendations represent a significant compromise. They find it difficult to make recommendations for the general population that are so at variance with the deeply ingrained eating patterns of the entire population. They feel it might set the entire economy into a tailspin. Frankly, I think they overestimate the impact such recommendations would have, at least economically (they would have dramatic health benefits, however). After all, about 50 million Americans still smoke, despite the very clear-cut and uncompromising recommendations from the medical community that have been aggressively delivered through many channels.[42]

The most common argument for these watered-down recommendations on the ideal fat level is the theory of maximum compliance. The 30-percent-calories-from-fat recommendation is supposedly easy to follow. Just make a few minor adjustments, remove a few items from your diet, add a little fiber, and so on. The effect of the 30-percent-calories-from-fat diet is a reduction in heart disease risk of about 30 percent compared to a diet of 40 percent calories from fat. The 10-percent-calories-from-fat diet, on the other hand, if sustained over a period of several years, results in a reduction of risk of at least 90 percent. In my own case, the reduction of risk, as indicated by my cholesterol, HDL, and other measurements, was more than 97 percent, according to the statistics of the Framingham Study.[43] The likelihood of my having a heart attack during my lifetime fell from more than 90 percent (with a high likelihood of it occuring during middle age) to just a few percent. Personally, I would rather make a significant change in my eating habits for a 97 percent reduction in the risk of contracting heart disease, as well as comparable reductions in the risk of major cancers and other diseases, than make a moderate change for a 30 percent improvement in risk. Also, although it sounds counterintuitive, the major change is, I believe, easier to make and to stick to. I'll explain more about that later in this book (see chapter 3, "The Benefits"). But the maximum compliance argument is that more lives will be saved by having relatively large compliance with a 30 percent reduction in risk than by having fewer people comply with stricter guidelines, even if the individuals following the stricter guidelines achieve virtual elimination of their risk.

Isn't there some logic to that?

The logic is there, but I believe the recommendations are nonetheless misleading and ultimately not in the public interest. First, they are certainly not in your own private interest, in that you can achieve virtual elimination of the risk of heart disease and most cancers. That fact is not generally communicated.

My second objection is that they are precompromised. They are presented as the ideal recommendations based on what we know, and that is clearly not the case.

Third, a lot of people compromise these recommendations on their own anyway. Either they don't fully understand and follow them or they think that the public-health recommendations must represent perfection and it is not their intention to achieve such perfection.

Thus, a typical person who takes these recommendations at all seriously figures, if perfection is 30 percent calories from fat, then it must be good enough to be at 35 percent. Often through ignorance or inattention, they end up even higher than that. Then the reduction in risk is almost nonexistent.

This leads to a fourth objection to the 30-percent-calories-from-fat recommendation, which is that it is subject to criticism of its effectiveness. Studies have shown that it is effective, but the effects are not overwhelming. Some critics have said, "Why bother? It's not worth the trouble." Recently there has been publicity about this debate between the cholesterol interventionists and their critics. But the two sides in this so-called debate are really on the same side, with *neither* side calling for meaningful changes. One side calls for very minor changes, although they certainly don't refer to them that way. The other side says that the results from these changes are not worth the effort. Studies show that reducing fat consumption to 30 percent of calories does slow down atherosclerosis to some extent, but doesn't stop it, let alone reverse it. The risks for heart disease are diminished, but by only a modest 30 percent or so. It's as if there were a debate between those advocating that two-pack-a-day smokers cut down to a pack and a half a day versus those who said that cutting down by a half pack a day is too difficult and not worth it. Overlooked in this debate is the case for truly meaningful changes. Human population studies as well as human intervention studies have clearly demonstrated the *dramatic* benefits of a *dramatic* reduction of fat intake. Cholesterol levels do drop significantly, and actual measurements of the plaque development show that not only is atherosclerosis completely halted in most individuals but can be reversed. Thus the results for greater restrictions on fat intake do show results that can withstand the objections.

Finally, those individuals who take these guidelines very seriously (I know people who have actually written to obtain the guidelines in great detail and attempt to follow them very carefully) would be willing to follow stricter guidelines, but they are not being informed of their alternatives.

What initiated this controversy?

An article, "The Cholesterol Myth," written by Thomas J. Moore (a condensation of Moore's book *Heart Failure*), published in *The Atlantic,* attempts to makes the case that it is not worth the trouble to reduce your blood cholesterol.[44] A great deal of his argument is based on a discussion of the MR FIT (Multiple Risk Factor Intervention Trial) study, which he claims "failed completely." For seven years, MR FIT followed two groups totaling fifteen thousand men who were at high risk for heart disease. One group was given instructions to quit smoking, alter their diet (to the usual 30-percent-calories-from-fat recommendation), and control their blood pressure. For ethical reasons, those in the other group were also told of their high-risk situation and referred to their own physicians for treatment. In the end, the two groups did not differ significantly from each other in mortality or number of cardiac events, which led to Moore's charge that the recommendations were ineffective.[45] As it turns out, the so-called control group went to their physicians as instructed and, not surprisingly, received the same recommendations, since the MR FIT recommendations were identical to standard medical practice. Being in the study alerted both groups to their precarious situation, and both groups apparently took the recommendations equally seriously. Thus both groups changed their diet and life-styles to the same degree. And both groups benefited to the same limited extent. The number of coronary deaths and events was 30 to 40 percent lower in both groups, compared with statistics for other men at the same ages and with the same risk factors. Critics of MR FIT have pointed out several other serious design flaws. The study does show, however, the modest improvement that can be obtained by following the standard health recommendations. Neither Moore nor the MR FIT researchers examined the benefits of a more extensive diet and life-style change.

Moore also points out the side effects and dangers of some of the cholesterol-lowering medications, and here his criticisms have some validity.

So why don't they put out multiple recommendations? They could put out the 30-percent-calories-from-fat guideline which gives you some benefit, and a 10-percent-calories-from-fat guideline for those who really want to do everything they can to eliminate their risk.

That's not an unreasonable suggestion. There is something along these lines in that the so-called phase 3 American Heart Association guideline for adults with hyperlipidemia (elevated cholesterol levels) is 20 percent calories from fat.[46] But this doesn't go far enough either and is limited to people with advanced disease. Ten percent calories from fat is the ideal level for most any adult, specifically to avoid getting to the point of having advanced disease.

The objection I have heard against multiple recommendations is that they would be confusing. People want recommendations that are straightforward and want to believe that they reflect the ultimate wisdom on the subject. The policymakers are concerned that people would reject the 10 percent guideline as too radical and then also reject the 30 percent guideline because there would be no point in following it since it would be clear that it is a compromise.

So what should the guidelines reflect?

I believe that the guidelines should reflect everything that is known. Let people judge for themselves what they want to do. Those who wish to follow such guidelines carefully will have the opportunity for a dramatic improvement in their health. The compromisers will at least be departing from a position that is not already severely compromised to begin with. And the great unwashed majority who ignore such counsel regardless of its merit will be no worse off.

The saddest thing to me are people who desperately need such information, people who have passed the 70 percent occlusion level, have angina pain, or have had a heart attack or bypass surgery (or have had a bypass operation recommended), and are not informed that there is a way to reverse years of atherosclerotic neglect. Many would be willing to go to the ends of the earth to regain their health, but they're not pointed in the right direction. Then there are others who, even after becoming ill, don't take any advice they get seriously. But these individuals are probably hopeless anyway. In many cases, though, people ignore the advice they get because the advice is not presented in a convincing or effective way. The enormous impact of diet and life-style on health is often presented in a low-key, ineffectual way, which invites people not to take it seriously.

You know, pain has value. Discomfort can make us aware of a situation and cause us to take remedial action. I've always thought it tragic that atherosclerosis is painless.

I understand that women don't get heart disease very often. So this stuff is mainly of concern to men, isn't that right?

It is true that women have some protection from heart disease prior to menopause. High levels of estrogen prior to menopause are linked to relatively high levels of HDL (the "good" cholesterol) and this reduces the rate of atherosclerosis.[47] Also, menstruation reduces the level of iron in the blood. Iron facilitates the oxidation of LDL (the

"HEART DISEASE IS 70% GENETIC"

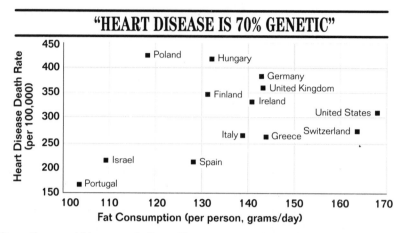

Or so they would have you believe. This common misconception is based on the observation that there is no clear trend shown on the above chart. If you only consider going down to 30 percent calories from fat (100 grams for 3,000 calories) then the trend is, in fact, muddled and, indeed, your genetic disposition will appear to be the most important factor.

BUT LOOK AGAIN

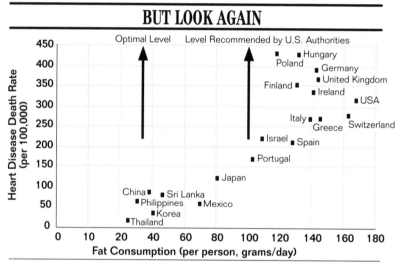

If we open up our vision and consider going to an optimal 10 percent calories from fat, then the picture becomes dramatically clearer. Now we see a very obvious trend. Lower fat consumption (around 10 percent calories from fat) does result in dramatically lower rates of heart disease. At this level, deaths from heart disease are cut by close to 90 percent.

Furthermore, population migration studies show that people who move to another society (Japanese who move to the United States, for example) take on the disease patterns of the society to which they move and whose eating patterns they adopt. Genetics is, therefore, a much less important factor when a truly healthy diet is consumed.

Data from: World Health Organization, 1982, 1988, 1989. Food and Agricultural Organization, Food Balance Sheets, 1979–81.

"bad" cholesterol), which is an early step in the process of atherosclerosis. Thus reducing iron levels may slow atherosclerosis. But most pre-menopausal women still have atherosclerosis. The lower rate of plaque buildup prior to menopause (compared to men) results in a much lower rate of coronary heart disease during that period, but it also means that once menopause is reached, a woman's arteries have already made substantial progress toward reaching the level at which a heart attack will occur. Women catch up quickly to men after menopause, and heart disease is the leading cause of death in women during these later years. There are other dangers that result from any rate of atherosclerosis, which we will discuss a little later.

Perhaps the most important reason that women should take this "stuff" very seriously is cancer. The rate of breast and other cancers is rising dramatically. I believe that a major reason for this may be the current preoccupation with so-called "heart-healthy oils" that are high in polyunsaturated fats, which accelerate the progression of cancer. As we will discuss in some detail, eating a diet that is very low in fat reduces the risk of most major cancers by 90 percent or more.

Hypertension, stroke, type II diabetes, and many other health concerns are equally important to both sexes, and the risk of all of these is dramatically reduced by this program. Also of interest to both sexes are the immediate benefits, including delaying the aging process, having smoother skin, and avoiding excess weight.

2
■
What Does This Mean?

Fat

So what does this mean? Ten percent calories from fat? How do I translate that into practical terms?

Each gram of fat has 9 calories. If you eat, let's say, 2,000 calories each day, then you want 200 calories from fat. Divide 9 into 200 and you get 22 grams of fat per day. Twenty-two grams of fat is equivalent to about 5 teaspoons of oil (or butter, margarine, fat from meat, etc.). Note that we are talking about all the fat in your diet, not just the added fats, such as oils. In fact, to achieve this level, you will want very little or no added fats.

That's great. How many fat grams did you say were in an apple?

There is about half a gram of fat in an average apple.

So I can have forty-four apples per day.

Well, that would comply with the fat guideline, all right, but you would not be getting the balance of nutrients that you need. Eating forty-four apples is also not the most interesting diet one could have. If you substituted some potatoes for some of the apples, you would be better off nutritionally, although that would be only slightly more appetizing.

So besides apples and potatoes, just what does 22 grams of fat a day mean, in terms of what I can eat?

To give you a brief overview, let's start with breakfast. You can eat many varieties of cereals, both hot (e.g., oatmeal, Cream of Wheat, Wheatena, other hot grain cereals) and cold (e.g., shredded wheat, Grape Nuts, puffed wheat, natural grain cereals), with skim milk, fruit, and fruit juice. You can have various breads, bagels, and English muffins, but avoid cakey muffins and croissant-type pastries, which are full of butter. You can have jams, although avoid the high-sugar ones. Ideal are fruit spreads without added sugar. You can have omelettes made with egg whites or low-fat (and non-fat) egg substitutes. You can have cheeses and spreads that are made with skim milk, but not your usual high-fat cheeses. Of course, avoid butter and margarine, which are all fat.

That sounds like a pretty big breakfast. What about lunch and dinner?

You can eat any fruit. Virtually all vegetables are good, except avocados and olives, which are 90 percent fat, although the type of fat in them is monounsaturated, which is not the worst type. Grains, most breads, beans, and legumes are ideal. But don't drown these foods in fat—no butter or cream sauces or oil-based dressings. So you can have vegetable and grain casseroles of various kinds, pastas with tomato-based sauces, and salads. Try balsamic vinegar as an easy no-fat salad dressing. Also, many non-fat and very low fat salad dressings are in the supermarket today.

What about meats and fish?

Many types of fish, such as sole and swordfish, are low to moderate in fat content. Some varieties, such as salmon, are fairly high in fat, but the fat in fish is of a special type called omega-3 fat or fish oil, which is beneficial to some extent.

A good fat?

Yes, for many people, it appears to be beneficial in moderate quantities. With meats, you have to be very careful. The type of fat in meat is high in saturated fat, which is the most damaging type of fat. Meat is also high in cholesterol.

So I have to become a vegetarian?

No, that's not necessary. But you do have to limit both the type and quantity of meat. You need to change the idea of a big slab of meat as the centerpiece of each meal. Limited quantities of white meat of chicken or turkey cooked without the skin or very lean grades of beef or pork are acceptable. I generally recommend limiting meat or poultry to about 4 ounces per day. But if eating meat is important to you, then it is possible to go as high as 8 ounces per day, as long as the meat is lean, and you otherwise eat very little fat. For example, 8 ounces of the light meat of chicken roasted without the skin has about 10 grams of fat. So it is possible to eat 8 ounces of meat and still stay within 22 grams of fat per day (which is the right level for 2,000 calories). Note that 8 ounces of light meat of chicken roasted *with* the skin has 25 grams of fat and is clearly not acceptable. Another option is to eat no meat on one day and a larger portion of lean meat on the next day.

This limitation of 22 grams of fat—is that it? Is there anything else I have to worry about?

That is by far the most crucial guideline. If you can eat a level of fat that low over a sustained period of time you have a very high like-lihood of stopping and even reversing atherosclerosis. And athero-sclerosis is the cause of almost all heart disease.

There are a few individuals—less than 5 percent of the popula-tion—that have a cholesterol-handling problem not caused by diet who will continue to have high cholesterol levels despite a very low fat, low cholesterol diet. This may be due to genetic factors or may have been self-induced, through alcohol abuse or use of other substances and medications. In these cases, diet plus an appropriate cholesterol-lowering medication may be recommended by that person's physi-cian. But what often happens, unfortunately, is that the principle of "try diet first" means trying the 30-percent-calories-from-fat diet and then going to medication when that fails. Individuals have not really tried an effective dietary approach unless they try levels closer to 10 percent calories from fat. So fat is by far the most important factor.

What about cholesterol in food?

Cholesterol

Limiting cholesterol to around 100 milligrams per day is also very important. This guideline is also stricter than the 300 milligrams recommended by the American Heart Association. Ten percent calories from fat and 100 milligrams of cholesterol have been shown to reduce both cholesterol levels and atherosclerosis far more dramatically than 30 percent and 300 milligrams. Following the 100-milligram-cholesterol guideline does not add a lot of restrictions. By avoiding fat, you are also avoiding most sources of cholesterol. There are a few exceptions. Lobster and shrimp are low in fat, but contain moderate amounts of cholesterol, so should be eaten in limited amounts. Egg yolks (as opposed to egg whites) are also low in fat, but very high in cholesterol—more than 200 milligrams in a single yolk—and so should be avoided altogether. Organ meats and brain in particular are spectacularly high in cholesterol and should never be eaten.

I've heard that it's important to eat fiber.

Fiber

The best way to avoid fat and cholesterol is to eat a diet high in complex carbohydrates. That automatically means a lot of fiber, which itself has many health benefits. Fiber is filling, aids in weight loss, improves digestion, elimination, and blood sugar regulation, and lowers cholesterol. The soluble fibers found in legumes such as peas and beans may be effective in lowering the LDL, or "bad" cholesterol, levels. The insoluble fibers found in most fruits and vegetables are effective in improving elimination and lowering the risk of cancer.[1]

I've also heard that iron may cause heart disease.

Iron

There are studies that suggest that an average or higher blood iron level is a risk factor for heart disease. A recent study of 1,931 Finnish men, reported by Dr. Jukka Salonen and his associates at the University of Kuopio, showed elevated risk of heart disease with elevated ferritin (a protein that carries iron in the blood) levels.

It should be noted that blood levels of cholesterol and iron are highly correlated. Also, these results in no way alter the role of cholesterol, particularly LDL (the "bad" cholesterol), as a major independent risk factor for heart disease.

The two substances may work together to promote atherosclerosis. It is known that iron promotes oxidation (combining with oxygen). The process of artery plaque formation appears to start with the oxidation of LDL, a process that may be accelerated in the presence of iron. This is consistent with the study's finding that the most dramatic increase in risk was noted for those men with elevated levels of both LDL cholesterol and ferritin.

If iron is a risk, what would that mean?

The dietary implications of avoiding fat and cholesterol and of avoiding iron are similar. Avoiding foods that are high in fat and cholesterol, particularly red meat and other foods of animal origin, will automatically avoid foods that are high in iron. So following the guidelines of the 10% solution for dramatically reducing the level of fat and cholesterol in the diet will automatically avoid concentrated sources of iron. Liver, which in any event is high in fat and cholesterol, is particularly high in iron. It would also be a good idea to avoid iron supplements (unless you have a significant deficiency of iron), vitamin and mineral supplements that include iron, and so-called "fortified" foods which have added iron.

Is there anything else one can do to lower one's level of iron in the blood?

Exercise appears to cause changes in metabolism that interfere with the ability of iron to accelerate damaging oxidation. Also, menstruating significantly lowers the level of iron. This has been proposed as an additional reason that women are protected from heart disease prior to menopause.

Not all of us have that opportunity.

For men and post-menopausal and other nonmenstruating women, donating about three units of blood each year would have a similar effect on iron levels. You should check with your physician to make sure that you are not prone to anemia or other medical conditions that would prevent your donating blood.

So menstruating or giving blood can protect one from heart disease.

Additional studies are needed to clarify the independent role of iron. Donating blood will lower one's iron level and may help to protect you from heart disease. We do know, however, that it can help save the lives of others.

Following the nutritional guidelines of the 10% solution will lower blood and bodily stores of both LDL cholesterol and iron and is by far the most effective way to reduce heart disease risk. In the Finnish study, those with the lowest levels of ferritin had half of the heart disease risk compared to those with the highest levels (above 200 micrograms per liter). Following the guidelines of the 10% solution for a sustained period substantially reduces both LDL and iron levels and can reduce the risk of heart disease by 90 percent or more.

The evidence for a direct link between dietary fat and the development of both heart disease and most cancers is very extensive. Avoiding fat and cholesterol in the diet (which automatically avoids concentrated sources of iron) will provide a very high level of protection from all of these diseases.

What about salt?

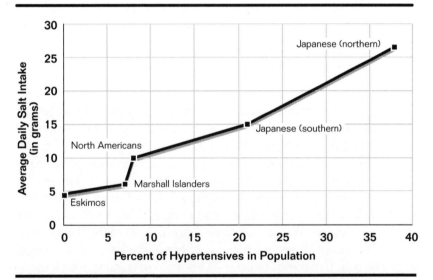

Data from: L. K. Dahl, "Possible Role of Salt Intake in the Development of Essential Hypertension," in Essential Hypertension, ed. by K. D. Bock and P. T. Cottier (Berlin: Springer-Verlag, 1960), 53–65.

Sodium

Another important dietary guideline is to restrict the intake of sodium, which can contribute to hypertension and other conditions. An excessive level of sodium can cause your blood volume to increase. This increases blood pressure, promotes atherosclerosis, and can increase the risk of a stroke or a heart attack. Staying below 2,000 milligrams per day is safe. Since salt is half sodium, that means less than 4,000 milligrams (4 grams) of salt.

Persons with normal blood pressure and no history of hypertension or coronary heart disease can probably stay healthy at a level of 3,000 milligrams of sodium (or 6 grams of salt) per day.

Without any known exceptions, in societies that have diets very low in fat and sodium, individuals have lifelong low blood pressure.[2]

It is advisable to add no salt to your food at all. Many packaged foods contain a large amount of added salt. Tomato juice, for example, typically has about 600 milligrams of sodium in a 6-ounce serving. You will, of course, be avoiding such salty snacks as potato chips for their fat content if nothing else. A 2-ounce bag of potato chips can have 20 or more grams of fat, which is your whole day's allotment. They are also very high in sodium. In general, pretzels are usually not that high in fat, but you should brush off most or all of the salt.

But that's what makes them taste so good.

Sugar

Well, you will change your ideas about that before long. Salt is actually a taste killer. And the more you use it, the more you need it for taste. Sugar is also worth avoiding. Unlike the more complex carbohydrates, sugar is digested very quickly and results in a sudden increase in blood insulin levels to process the extra sugar. The insulin processes the sugar and, ironically, often leads within a few hours to rapidly falling and low levels of blood sugar. This leads to further cravings for sugar. When combined with high-fat diets, this pattern can lead to chronic sugar imbalances, either hypoglycemia (low blood sugar) or type II diabetes (sustained high blood sugar). Even if these extremes in sugar metabolism are avoided, concentrated ingestions of sugar and fat can lead to a recurrent cycle of low blood sugar causing sugar cravings leading to further large ingestions of sweets. Usually these sweets are also high in fat, which is the most damaging aspect of indulging in them. If you eat sweets that are low in fat, such as non-fat frozen yogurt (low-fat frozen yogurt may be okay depending on the fat content, but remember to keep track of the fat grams it contains), frozen fruit desserts, and the like, in moderate quantities, then the health problems associated with sugar are limited. It is sugar combined with fat that causes the most significant problems. In fact, serious, chronic problems with sugar metabolism, such as type II diabetes, are caused primarily by fat (and calories) in the diet, not sugar.[3]

The sugar and salt guidelines sound fairly moderate. The cholesterol guideline seems to affect mostly the same foods as the fat guideline. So the 10-percent-calories-from-fat guideline seems to be the heart of the matter.

Indeed that is well put.

It may be the heart of the matter, but it also seems a bit extreme. It sounds quite different from the way I am now eating. I mean, no ice cream? None of the desserts I am used to eating? No steaks? No french fries? No potato chips? What happened to moderation? Moderation in all things—isn't that also a reasonable guideline?

It is true that there are a lot of things you cannot eat following the 10% solution. But there is an equally long list of things that you can eat. And society is beginning to respond. Our Yankee ingenuity is being applied and there is an increasingly large array of prepared foods from entrees to desserts that are very low in fat (or even non-fat) that are quite appealing. The chairman of Con Agra, one of the nation's largest manufacturers of food, after suffering a heart attack, directed his firm to develop a low-fat line of frozen dinners, which resulted in the successful Healthy Choice series. You can now find very low fat and non-fat varieties of many foods, including frozen desserts, puddings, mayonnaise, even hamburgers. It does take time to discover the foods that appeal to you and that comply with these guidelines, but you would be surprised how much variety you have.

As for moderation, I tend to be a moderate person. But the more I have studied this issue, the more it has become apparent that it is our society that is not moderate. Somewhere along the line, our dietary habits diverged from what is healthy for the human species. We may have evolved intellectually from animals, but our digestive system is not that different from many other mammals, particularly other primates. You have only to examine what chimpanzees and other primates choose to eat when left to their own devices in the wild to obtain one example of a healthy diet.

The divergence of the (primarily Western) "civilized" diet from the diet on which we evolved and thrived began to pick up steam with the advent of the Industrial Revolution. Prior to the Industrial Revolution, such luxuries as rich cakes and large slabs of meat were simply not available to the masses. Even refined sugar was a delicacy available only to nobility and the wealthy. As the Industrial Revolution made the mass production of these items possible, the rich food of the upper class became available to the common man.[4] This divergence accelerated after World War II when modern production methods led to such innovations as fast food and other manufactured foodstuffs that are typically extremely high in fat, and often salt and sugar as well.[5] The typical fast-food hamburger is more than 50 percent fat, much of which is saturated, with a very high sugar content in the bun.

It is our society that is radical, unfortunately in a very negative direction. We have thousands of people having heart attacks, with nearly three thousand losing their lives from heart and cardiovascular disease each day. Almost all of this destruction is preventable. We know what to do and how.

With the American diet so drastically off the mark, moderate changes won't make much of a difference. It is similar to saying "be moderate" to a smoker: "Don't cut out cigarettes, just cut down a bit, maybe switch to a lower tar and nicotine brand." That, in fact, was exactly the approach to smoking that was taken by the medical community after World War II. But as the evidence mounted, it eventually became irresistible and the recommendations today are to avoid cigarette smoke altogether, even in the air around you. But it took more than forty years for that position to be accepted.

So the 10% solution is extreme only in comparison to the extremely devastating diet that people now follow.

Wasn't primitive man a carnivore? You know, the hunter and all that.

Primitive Man

Yes, primitive man ate meat, and so can you. But our hunting forebears did not buy one-pound slabs of meat in the grocery store. The amount of work and expenditure of energy involved to hunt a small animal was usually enormous. And this animal was then shared by several families or a whole community. So the amount of meat eaten was generally limited. The meat was also much leaner. Wild animals are usually no more than 10 to 15 percent fat, whereas our genetically altered, hormone-induced livestock are closer to 30 percent fat (by weight). A survey of fifteen different species of African animals in the wild found an average carcass fat content of about 4 percent. While it is hard to generalize about many scattered primitive communities over thousands of years, meat was usually not the primary constituent of the diet. The small amounts of lean meat that were shared by a community were generally supplemented by larger amounts of roots, beans, nuts, tubers, and fruits, which were gathered. Recent studies of primitive man have estimated his fat consumption at no more than 20 percent of his calories, and often less. Also, his physical activity level went way beyond that of even our more avid fitness fans, and everyone was involved.[6]

Degenerative diseases that are still unknown to primates in the wild include heart disease; stroke; type II diabetes; breast, colon, and other cancers; arthritis; gallstones; hypertension; glaucoma; and cataracts. The available evidence appears to suggest that primitive man was also free of heart disease. Interestingly, if we subject the primates in captivity to our civilized diet, they do develop heart disease and these other degenerative diseases.[7]

Okay, so dramatically lower the level of fat in the diet, watch those high-cholesterol foods that are not otherwise eliminated by way of their fat content, control salt, and watch sugar to some extent. Iron is largely avoided by avoiding fat and cholesterol, but avoid iron supplements and "fortified" foods. Is that it?

Exercise

The other crucial issue is exercise. Numerous studies have shown the effectiveness of exercise in reducing heart disease, cancer, hypertension, diabetes, obesity, osteoporosis, and other ailments, particularly when combined with a healthy, that is, low-fat, diet. We do not understand all of the mechanisms for this, but several are apparent. Exercise is one of the few ways to increase the level of "good" cholesterol, or HDL, in the blood.[8] HDL mitigates some of the damage done by LDL. One of the primary findings of the Framingham Study showed that a primary risk predictor for heart disease was the ratio of total serum cholesterol to HDL. So increasing HDL reduces heart disease.

There is also evidence that exercise thins the blood, thus reducing the likelihood of clotting.[9] Once your atherosclerosis has gotten to the point that your arteries are blocked in that 70 percent-plus danger zone, the factor that actually causes the heart attack or stroke or other catastrophic event is a blood clot developing on or getting stuck in the plaque-clogged artery. Reducing spontaneous clotting thus at least reduces the likelihood of this final coup de grace.

Exercise also improves bowel function. The more rapid transportation of food through the digestive tract reduces the likelihood of colon cancer, one of the most prevalent and deadly cancers in American society.[10]

Exercise improves body composition and shape. It also greatly assists with weight loss. If you exercise properly, you tend to burn fat rather than sugar and glycogen stores. Exercise suppresses appetite and increases your metabolism, even after you finish exercising. It also strengthens your bones and support tissues and can slow or prevent the development of osteoporosis, which is a loss of bone calcium.[11] Eating a sufficient amount of calcium is important, but by itself is not sufficient to prevent this condition.

Regular aerobic exercise also strengthens the heart and enlarges the diameter of the arteries to handle the increased blood flow. This means that atherosclerosis will take longer to clog up the artery.[12]

There is also literature indicating that exercise may increase the development of collateral circulation.[13] Collateral circulation is the development of additional arteries to supplement the crucial coronary arteries. Collateral arteries tend to develop later in life in the presence of artery disease and often enable an older person to survive a heart attack. But at any age, exercise will promote the collateral circulation process. The development of collateral circulation is a primary hope for people whose arteries are approaching complete blockage. If there is still blood flow through a partially occluded artery, then it is possible through the 10% solution to begin a reversal of the atherosclerotic process and start reducing the occlusion. If an artery is completely blocked, however, then collateral circulation would be the mechanism for maintaining a healthy flow of blood. It is possible over time to develop sufficient collateral circulation to restore blood flow to near the level provided by the original coronary artery.

Exercise increases blood flow to the brain, providing better mental functioning and alertness.[14] Perhaps most interesting is the contribution of exercise to mood. An evolutionary adaptation is the release of natural tranquilizers called endorphins during aerobic exertion.[15] These tranquilizers permit sustained physical activity and thus block the level of stress and even pain that might otherwise accompany such activity. It allowed our ancestors a sustained flight from a hungry predator. These endorphins, chemically related to morphine, result in a natural high that elevates mood for a sustained period of time. It is actually a wonderful treatment for mild depression. It is a chemically induced high that is legal, healthy, and always available.

One thing that exercise will not do is lower the level of LDL, the "bad" cholesterol, in the blood. For that you need a diet low in both fat and cholesterol.

3
■
The Benefits

Heart Disease

So, a diet low in fat, cholesterol, and sodium, plus regular aerobic exercise, produces a dramatic reduction in artery and heart disease. Are there any other benefits?

As a matter of fact, reduction in heart disease risk is just the first in a long list of benefits. I mentioned it first because it is the primary health risk in our society and is by far our biggest killer.

Stroke, Aneurysms, Claudication

In terms of other diseases, consider first the diseases caused by the same atherosclerotic mechanism. When the coup-de-grace event—a blood clot forming on or getting stuck in an advanced atherosclerotic plaque formation—occurs in the coronary arteries, that's a heart attack. When it happens in the arteries feeding the brain, you have a thrombotic or embolic stroke.

When atherosclerosis occurs in the aorta, which is the largest artery leaving the heart, or in other large arteries that feed the rest of the body, it can cause an aneurysm, which is associated with swelling, weakness, and clotting in the damaged artery wall. The clot can break off and subsequently lead to a stroke. Expanding aneurysms tend to rupture, and surgery is generally indicated to avoid these events, although the operation is fatal in a significant fraction of cases.

Atherosclerosis in the leg arteries can cause claudication (a symptom of peripheral vascular disease), a painful condition. Claudication is dangerous for the same reasons that an aneurysm is dangerous. There are many other variations of the problems that can be caused by atherosclerosis, which account for enormous suffering in addition to the rising death toll.

What about cancer?

Cancer

Good question. Cancer is another prevalent disease that is dramatically reduced by a low-fat, low-cholesterol diet. The nutritional issues of cancer are not identical, however, to that of heart disease. Cancer and heart disease have different sensitivities to dietary fiber and polyunsaturated fat, as we will discuss.

Cancer progresses in several stages: initiation, promotion, and progression. Initiation happens quickly and may be caused by a carcinogen casually introduced to the body's tissues. For most adults, this step has already taken place somewhere in the body. In other words, most of us have potentially precancerous lesions. For most women, initiation of cancer in their breasts takes place during puberty. These lesions are not detectable and will not evolve into full-blown cancer without the growth or promotion phase in which a precancerous growth evolves into a cancerous tumor. The final and usually fatal stage is progression, in which a tumor metastasizes (spreads from its original site) causing the creation of new tumors throughout the body. Fat is the primary fertilizer or growth promoter advancing the development of a tumor during the crucial promotion stage. It also assists the progression stage.[1]

There is a direct, almost linear, relationship between the percentage of fat in the diet and the risk of a wide variety of cancers. If we examine different societies around the world, we find the lowest rate of cancers such as breast, ovarian, colon, uterine, and prostate among the societies that eat a very low fat (i.e., 10-to-14-percent-calories-from-fat), low-cholesterol diet (see chapter 15, "Ranking the Killers: How to Save a Million American Lives a Year").[2] Indeed, in these societies, these cancers are almost nonexistent. At the other extreme is the United States, with its extremely high level of fat in the diet and extremely high level of these cancers.

THE LINEAR RELATIONSHIP BETWEEN FAT CONSUMPTION AND THE INCIDENCE OF BREAST CANCER

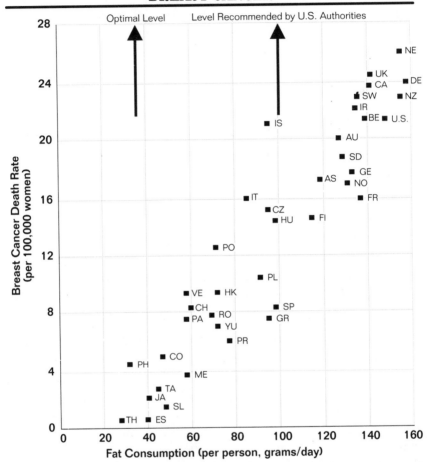

The greater the intake of fat, the greater the risk of breast cancer. In societies that eat very low fat diets, breast cancer is very rare. However, if we restrict our view only to levels at or about 30 percent calories from fat (about 100 grams), then the pattern is much less clear (and the rates are, of course, much higher).

AS	Austria	FR	France	NE	Netherlands	SP	Spain
AU	Australia	GE	Germany	NO	Norway	SD	Sweden
BE	Belgium	GR	Greece	NZ	New Zealand	SW	Switzerland
CA	Canada	HK	Hong Kong	PA	Panama	TA	Taiwan
CH	Chile	HU	Hungary	PH	Philippines	TH	Thailand
CO	Columbia	IR	Ireland	PL	Poland	UK	United Kingdom
CZ	Czechoslovakia	IS	Israel	PO	Portugal	U.S.	U.S.A.
ES	El Salvador	IT	Italy	PR	Puerto Rico	VE	Venezuela
DE	Denmark	JA	Japan	RO	Romania	YU	Yugoslavia
FI	Finland	ME	Mexico	SL	Sri Lanka		

Data from: B. S. Reddy et. al., "Nutrition and Its Relationship to Cancer," Advances in Cancer Research 32 (1980): 237–345.

THE LINEAR RELATIONSHIP BETWEEN FAT CONSUMPTION AND THE INCIDENCE OF COLON CANCER

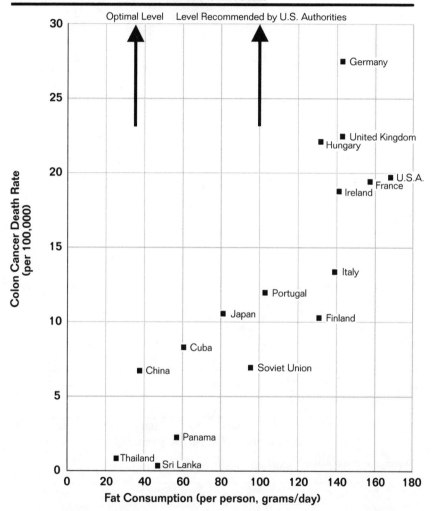

The strong linear relationship between fat consumption and the incidence of colon cancer is remarkably similar to that for breast cancer.

Data from: World Health Organization, Statistics Annual, 1982, 1988, 1989. Food and Agricultural Organization, Food Balance Sheets, 1979–81.

THE LINEAR RELATIONSHIP BETWEEN FAT CONSUMPTION AND THE INCIDENCE OF PROSTATE CANCER

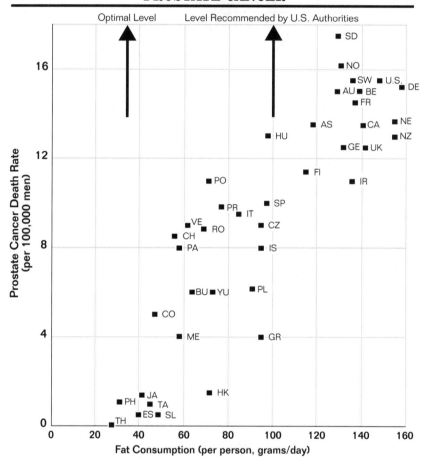

Again, the same relationship between fat and cancer.

AS	Austria	**FI**	Finland	**ME**	Mexico	**SL**	Sri Lanka
AU	Australia	**FR**	France	**NE**	Netherlands	**SP**	Spain
BE	Belgium	**GE**	Germany	**NO**	Norway	**SD**	Sweden
BU	Bulgaria	**GR**	Greece	**NZ**	New Zealand	**SW**	Switzerland
CA	Canada	**HK**	Hong Kong	**PA**	Panama	**TA**	Taiwan
CH	Chile	**HU**	Hungary	**PH**	Philippines	**TH**	Thailand
CO	Columbia	**IR**	Ireland	**PL**	Poland	**UK**	United Kingdom
CZ	Czechoslovakia	**IS**	Israel	**PO**	Portugal	**U.S.**	U.S.A.
ES	El Salvador	**IT**	Italy	**PR**	Puerto Rico	**VE**	Venezuela
DE	Denmark	**JA**	Japan	**RO**	Romania	**YU**	Yugoslavia

Data from: B. S. Reddy et. al., "Nutrition and Its Relationship to Cancer," <u>Advances in Cancer Research</u> 32 (1980): 237–345.

With regard to colon cancer, a high-fat diet creates a hospitable environment for anaerobic (literally, "living without oxygen") bacteria in the large intestine. These bacteria are good at converting bile acids from the intestinal tract into such potent cocarcinogens as deoxycholic and lithocholic acids as well as estrogenlike breast carcinogens.[3] Conversely, a low-fat diet creates an inhospitable environment for anaerobic bacteria and instead encourages aerobic ("with oxygen") bacteria that do not produce cancer-causing chemicals and have other benefits. A collaborative study conducted in the United States, Canada, and China found that consumption of saturated fats in meat and dairy products was linked to a four-to-seven-times-higher rate of colon cancer among Chinese-Americans than among their counterparts in China.[4]

The high-fiber content typical of most low-fat diets reduces the transit time through the intestines. This also inhibits the creation of carcinogens.[5] The high-fat, low-fiber American diet is particularly conducive to the development of colon cancer, the second most common cancer in the United States. In comparison, the Finns, who eat a high-fat but high-fiber diet, have a high rate of coronary heart disease but a low rate of colon cancer.[6]

In a study of Italian women, conducted by Dr. Paolo Toniolo of New York University Medical Center, it was found that those eating a 26-percent-calories-from-fat diet had one-third the incidence of breast cancer as those eating a diet of 40 to 50 percent calories from fat.[7] Because few women in the study ate a diet lower than 26 percent calories from fat, the study did not examine lower levels. Other studies, however, have shown that the incidence of breast (and other) cancer for women who eat a diet that is 20 percent calories from fat is again significantly lower than women who eat 26 percent calories from fat. Other population studies show that the trend continues on down to 10 percent, where the incidence of these cancers is virtually nil. Extensive animal studies have shown the same findings. In addition to inhibiting the crucial promotion phase of cancer, a low-fat diet boosts the immune system, which helps to combat cancer as well as other diseases.

Lung cancer is primarily a result of smoking, isn't that right?

Only in part. A dramatic indication of the impact of fat in the diet on cancer risk can be seen in the rate of lung cancer in Japan. Smoking is extremely prevalent in Japanese society, far more so than in American society. Two out of three Japanese men smoke (compared to one out of three American men), yet the rate of lung cancer in Japan is the *lowest* in the industrialized world![8] This is a result of the low level of fat in the Japanese diet. Heart disease is also very low in Japan, despite the high rate of smoking. Interestingly, vegetarian smokers in the United States also have lower rates of lung cancer.[9]

So you can smoke if you eat a low-fat, that is, 10-percent-calories-from-fat, diet?

No, not at all. The very high level of tobacco usage in Japan does contribute significantly to the health problems that do exist there, most notably their high rate of hypertension. This condition, which is caused by the high levels of both salt in the diet and smoking, leads to intracerebral hemorrhage, a form of stroke and a major cause of death in Japan. There are other serious health problems, such as emphysema, which are related to smoking in the Japanese people. But the low incidence of lung cancer and heart disease in societies that smoke but eat a very low fat diet is just another piece of evidence of the powerful beneficial effects of reducing fat in the diet.

Are there cancer studies that looked specifically at Americans?

Yes, a particularly interesting study, conducted at Harvard University's School of Public Health and reported in the January 1992 issue of the *Journal of the National Cancer Institute*, studied more than 7,000 male health professionals since the mid-1980s.[10] It found that the men who ate the highest proportion of low-fat and high-fiber foods were 3.6 times less likely to develop precancerous colon polyp growths, as compared to men who ate a high-fat, low-fiber diet. It also reported that the men who ate red meat on a regular basis instead of chicken and fish had an 80 percent greater risk of developing polyps. An editorial accompanying the report suggested that high-fat, low-fiber foods may damage genes that are responsible for preventing the uncontrolled growth (i.e., cancer) of the colon and rectum cells.

The Low-Cholesterol Controversy

I have heard that while high blood cholesterol levels are bad, that very low levels are also bad.

There have been reports in the news media of correlations between low levels of blood cholesterol and the incidence of certain diseases, including certain cancers, alcoholism, and even suicide.

However, these reports totally mix up cause and effect. High blood cholesterol levels do cause significantly increased rates of atherosclerosis, which is the cause of almost all heart disease. But low blood cholesterol levels, on the other hand, do not *cause* cancer or alcoholism. The opposite is the case—certain cancers, such as colon cancer, can cause low blood cholesterol levels. This often occurs at a very early stage of the cancer, even years prior to diagnosis.[11] It seems that the cancer cells are voracious consumers of cholesterol in the blood and effectively cleanse the blood of cholesterol.[12]

How do we know that it is the cancer causing the low cholesterol level and not the other way around?

The direction of the causality is clear from examining both population studies and cancer studies and is well accepted by cancer specialists. Consistently, societies that eat diets very low in fat have very low cholesterol levels. And, equally consistently, these societies have extremely low rates of both heart disease *and cancer.* The same result is found for Americans who eat very low fat diets. The typical pattern that is found for persons in the United States who do develop certain cancers, such as colon cancer, is that the person was eating the "normal" American diet (i.e., high in fat and low in fiber) and had a *high* serum cholesterol level. Then only as the preclinical cancer developed did their cholesterol levels decline.

So cancer of the colon is a cure for heart disease?

It does appear to be an effective way to slow down or even halt atherosclerosis. The cancer can dramatically lower cholesterol levels, and if the patient lives long enough may cause a regression of the atherosclerotic plaque. But this is not the way you want to ameliorate your atherosclerosis, by replacing one life-threatening disease with another. A diet low in fat and cholesterol will dramatically lower the risk of *both* heart disease and cancer.

So these people who have very low blood cholesterol levels and get cancer were eating high-fat, as opposed to low-fat, diets?

That's exactly right. If someone is eating the "normal" American diet (i.e., high in fat) and has a very low cholesterol level (150 or less), then that might be an indication of a developing cancer; one that may not be diagnosed for several years.

If the person has always had a low cholesterol level, then it could just be "tolerant" genes. A pattern that might cause concern would be high blood cholesterol levels that fell significantly for no apparent reason, that is without the person having changed their diet. Indeed, that is the pattern we see in those individuals that have low cholesterol levels and develop cancer. You have to keep in mind that this is an odd group: people who are eating high-fat diets and then develop low cholesterol levels without altering their eating patterns.

Another unhealthy cause of low cholesterol levels is alcoholism.

You mean that excessive consumption of alcohol can also improve one's cholesterol levels?

Yes, alcohol damages the liver which is responsible for regulating blood cholesterol levels. The impact of damaging one's liver is unpredictable, but in certain individuals it appears to result in very low levels of cholesterol in the blood. Note, that among its many negative consequences, alcoholism is associated with high levels of violence including suicide. Cancer is also associated with higher levels of suicide. But in both these cases, low blood cholesterol is the result of these diseases, not the other way around.

Has there also been something about a link between very low blood cholesterol and stroke?

There have also been reports of an association between very low blood cholesterol levels and intracranial hemorrhage, a form of stroke. People with very low blood cholesterol levels have a small increased risk of intracranial hemorrhage only in the presence of very high blood pressure (hypertension). This has been noted in societies that eat extremely high levels of sodium such as Japan.

Following the guidelines of the 10% solution (which includes low-fat consumption, moderation of sodium intake and exercise) is very effective in *lowering* blood pressure levels. There is no increased incidence of intracranial hemorrhage in individuals (or societies) that have very low blood cholesterol levels and *normal (or low)* blood pressure. In fact, we see the opposite: dramatically *reduced* levels of stroke, particularly the forms of stroke caused by atherosclerosis, which are dominant in this country.

In societies that eat diets that are low in both fat and sodium, such as many of the counties of China, we find that the individuals have lifelong low blood pressure levels, and have extremely low rates of all forms of stroke.

What about polyunsaturated fat—isn't that better than saturated fat?

Polyunsaturated Fat

Another major issue in the relationship between fat and cancer is the role of polyunsaturated fats. Polyunsaturated fats are often promoted as "good" fats, and that represents another important misconception. The conception of polyunsaturated fat as good, or perhaps benign, stems from the observation that people who substitute polyunsaturated fat for saturated fat lower their total serum cholesterol levels. Thus, it is said that polyunsaturated fat "lowers" cholesterol. This point is heavily promoted in advertisements for corn oil and other products that are high in this type of fat. In actuality, polyunsaturated fat *raises* serum cholesterol levels; it just does this less than saturated fat does. Consequently, substituting polyunsaturated fat for saturated fat will cause cholesterol levels to go down somewhat, but not nearly as much as cutting out both types of fat.

Okay, so polyunsaturated fat is not good, per se, but if it does indeed raise cholesterol levels less than saturated fat, it would seem at least a step in the right direction to use polyunsaturated fat rather than saturated fat.

Not exactly. The effect on total cholesterol level is only a small part of the story of polyunsaturated fat. In this one regard, polyunsaturated fat is somewhat "less bad" than saturated fat. But in a number of other aspects, it is actually worse. First of all, polyunsaturated fat causes a significant reduction in the level of HDL, the good cholesterol, in the blood.[13] Saturated fat also does this to some extent, but polyunsaturated fat is substantially worse than saturated fat in this regard. Thus, while substituting polyunsaturated fat for saturated fat does cause some reduction in the total level of cholesterol in the blood, some of this is a reduction in the good cholesterol. Therefore, the ratio of total serum cholesterol to HDL, which, as I mentioned, is a key predictor of heart disease risk, does not necessarily improve at all. Now, if we regard saturated fat as being devastating to one's health, which is correct in my view, and if polyunsaturated fat causes a ratio of cholesterol to HDL that is not significantly better, then on these grounds alone, we can consider that eating polyunsaturated fat is also devastating.

A seven-year study conducted by Dr. David H. Blankenhorn at the

THE RISE IN BREAST CANCER: WHY?

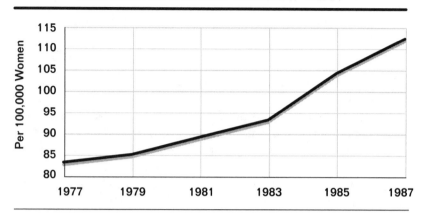

A major factor in the increase in breast cancer over the past ten years may be the increasing use of so-called heart-healthy oils, which are composed primarily of polyunsaturated fat (PUFA). PUFA is strongly linked to promoting cancer during the crucial growth and progression phases. PUFA accelerates cancer growth even more than saturated fat. Its "beneficial" impact on heart disease is also dubious: While it does cause less increase in total cholesterol levels than saturated fat (and thus replacing saturated fat with PUFA does result in a reduction in total serum cholesterol), much of the observed decrease results from lower levels of HDL, the "good" cholesterol.

Data from: National Cancer Institute.

Atherosclerosis Research Institute of the University of Southern California School of Medicine in Los Angeles, and published in the *Journal of the American Medical Association*, found that the more polyunsaturated fats were consumed by a group of middle-age men who had undergone coronary bypass surgery, the greater was their risk of developing new lesions in their arteries. Conversely, reducing all fats, including polyunsaturated fats, was found to provide significant protection against heart disease.[14]

But there's more. While saturated fat is a significant contributing factor to the development of cancer, polyunsaturated fat is actually worse.[15] This is widely recognized by cancer specialists and is one reason that the fat guidelines that are promulgated restrict the level of polyunsaturated fat. Polyunsaturated fat also appears to suppress the immune system more than saturated fat.[16]

Are there short-term impacts of eating fat?

Blood Sludging

Fat causes blood cell aggregation or blood sludging. Within hours of eating a meal with a significant fat content, red blood cells begin to stick to one another, making it impossible for them to pass through the smaller capillaries that provide oxygen to the body's tissues.[17] If you eat a meal that is high in fat, you will temporarily deprive your brain of significant oxygen, which is one reason that people often feel groggy after eating a meal rich in fat.[18]

The difference between saturated and polyunsaturated fat in this regard is that the declogging of the capillaries appears to take significantly longer with polyunsaturated fat.[19] Thus, it is quite possible when eating a daily diet high in polyunsaturated fat to have a semipermanent condition of clogged capillaries. This clogging is a different mechanism than the clogging of our arteries. It is caused by blood cell aggregation rather than formation of cholesterol-rich plaque deposits, but the effects are also quite negative on our health.

It sounds as if polyunsaturated fat is as bad as saturated fat.

Wait, there's more. Polyunsaturated fats are also known to interact with oxygen to form free-radicals (powerful molecules that can damage cell membranes), which are associated with premature aging and the development of cancer.[20] They are also associated with the formation of gallstones.[21] Recent studies have also shown that margarine (which is high in polyunsaturated fat) actually raises LDL levels the same way saturated fat does, because of the hydrogenation process (a chemical process that converts liquid fats to solid fats).[22] Hydrogenation causes naturally occurring cis–fatty-acids to be converted to trans–fatty-acids, which have been indicted in raising LDL levels and lowering HDL (the good cholesterol) levels and have caused cancer in animal studies. There are no human societies that have anything approaching a good record of health while eating a diet that is high in polyunsaturated fat.

With all of these effects, I find the ads for products high in polyunsaturated fat both misleading and disturbing. Corn oil, which is very high in polyunsaturated fat, is far from a benign substance. The widely promoted fact that it is "low in saturated fat" and "has no cholesterol at all" does not change the fact that its high–polyunsaturated-fat content is in at least some ways *worse* than saturated fat. Yet people are under the impression that they are eating more healthily by choosing products with polyunsaturated fat.

So no fat is really good for you, then.

Monounsaturated Fat and Omega-3 Fat

There are two fats that are better than either saturated fat or polyunsaturated fat. Monounsaturated fat, which is the primary fat in olive oil, for example, also raises cholesterol levels less than saturated fat. So substituting it for saturated fat does bring down total serum cholesterol levels. Unlike polyunsaturated fat, however, it does not suppress HDL levels, so total cholesterol-to-HDL ratios do improve.[23] It is definitely not as good as cutting out added fats altogether, but it is indeed a "less bad" fat. It also does not clog capillaries as badly as polyunsaturated fat. The term *polyunsaturated* comes from the fact that in polyunsaturated fat there are many unsaturated links in the long fat chains. This often does not occur naturally in food, but can be the result of the manufacturing process used to make these oils. Monounsaturated fat means there is a single unsaturated link in the fatty acid chain. This is the fat that occurs naturally in such foods as olives and avocados. If olive oil is made simply by squeezing the olives, then the product is high in these monounsaturated fat molecules. Not being bound together in these long chains, it is more easily digested and does not cause as much blood cell aggregation. It is also not implicated as much in the promotion phase of cancer.

For these reasons, the southern Europeans, who use a lot of extra virgin (i.e., first-pressed and unrefined) olive oil, rather than corn oil or saturated animal fats, do have significantly lower rates of heart disease and cancer than people in the United States or other parts of Europe. But their rates are not nearly as low as Asian societies that restrict all forms of added oils and fats.

As I discussed before, the special type of fat in certain fish, called omega-3, appears to have beneficial properties in most—but, unfortunately, not all—people. For many people, it is indeed a "good fat," but only in limited quantities.

Are cancer rates low in Japan?

Breast, colon, and prostate cancers, all of which are at high rates in the United States, are very low in Japan, although rates have increased since World War II as a result of the rising level of fat in the diet. The one cancer that is prevalent in Japan—stomach cancer—is linked to two aspects of the Japanese diet that are not healthy and that do not follow the recommendations of the 10% solution. First of all, their extremely high salt level—even higher than the excessive sodium level of the American diet—appears to contribute to stomach cancer. The Japanese consume a lot of salt in soy sauce and preserved foods, which not only contain high concentrations of sodium but nitrates and nitrites, which are also linked to stomach cancer. Furthermore, the Japanese eat a great deal of dried, salted fish, smoked fish, pickled vegetables, and charcoal-cooked foods, all of which have been found to have a significant correlation with stomach cancer.[24] In other societies in which people eat a diet low in fat and sodium and do not smoke, charcoal-broil, or extensively pickle their foods (such as rural counties of China), stomach cancer is virtually nonexistent, as are these other cancers.

Any other diseases on your list?

Hypertension

The next issue is hypertension, that is, high blood pressure. Both people in our society who follow the dietary recommendations we have been discussing and whole societies that follow them rarely have hypertension. In fact, following this life-style is the best possible treatment for hypertension. Many of the drugs that are prescribed are very dubious in their effectiveness. They do reduce the measured blood pressure levels, but do not affect the underlying conditions that caused the hypertension in the first place. Diuretics, for example, have actually been found to increase the risk of heart disease when compared to no treatment at all for hypertension![25] Since one of the main reasons for treating hypertension is that high blood pressure is a significant additional risk factor for the development of heart disease, this is a disturbing finding. The MR FIT study, which followed 13,000 men, found that after 7 years, men on hypertension drugs, particularly diuretics, had a substantially higher level of electrocardiogram abnormalities and had a death rate 50 percent higher than expected.[26] The thiazide-type diuretics have also been found to increase cholesterol levels, increase glucose levels, and increase triglyceride levels, all of which are implicated in the risk for development of atherosclerosis. They also increase uric acid levels, which can cause gout and other problems.[27] Many hypertensive drugs also have significant side effects that reduce the quality of life and sense of well-being. For example, diuretics have been found to decrease potassium levels, which can make you tired, cause cramps in the legs, cause heart arrhythmias, and increase the likelihood of cardiovascular mortality. Increased levels of impotency have also been found with the diuretic drugs. Beta blockers, another class of hypertensive drugs, have been found to decrease levels of HDL (the good cholesterol), increase levels of glucose, and have been linked to an increased incidence of impotence. Doctors frequently complain that their patients fail to take their hypertension medicine. The reason for this is not that these patients are lazy or inattentive. It is not simply a matter of finding it too much trouble to take a pill. The resistance has more to do with the fact that very often a patient's body knows better than anyone else what is best for it.[28]

In our society and other societies that eat a similar diet, it is considered "normal" for a person's blood pressure to rise with age, but this does not occur in societies that avoid our high-fat, high-salt diet. In societies that eat a low-fat *and low-sodium* diet, such as the peoples of New Guinea and Botswana and the Yanomamo of Brazil and Venezuela, blood pressure stays at the same low rate throughout life.[29] Other examples include unacculturated populations of the Pacific islands, Central and South America, Africa, and Australia.[30] It is not the case that blood pressure must necessarily increase with age. One of the reasons for the increasing level of blood pressure with age in our society is that increasing levels of arterial plaque result in increasing resistance to blood flow.

High blood pressure is a common medical problem of Japanese people because of the extremely high level of sodium in their diet. But despite their hypertension, Japanese people have low rates of heart disease because of the low fat level of their diet. However, their high blood pressure levels contribute to another medical problem, that of intracerebral hemorrhage, a form of stroke caused by the high blood pressure itself, even in the absence of atherosclerosis.[31] (This is different from the thrombotic and embolic forms of stroke, which are common in the United States.) The pressure simply causes a blood vessel to rupture, and the hemorrhage of blood into the brain can cause massive damage. This type of stroke is one of the leading causes of death in Japan and is also common in this country. A low-fat, *low-sodium* diet prevents hypertension and *all* forms of stroke.

Okay, what's next?

Type II Diabetes

Another major issue is type II diabetes, which is an inability to properly control blood glucose or sugar levels. Type I diabetes, formerly called juvenile-onset diabetes because it primarily strikes during childhood, is caused by the failure of an abnormal pancreas to produce a sufficient quantity of insulin (a hormone, secreted by the pancreas, that controls the level of glucose in the blood).[32] Failure to control blood glucose at near normal levels can result in multiple organ damage and even death, and until the availability of insulin earlier this century, the life expectancy of children with diabetes was limited. Type II diabetes, previously called adult-onset diabetes because it usually develops after the age of 40, has a completely different origin. It is caused by the inability of the cells to properly utilize insulin for the metabolism of glucose; the cells become relatively insensitive to the insulin that is in plentiful supply in the bloodstream.[33] In fact, the insulin levels of a type II diabetic are often higher than that of nondiabetics.[34] In particular, individuals with glucose intolerance, considered an early form of type II diabetes, typically have insulin levels several times the normal level.

The early symptoms of type II diabetes can be subtle—frequent urination and thirst, for example—and are often overlooked. The long-term complications can be severe. Diabetes is a significant independent risk factor for the development of coronary heart disease and can lead to other complications such as visual impairment and kidney damage.[35] Treatment is generally either insulin injections, similar to the treatment for the type I diabetic, or oral medications to control blood glucose levels.

Yet there is a treatment, generally overlooked, that allows most individuals with type II diabetes to respond far more effectively than they do to either injections or medications. Indeed, in many individuals, this approach appears to significantly reduce or eliminate all symptoms or indications of diabetes. The treatment is, again, the 10% solution. The most important aspect of this treatment is limiting fat to 10 percent of calories. Eating a low-fat diet will significantly improve the body's ability to utilize insulin to control blood sugar levels naturally. Limiting the consumption of simple sugars is also worthwhile so as not to overly tax the body's ability to process sugar.

The bulk of the recommended diet consists of complex carbohydrates. While complex carbohydrates are converted to sugar in the body, this process is a gradual one and, thus, sugar and insulin peaks are avoided.

In several studies of type II diabetics who undertook a four-week course in life-style adjustment that emphasized the type of diet and exercise described here, most individuals were able to terminate their usage of diabetes medication while achieving normal blood glucose levels. These studies, conducted at the Pritikin Longevity Centers, which incidentally are noted for having pioneered this dietary and life-style approach to treating and averting disease, included a three-year follow-up study. This study indicated that those diabetics who continued to adhere to the guidelines—which was an encouraging 50 percent of the original sample of subjects—were able to control their blood glucose levels *without medication*. Those that reverted to the "normal" American life-style also returned to dependence on medication because of high blood sugars and the return of multiple features of diabetes.[36]

Well, what's wrong with dependence on medication? Isn't that easier than the type of life-style modification you're advocating?

That's a very good question, actually. I'm definitely not antimedication in general. There are many conditions for which medications are quite literally lifesavers or help an individual avoid great suffering. On the other hand, it is often the case that the available medications are not as effective as we would like, or they have undesirable side effects. These issues are of particular concern when talking about medications that must be taken for a lifetime.

Consider type II diabetes. Research by Dr. George King at the Joslin Diabetes Center in Boston and other researchers has discovered that one of the causes of increased atherosclerosis in type II diabetics is not the glucose imbalance at all, but rather the increased level of insulin. Insulin is a growth promoter and speeds up the atherosclerotic process. While the sugar imbalance, itself, does cause other problems, the mechanism underlying the worst effect of diabetes, the accelerated onset of coronary heart disease, appears to be caused by the greatly increased levels of insulin in the blood.[37] The pancreas of the type II diabetic is essentially pouring out large amounts of insulin to try to overcome the resistance of the cells in using the insulin. Thus, the use of insulin injections to further increase the level of insulin would appear to be counterproductive in this regard. If administered in high enough doses, it can bring down the glucose level in the blood, but, obviously, it also further increases the insulin level. It reminds me of the recent findings on some of the hypertensive medicines: they do indeed bring down the measured levels of blood pressure, but actually make coronary heart disease risk higher than no treatment at all.

Well, what about those noninsulin medications?

While they are not increasing insulin levels, they also are not bringing down the levels of insulin, which, as I mentioned, can be substantially higher than normal. They also have side effects and can reduce the quality of life and the sense of well-being, which is also a factor in some of the hypertension medicines.

So why isn't the dietary approach more widely prescribed?

It is followed to some extent in some places. For example, the Joslin Center of the Joslin Diabetes Foundation has been a pioneer in the use of dietary treatment of diabetes, following a tradition set by Dr. Elliott P. Joslin, himself, around the turn of the century, when he treated type I diabetics with a low-calorie diet. While Elliott Joslin's diet was not specifically low fat, its very low calorie level (under 800 calories per day) did have the effect of reducing fat grams. This reduction in both calories and fat grams made whatever level of insulin these children did have more effective and significantly extended their lives. Today, doctors at the Joslin Center recommend a 20-percent-calories-from-fat diet (for patients with type II diabetes and elevated cholesterol levels), which is an important step in the right direction, although the evidence strongly suggests that even greater results could be achieved by adopting a 10-percent-calories-from-fat diet.

A doctor at the Joslin Center has described to me some of the challenges in using a dietary treatment. Dietary counseling is generally not recognized as a medical treatment and, thus, is usually not reimbursed by medical insurance and other third-party providers of medical funds. Yet, it is often not effective to simply give someone a pamphlet and say, "Cut your fat intake to 10 percent of calories"—or even 20 percent.

If a pamphlet doesn't work, maybe this book will.

Let's hope that's the case. That is why I wrote it.

It is interesting to note that the approach to nutrition for treatment of diabetes has changed direction 180 degrees over the last several decades. Since diabetes is primarily known as an inability to digest sugar, it was originally felt that people should, therefore, avoid sugar. In addition to sugar, it was recommended that people should avoid complex carbohydrates as well, since complex carbohydrates are composed of complicated arrangements of simple sugar molecules. That leaves only protein and fat as sources of nutrition. We now understand that fat is a primary causative agent for type II diabetes. In the susceptible individual, high fat levels in the diet and in the blood cause the insulin receptors on the cells to become relatively insensitive to insulin. In most type II diabetics, a low-fat diet, along with elimination of excess weight, restores the sensitivity to insulin and eliminates the metabolism profile associated with diabetes. With relatively normal glucose metabolism restored, insulin levels come down as well. So the 1950s diet for diabetics was the perfect diet to make their diabetes as bad as possible.

Any other conditions worth mentioning?

Another form of glucose imbalance, called hypoglycemia, refers to blood glucose levels that are too low. This situation results in feelings of anxiety, ravenous appetite, and other, both short- and long-term, symptoms. Hypoglycemia also appears to be easily controlled by adopting the 10% solution, generally within a couple of weeks of dietary modification.

You haven't mentioned protein. Isn't it important to get enough protein in your diet?

Protein

Another misconception is that it is important to get "enough protein," and the label "high in protein" is often used on products as if that were a good thing. Protein insufficiency is almost unheard of in developed societies. In fact, even in undeveloped societies, the major dietary problem is not usually related to getting sufficient protein, but to getting sufficient calories.[38] Protein insufficiency in the absence of calorie insufficiency is rare anywhere in the world.

In fact, the American diet often contains about twice as much protein as is needed, and this high level is not benign.[39] An excess of protein in the diet leads to high levels of urea, which acts as a diuretic, depleting the body of important minerals such as calcium. This is a significant contributing factor to the development of osteoporosis and other conditions.[40]

Evidence strongly suggests that several forms of arthritis (particularly gouty arthritis) are also linked to the high levels of both fat and protein in the diet.[41] There are also links to gallstones, gout, glaucoma, cataracts, and other forms of hearing and vision impairment.[42] For example, cholesterol deposits can clog the blood vessels in the connective tissue between the small hearing bones, thus causing hearing loss.

That's quite an indictment.

It is as if we were running our engine on the wrong fuel. It's not going to run as well. In time, the engine will break down. Our genetic inheritance determines just how it will break down and when. Some of us are more impervious than others to the effects of the poisonous diet that our society eats.

In the case of atherosclerosis and the development of coronary heart disease, there are blood measurements that one can take, primarily of the total serum cholesterol and HDL levels, that provide a reasonable estimate of risk for that disease. This risk level is compounded further by other life-style and health indicators, such as smoking, diabetes, hypertension, and so on. But just because you have good levels of cholesterol and HDL does not mean you have a low risk of developing the other degenerative diseases caused by the civilized diet. For example, women tend to have high levels of HDL prior to menopause, and this provides a certain level of protection from heart disease during this period of time.[43] However, high levels of HDL are connected to high levels of estrogen, which appear to be linked to a high risk of breast, endometrial, and ovarian cancer.[44] The 10% solution provides protection from both heart disease and these cancers, so I feel it is a mistake to reject a healthy diet just because one's cholesterol levels are in the low-risk range.

You've mentioned diet and exercise and avoiding smoking. But what about stress? I hear a lot about that.

Stress

Stress plays a complex role and certainly can contribute to disease, particularly coronary heart disease, once the process of atherosclerosis is established. There is evidence that once atherosclerosis progresses to a certain stage, the activation of a syndrome called "fight or flight," which is the hallmark of stressful situations, can cause greater inflammation in the arteries and accelerate the process of atherosclerotic plaque formation.[45] It also can cause increased platelet clumping and vasoconstriction (narrowing of blood vessels) and, thus, induce the development of a blood clot, thereby causing the coup de grace of a heart attack, stroke, or other such incident.[46] There is also evidence that chronic stress can suppress the immune system, which is crucial in fighting cancer and other diseases.[47]

We will talk more about stress in chapter 8, "The Mind-Body Connection," because the kind of stress that is damaging is not necessarily the type that causes us to respond to a challenge we find meaningful, but rather the chronic kind that causes us to fight against ourselves. Note that the rate of heart attacks did not go up in Europe or the United States during the enormously stressful period of World War II. As I mentioned, the only change noticed was the dramatic drop in heart attacks in the rationing countries during the period of rationing.

Basically, if you build a strong foundation by eating the right diet and by exercising, you can withstand more stress, although, again, we have to distinguish between an unhealthy stress and an energizing challenge. For people who have developed atherosclerosis to the point where they have angina pain, then management of stress becomes very important in that they want to avoid both the angina pain and the potential for a heart attack. Stress produces adrenaline, which causes blood flow constriction and can trigger a heart attack. Thus, for such individuals, modifying one's life to avoid stress is as important as the other dietary and life-style recommendations.

Suppose I like my diet and life-style the way it is. If I die a few years early, so be it.

You have just articulated a very common attitude. I have three reactions to this point of view. First, the impact is often more than "a few years." Atherosclerosis and the heart attacks and strokes that result, plus the various forms of cancer that are among the degenerative diseases caused by the civilized diet, are the primary causes of *premature* death. We are often talking about decades lost, not a few years. Right now, a third of all Americans die in middle age (40 to 65). Almost all of these deaths are the result of atherosclerosis, stroke, or cancer, all degenerative diseases caused principally by a high-fat or high-salt diet and all largely avoidable through the dietary and life-style recommendations we have been discussing.

Second, don't count on dying.

Come again?

People imagine that the diseases caused by their high-fat diets and other negative life-style factors will simply reduce their life expectancy by a few years, and that's the end of it, so to speak. Now it's true that the first symptom of atherosclerosis is often sudden death. But more often we're talking about many years of gradual debilitation and suffering.

You sound like a fun guy.

What do you mean?

All this talk about dying and suffering. I mean, you can't go around worrying about this stuff all the time.

Okay, I'll grant you that these topics are not the most enjoyable things to talk about. But that brings me to my third reaction, which has to do with the *immediate* benefits of the 10% solution. We'll talk in more detail about that in a moment, but suffice it to say you will feel better immediately in a number of important ways.

Perhaps, but it still doesn't sound like fun. You know, people like to let loose and have a good time now and again.

Did I say you couldn't have a good time?

I'm not sure.

Do you have to eat fat to have fun?

Well, I do like to eat sweets occasionally.

You can still eat sweets, although not the ones you're currently used to. You'll have to take my word for it, at least for a little while, but this diet is a lot more enjoyable and diverse than it may appear at first. An important phenomenon is the profound change that actually takes place in your own tastes and preferences. You need to keep an open mind about this. The experience is likely to be different than you expect.

People sometimes act like I was suggesting that they give up sex. But sex is a natural desire.

So is eating.

Yes, the desire for food is natural. But the desire for high-fat, high-sodium foods is not. That desire is learned. And you can unlearn it.

Given your own dramatic improvement, why shouldn't everyone wait until they hit, say, 40, and then make the switch to the 10% solution?

You *do* cause permanent damage to your body the longer you eat the "civilized" way. The sooner you stop consuming toxic levels of fat and adopt a healthy diet and life-style, the greater the likelihood of avoiding heart disease, cancer, and other problems. Symptoms of aging, such as wrinkling of the skin, are greatly ameliorated. It also feels a lot better to be at your optimal weight.

Weight Loss

This is all very interesting, but I have to admit that the opportunity to drop some of these excess pounds would be particularly motivating. I'm not all that overweight, but I have been trying for more years than I can remember to get closer to my ideal weight.

Interesting you should say that, because high on the list of undesirable conditions caused by the high-fat, high-protein, high-cholesterol diet and frequently sedentary life-style that our society follows is varying degrees of obesity. Look around you and you will see an epidemic of obesity. In societies with a low-fat diet, such as Japan, there is virtually no obesity. In the United States, many people are overweight and a significant fraction of them are endangering their health in the process. Being 20 percent or more over your ideal weight is a significant added risk factor for heart disease, diabetes, and other illnesses. It is also, frankly, unpleasant to carry around all that extra baggage.

It doesn't look great to be overweight either.

It's useful to have vanity on the side of good health. This one factor is probably more motivating than everything else we have discussed.

All right, so what miracle weight-loss program do you have for me?

I have a "miracle" weight-loss program that immediately enables you to start losing weight *slowly* and *gradually*, a weight-loss program that requires you to make major changes in your eating habits and that requires you to maintain these changes long after the weight loss is completed.

Remind me not to have you write my advertising copy.

Okay, maybe the above does not make a good advertisement. But here is the good news. The diet is enjoyable. Unlike most other diets, you do not feel deprived. You will never feel hungry. Perhaps most important, it works.

There are other diets where people take off weight.

True, but do they keep it off? For most diet programs, more than 90 percent of the dieters put back the weight lost within a year.[48] With this program, you will take the weight off and never put it back.

Sure, if you keep on dieting forever, you can keep the weight off forever. What's the big deal with that?

The problem, perhaps, has to do with the word *diet*. The word implies a temporary period of deprivation in which you discipline yourself to gain some benefit, generally weight loss. The period is necessarily temporary because it is impossible to deprive oneself indefinitely. The word *diet* also refers to the normal eating patterns of a person or society. In this context, I am using the word in the second sense, although the association with the first meaning is never quite lost.

You're confusing me now.

My point is that the only way to take weight off and keep it off is by permanently changing your eating habits to a healthy pattern of eating.

And that, I suppose, means the 10% solution.

Yes, indeed. It is relatively easy to lose weight by following the guidelines of the 10% solution, and, assuming you maintain this lifestyle, relatively difficult to put the weight back on. Weight will come off gradually and naturally and you will gravitate toward a healthier weight.

So all you have to do is follow the guidelines of the 10% solution?

That's the most important thing, but there are some other considerations as well if you are going to lose weight. You will need to moderate your calorie intake to some extent. You will find, however, that you can eat a rather large quantity of food and still lose weight with this approach.

I'm sure you can eat a lot of lettuce and still lose weight.

True, lettuce has almost no calories at all. But I lost about two pounds a week, 40 pounds in all, while eating over 2,000 calories a day. And with low-fat foods, you can eat a large quantity for 2,000 calories. I never felt hungry or deprived. And I ate very little lettuce.

This is basically a calorie-controlled diet. And since the food is so low in fat, it tends to be low calorie, isn't that right?

It is true that you are losing weight by controlling calorie intake combined with exercise. It is also true that by avoiding excessive fat you are avoiding the largest source of calories. Fat has more than twice the calorie content per gram as carbohydrates or protein. But these are not the most important factors. Studies examining different groups of people eating the *same* number of calories but varying percentages of fat found that the groups eating a lower percentage of calories from fat lost significantly more weight.[49] Fat not only has more than twice the calories per gram, it is metabolized differently. Carbohydrates are stored in the body as glycogen and are more likely to be burned for fuel, whereas fat is much more likely to end up as, well, fat. The fat content of our diets is a major factor in controlling our set-point, which is the weight that our body tries to maintain.[50]

It sounds like more of a discipline, not less. With calorie-controlled diets, you only need to watch your calories. With the 10% solution, there are all these other guidelines as well.

Yes, there are more guidelines, but in an important way, they require less discipline, or at least involve less deprivation. If you simply control calories, you end up eating a rather small quantity of food. Also, there are some vicious cycles in the normal eating pattern that make discipline very difficult. The typical high-fat, high-sugar desserts often lead to a surge of insulin in the blood, which in turn leads to low blood sugar, which in turn leads to cravings for more sweets. In contrast, the low-caloric density and high-fiber content of complex carbohydrates enable you to eat a relatively large quantity of food and to feel full and satisfied while consuming a limited number of calories.

Your diet is high in complex carbohydrates. Those are sugar, too, aren't they?

Complex carbohydrates are composed of long chains of sugar molecules. They are broken down into sugars in the blood, but are digested slowly and, thus, do not stimulate the sudden high level of insulin that simple sugars do. The high level of fat in the "normal" diet also tends to interfere with glucose metabolism and is a primary factor, as I mentioned earlier, in type II diabetes and hypoglycemia.

Okay, but let's get back to discipline. Explain to me how this is not a huge discipline.

It certainly requires some discipline to start out. Your mission here is not a temporary diet, but something more profound: a permanent change in eating habits and attitudes. It requires a serious level of discipline for the first month, then less for the second, and so on. People who approach it with a serious commitment find it a lot easier than they expect. And something happens that most people don't expect: your tastes change. When you first start drinking skim milk or using it on your cereal, it tastes like water. After a while, it tastes like milk, and you find that whole milk is objectionable—it tastes too rich, too heavy. Your desire for foods you may now feel you could never do without— steaks, french fries, potato chips, fried foods in general, cakes and other rich desserts—gradually goes away.

I've tried changes that are much more limited than those you are recommending and found them very difficult to keep up. So I just don't know how successful I could be with such major changes.

I've had exactly the same experience with making minor changes before I made this fundamental change in my eating patterns. The minor changes are actually harder because they are not self-sustaining. They involve deprivation and can be enforced by personal discipline for only so long. The more meaningful changes I am recommending here do not result in deprivation. Even though they involve making a greater change in habits, they are not sustained by endless discipline. They are sustained because of the greater level of satisfaction and feeling of well-being they engender.

If I can sum up the approach you are advocating, you make the short-term sacrifice of changing your habits to attain long-term gains, which is to say weight loss as well as dramatically reduced risks of heart disease, cancer, and other diseases.

Immediate Benefits

The long-term gains are certainly there, but there are also very significant *immediate* or short-term benefits from the 10% solution— some of which I've previously discussed. I'll review a few of these.

I've mentioned that within hours of the typical high-fat meal in our society, massive aggregation of red blood cells, or blood sludging, occurs. The resulting blockage of the capillaries deprives the body's tissues and brain of oxygen, which can cause a wide range of symptoms, including difficulty in sleeping, irritability, and other unpleasant side effects. The improved circulation afforded by a low-fat diet has significant effects on energy level and alertness.

Since the 10% solution is very high in complex carbohydrates, it is necessarily high in fiber, which improves bowel regularity and digestion in general.

The exercise increases the intake of oxygen and stimulates the production of endorphins, which improves mood.

A high-fat diet suppresses the immune system. Conversely, following a low-fat diet, particularly in combination with exercise, encourages a strong immune system. This helps to fight diseases, both big and little.

Swings in sugar metabolism are eliminated, thus avoiding the anxious and run-down feeling that results from low blood sugar. Food cravings in general are replaced with a healthy and controllable appetite. Weight loss is much easier.

Even your complexion is greatly aided by a low-fat diet. Pimples generally clear up on a very low fat diet.

I have spoken with many people who have tried the 10% solution. Most report a greater sense of well-being within several weeks. Most people with conditions such as hypertension, type II diabetes, elevated cholesterol levels, and others that require medication, are able, with a doctor's supervision, to significantly reduce and usually eliminate these medications. Since many of these medicines have significant side effects that reduce the sense of well-being, eliminating their use also provides immediate benefits.

So you get long-term benefits by getting short-term benefits. There's got to be a cost in there somewhere.

Let's return to the analogy of fuel for your automobile. If you feed it the wrong fuel, it's not going to run very well, and eventually the engine will corrode and break down. If you change to the right fuel for that engine, you have the *immediate* benefit of the car running more smoothly, more efficiently, and with greater energy. You also have the *long-term* benefits of the car not corroding, and remaining in good condition for a much longer period of time. Our engines also require a certain type of fuel. We evolved over millions of years to eat a certain way. We have in recent centuries, and in particular in recent decades, departed quite dramatically from the right fuel.

There is a cost, of course, in adopting the 10% solution. It is the effort required to change your habits. It is time-consuming, in that you have to learn the guidelines and what they mean in your everyday life. You then have the emotional challenge of actually changing and sticking to it. It definitely takes effort. It's not a quick or effortless "cure." On the other hand, it is not as hard as you may think.

One counterintuitive, but psychologically sound, observation is that adopting the 10% solution is actually easier in a profound way than adopting a 20 or 25 percent solution or other halfway measures. If you are strict about the change during a period of transition, *your tastes actually change.* You lose your desire for high-fat foods and many of these will begin to appear unappetizing. You will discover the tastes of grains and vegetables that were previously smothered with high-fat, high-salt condiments and sauces. But if you make occasional exceptions in order to make the change "easier," your tastes will never change, and the new diet will continue indefinitely as a constant discipline, which will ultimately fail.

The dietary aspects of the 10% solution are similar in this regard to some of the other changes we have discussed. If you stop smoking, you get immediate benefits in that you breathe more easily and feel better in general. You certainly get long-term benefits, as well, in terms of dramatically reduced risks of a variety of diseases. But it does take effort in changing what is for many people a long-standing habit and addiction.

Consider exercise. There are immediate benefits in elevation of mood, improved breathing, improved ability to sleep, and so on. The long-term benefits are also well documented in terms of reduced risks of heart disease, cancer, and other diseases. Here again, you need to go through a period of adjustment. When you first exercise, just walking a mile can be strenuous and difficult. Yet the experienced jogger or walker can go three or four miles or more without any strain. These people are fit for exercise; their capacity to do it has been built up over time.

Similarly, your fitness for the dietary changes improves in the same way. People vary in their initial reactions. Some take to this dietary approach easily and quickly. Others struggle with it for a few weeks or months. But your "fitness" for proper eating improves over time, just as surely as does fitness for physical exertion.

I emphasize the dietary aspect of this life-style because it is the aspect most poorly understood and perhaps the most important. But the other issues of avoiding harmful drugs such as nicotine, as well as exercising, are also important parts of what I am calling the 10% solution.

It sounds like commitment is an important factor here.

Yes, commitment is certainly vital, especially in the beginning. One thing I have noticed is that these changes are easier to make if one's resolve is higher. Those who approach these changes with a very high degree of commitment usually report back that making the change was not such a big a deal after all. Those with less resolve find it much harder. If you're wishy-washy about it, you will probably find it impossible.

It is unfortunate that most people do not get the necessary level of resolve until some episode scares them into taking their health seriously. Not everyone is lucky enough to have some angina pain warn them of their advancing atherosclerosis. It is also easier to fight cancer before you get it. Of course, if you are fortunate enough to have fought a previous episode of cancer successfully, then the 10% solution is an ideal way to prevent its return.

It would be beneficial, though, if more people took these issues seriously before death stares them in the face. Granted, most people don't receive vital information on diet and life-style until they are at considerable risk—that is, if they receive any such information at all. But it still amazes me how many people choose to remain oblivious to these issues, even after a life-threatening episode.

4
■
A Parable

I can accept that not smoking and doing regular exercise are feasible, even enjoyable, ways to live. But just how habitable is this diet?

That is an excellent question, perhaps the most important question about the 10% solution that I will deal with. The health benefits of this approach are well documented, and the research on this question is getting stronger every year. The primary challenge and area of controversy is whether or not people would be willing to make this type of "radical" change. Many people dismiss this diet as "not palatable." These people have never tried it, of course, but they think about it for a few minutes and decide it's not for them, or for anybody.

Let me approach the issue by telling a parable. Suppose there was a society that added enormous amounts of curry to most of its food. To their meat dishes, they added curry. To their vegetables, they added curry. They put curry in fruit dishes, on bread, and so on. Now suppose curry caused a gradual deterioration of health and most people got sick and eventually died from diseases caused by curry. (I am not aware of health problems caused by curry, but let's just suppose there are.) Now some insightful people in this society are sufficiently motivated to realize the connection between curry and health problems.

They try eliminating curry from their diet and regain their health. However, this might be a coincidence, so some pioneering researchers thoroughly investigate the topic. They notice that societies that do not add significant amounts of curry do not get any of these diseases. Enough people are convinced to try a very low curry diet, and they also get well. Research studies are conducted that document the benefits of a low-curry diet. However, the recommendations for a diet very low in curry become controversial, not in their health claims, but in terms of their palatability. Others recommend a more modest 25 percent reduction in curry intake. The common wisdom is that food has no taste unless it is buried in huge amounts of curry. A modest reduction in curry is considered a healthy thing to do, but cutting down on curry dramatically is considered too radical.

If we now leave the parable, we realize that a high-fat diet, like a high-curry diet, is simply a matter of habit and acquired taste. There are societies that do use large amounts of curry or other spices in their food, and indeed these people find foods that are not saturated with these spices to be relatively tasteless. Similarly, we are used to drowning our foods in added fats of various kinds and find the idea of doing without these added fats unpalatable. But these habits, whether of curry or fat, are learned and can be unlearned. It is hard for people to accept that their tastes can actually be different than they are now, that they could find unpalatable things they now crave, and vice versa.

You're not suggesting eliminating fat, are you?

No, certainly not. Fat is a vital component of our diet, and we could not survive without it. Fortunately, it would be almost impossible to avoid it. Almost all foods, including grains, vegetables, even fruits, have small amounts of fat. If you get 10 percent of your calories from fat, you're getting a sufficient amount. In particular, the two "essential fatty acids" that we do need—linoleic acid and linolenic acid—are contained in more than sufficient quantity in vegetables, grains, and legumes, which are the quintessential foods of the 10% solution. The problem with fat in the diet for most people is the vastly excessive quantity that they ingest. I am suggesting eliminating the *added* fats: oils, butter, margarine, mayonnaise, whole-milk and cream-based sauces and dressings, and so on.

I like to compare this diet to a picture of autumn hues or spring pastels—subtle but still intense, with meaningful shadings, as opposed to the usual fare, which is more like a picture of saturated primary colors.

On this diet, I have rediscovered the many diverse tastes of vegetables, grains, and fruits, which are quite delightful once they are freed from high-fat, high-salt sauces, condiments, and preparation methods.

Who were these people in the parable?

The first person to pioneer a diet that is 10 percent of its calories from fat, and to methodically document its health benefits, was Nathan Pritikin.[1] The health centers that he founded are still the best places to obtain a thorough education in these nutritional and life-style principles. But today, the medical and scientific documentation of the benefits of the 10% solution are widely corroborated.

The parable was interesting, but it still doesn't convince me that I will enjoy this diet. Well, I know "diet" isn't the right word....

Yes, unfortunately, we don't have a better word for it. With regard to really convincing you that this way of eating is palatable, I could point out the tens of thousands of people who do eat this way in this country, not to mention many millions around the world, and who enjoy it. But the only way to really convince yourself is to try it.

Sure, just try it. That's always the come-on. And once I've made all that investment in trying it, I'll be likely to stick with it.

Perhaps. It is difficult to convince someone of a subjective experience without sharing that experience. Actually, I have found that it is not that difficult to convince people intellectually that this dietary approach is enjoyable and easily sustainable once your habits and tastes have changed. But translating that intellectual acceptance into emotional readiness for change is another matter. People have to be ready, either because they accept the links between their bodies, health, well-being, and nutrition, or because they have had some experience that generates fear for the loss of their health. Sometimes it is just a test for high cholesterol, sometimes it is an actual episode.

Probably the biggest reason that people resist this type of change is that they think they are going to be deprived. They look at all the things they like to eat and feel they will be bereft without them. They don't realize that they *will* get through the knothole, that they will not miss these items once their tastes and orientation to food change. But you have to have this experience to be really convinced of it.

The only other way I can convince you of the palatability of this life-style is with the rest of this book, with examples that illustrate the enormous diversity of texture, color, shape, and taste of what you *can* eat.

Perhaps you are right, but it does sound time-consuming. I have to learn or relearn all about foods, understand their nutritional content, figure out what I like and don't like, rearrange my meal preparation and eating schedules, struggle with restaurants, find time to exercise. I'm not sure I have all that time.

Well, if you try it, I'll give you an extra ten to thirty years to work on it.

You will?

Not me, actually, but your body just might. Also, many of the benefits come quickly, so you don't have to wait the five or ten or twenty years to not get heart disease or cancer to begin reaping some of the rewards.

You know, it seems amazing to me that fat can be the cause of so much death and suffering, yet there is only a dim recognition of that fact.

It's a little bit like those primitive societies that do not understand the link between sex and babies. There is a lot of sex and there are a lot of babies, and they just never realize the connection. We have a lot of fat and a lot of degenerative disease. The portion of the population that eats a truly healthful level of fat, cholesterol, and sodium is fairly small, so the connection is just not obvious. There are a lot of people who think they are eating a "low" level of fat and cholesterol, whereas their diets are still very excessive in these substances because the generally promulgated guidelines are inadequate. But fortunately, we do have respect in our society for the scientific method, and that will be our saving grace. Because the evidence is now mounting up. But moving the recommendations in the right direction will be a gradual process. If it takes as long as the recommendation against smoking, it will be another thirty years before the optimal recommendations are public policy. But you, personally, don't have to wait that long.

The "French Paradox"

What about the French? I understand that they eat a lot of cheese and foie gras, both high in fat, yet they don't get heart disease.

First of all, they do get heart disease. It's their leading cause of death. Their heart disease rate is half of ours, and the reasons are not particularly hard to understand. One very significant factor in my view is their lack of obesity. The French do not overeat; they eat three reasonably sized meals a day. When was the last time you saw an obese French man or woman?

Yes, there does seem to be more obesity among Americans than among the French.

That's for sure. The French are also avid consumers of fresh fruits and vegetables as well as French bread, which is made without added fats.

There has been significant attention paid recently to two other issues: the calcium content of cheese and the possible protective effect of wine (and alcohol in general) on coronary artery disease (atherosclerosis). Research conducted by a French scientist, Dr. Renaud, suggests that the calcium in cheese binds with and neutralizes the fat. Thus, according to Dr. Renaud, some of the fat (as well as the calcium) is eliminated from the body rather than absorbed. This research has not yet been published and, thus, should be considered speculative, although that has not prevented widespread publicity of his findings. If true, the calcium binding is preventing absorption of a portion of the fat, but the majority of the fat is still absorbed. This would make cheese less of a contributing factor to heart disease than other high-fat foods, but still not healthy.

With regard to alcohol, the research is still unclear. Moderate use of alcohol does appear to increase levels of HDL (the good cholesterol), but recent research indicates that it may be a nonprotective component of HDL that is being increased. There are also indications that alcohol thins the blood and therefore reduces the likelihood of a blood clot causing a heart attack. We will discuss the issue of alcohol and heart disease in more detail in chapter 8, "The Mind-Body Connection."

As for foie gras, although it is of animal origin, its chemical composition appears to be closer to olive oil and is rich in monounsaturated fat, which is a "less bad" fat.

The French rate of heart disease only seems low in comparison to the American rate. While it is half of ours, it is still dramatically higher than Asian rates. Also, the French rate of breast and colon cancer is equal to ours, which is very high. Their rate of stroke and cirrhosis of the liver is about double ours (due to their alcohol consumption). So their overall health pattern is not much better than ours, which is pretty bad.

If I adopt these recommendations that you are calling the 10% solution, then I'm not likely to die of heart disease or most cancers. So just what am I going to die of? I mean I'm just shopping around here, you know, for a desirable way to die.

It is impossible for anyone to predict what is going to happen to any individual. If you look at societies that follow these guidelines, it is not uncommon to find individuals who live long lives and are remarkably free of disease and the other degenerative processes that we associate with the "normal" aging process. Individuals in these societies do not develop atherosclerosis, cancer, hypertension, diabetes, arthritis, hearing and vision loss, and the other physical and sensory losses we associate with aging. They tend to remain in good health throughout their senior years.

We are now recognizing that much of the deterioration that we normally associate with old age is not normal to the human species, but is the result of decades of consuming a toxic, high-fat diet. Fat plays a role in some of the mechanisms that underlie the most common forms of hearing and vision loss.[2] The same appears to be true of rheumatoid and gouty arthritis.[3] Beyond the loss of life, strokes, heart disease, diabetes, and cancer are responsible for much of the suffering seen in the aged (as well as in millions of middle-age individuals).

Living in an "advanced" society, we have an opportunity for the best of both worlds: a nontoxic diet and life-style that can avoid these major degenerative diseases and processes, combined with good basic medical care, which is often unavailable in nonindustrialized societies. Research has indicated that the human body can live in a healthy state past the age of 100—some scientists say longer. But the main point is to delay morbidity, not just mortality. As anthropologist Ashley Montagu once said, "The goal of life is to die young—as late as possible."

People are realizing the need to cut down on cholesterol and fat, particularly saturated fat, aren't they?

Yes and no. There is certainly a lot of consciousness of some connection here. A substantial fraction of the food ads talk about fat, cholesterol, and sodium. But, again, the understanding is greatly watered-down. People think they will make a big difference by making a modest change. Yet modest changes produce only modest gains. There is not an understanding of just how far off-base our eating patterns have become.

There is a high degree of understanding about certain aspects of the connection between life-style and disease. President Kennedy raised our consciousness with regard to fitness and exercise. Ever since he mobilized the nation for exercise, we have put a high priority on fitness. It shows you the enormous impact that presidential leadership can have if applied to the right issues. We do now have the right guidelines on smoking. People understand the connection between weight and health.

Unfortunately, those people who are motivated enough to try to optimize their life-styles for health reasons usually do everything *except for the most important thing of all.* They watch their weight, they don't smoke, they exercise regularly, and they may even "watch" their fat and cholesterol intake. But their intake of fat and cholesterol, while perhaps better than the norm, is still extremely high, judging by the standard of what is actually good for our bodies.

As I will document later in the book, our dietary excesses, particularly our high-levels of dietary fat, kill more than one million Americans each year (see chapter 15, "Ranking the Killers: How to Save a Million American Lives a Year"). It is by far the biggest killer, exceeding smoking or any other life-style factor. It always saddens me to hear of someone dying from a heart attack, or breast cancer, or any of the degenerative diseases, because I know that in all likelihood it could have been avoided.

In a restaurant the other day, I overheard several people at the next table talking about a friend who had just died of a heart attack. They spoke about it as if it were just one of those tragic things that randomly happen. He was perfectly "healthy." "Ask not for whom the bell tolls," and all that. Meanwhile, they were devouring the usual fare: hamburgers, french fries, cheesecake, and so on. That there was any connection at all between what they were doing at that table and what they were talking about never seemed to occur to any of them. It was also clear that they really believed that this person had been in good health. We now know that if someone dies from a heart attack they were silently ill for years, their arteries gradually occluding. It is, of course, a disease that the great majority of Americans and Europeans live with and die of.

What is most frustrating for me are the people who are still alive and who are in need of this information. You don't have to look very far to find someone who desperately needs this knowledge. Yet, I cannot just tell someone who has just had an episode of angina, "Hey, eat ten percent of your calories from fat, and cut down on cholesterol, sodium..." It's a very long discussion: the benefits, the evidence, the guidelines, why this diet is a lot more palatable than it might sound, and so on.

So who is this book for?

It's for all adults who take their health and their sense of well-being seriously. Someone who has had an episode related to atherosclerosis is perhaps easier to influence because they have been forced to understand that their health is in jeopardy. Someone with high cholesterol is perhaps next. If they are sufficiently educated to understand the issues, they understand that they are at risk. But even if your cholesterol levels are fine (by my standards, 160 mg/dl or less), that doesn't say anything about your risk of cancer or the many other conditions caused principally by excessive levels of dietary fat, cholesterol, and sodium.

But perhaps the most important reason the 10% solution should be considered by all adults is the immediate benefit to that ineffable and elusive sense of well-being. Everyone I know who has ever tried this life-style has described how much better they feel.

You say adults. What about children?

Children

Teaching children about nutrition and its importance to health is very important. Childhood is, after all, when we develop our habits. And generally, the habits we develop are very poor ones. In the United States and Europe, we have found that atherosclerosis starts at an early age.[4] But I don't necessarily recommend 10 percent calories from fat for most children. Most children need more caloric density for growth, particularly if they want to keep up with their American peers in height. For children, I would recommend that 20 to 25 percent of their calories come from fat, which is still substantially less than is typical. For children under 2 years of age, there should be no restriction on fat, as adequate caloric intake is crucial during this phase of life.

It is also remarkable that we allow children free access to caffeine, a rather powerful drug, particularly for small developing bodies. A 50-pound child drinking 3 cans of caffeinated cola is equivalent to a 150-pound adult consuming more than 7 cups of coffee (both are ingesting 2.76 milligrams of caffeine per pound of body weight).[5]

Are children the only exception to your recommendation of 10 percent calories from fat?

Exceptions

Another exception would be adults who are chronically thin and have great difficulty maintaining adequate weight. It is possible to gain weight following the 10% solution. There are foods that are reasonably high in caloric density but low in fat. But if someone is struggling to maintain sufficient weight, then they may wish to increase the percentage of fat in their diet to 20 percent or even 25 percent. Otherwise, I strongly recommend 10 percent of calories from fat. The incidence of all the degenerative diseases is substantially less at 10 percent fat than at 20 percent.

What about pregnant women?

Pregnancy

During pregnancy, women need higher levels of protein, calcium, and calories. I would be concerned about a woman starting on this program during pregnancy, in terms of her obtaining sufficient nutrition for herself and her developing fetus. It would be reasonable to eat closer to 20 percent of calories from fat during this period for this reason. However, it is certainly true that women in societies that naturally eat very low fat diets (such as rural areas of China) have no nutritional difficulty during pregnancy as a result of their low-fat diet.

The key nutritional issue during pregnancy is obtaining sufficient calories. A recent study of 2,000 pregnant women, conducted by Dr. Theresa Scholl at the School of Osteopathic Medicine at the University of Medicine and Dentistry of New Jersey, found that gaining insufficient weight during the first two trimesters of pregnancy was a principal cause of low birth weight in newborns.[6] The study recommended that a woman gain approximately 10 pounds during the second trimester of pregnancy, and 24 to 30 pounds overall.

Is that it for exceptions—children, pregnant women, and thin people?

Those are the primary categories of people who under certain circumstances *should* eat a somewhat higher percentage of calories from fat. There is another category of people who *may* eat a slightly higher percentage of fat: Persons without any major risk factors, that is to say, persons who do not have diabetes or hypertension, who have never had coronary heart disease, cardiovascular diseases (such as stroke), angina, cancer or any indications of these diseases, who have no immediate family members who have had these diseases, whose lipid cholesterol is under 160 and whose cholesterol-to-HDL ratio is less than 3.5, whose weight is no more than 105 percent of their ideal weight, who exercise regularly, who do not smoke, abuse alcohol, or other drugs, and who would prefer to eat 15 percent of their calories from fat may do so.

That's quite a list of requirements.

I'm sorry, but this stuff is sometimes inherently complicated.

Your last "requirement" seems unnecessary. Wouldn't everyone prefer to eat 15 percent calories from fat, rather than 10 percent, if they could?

That view reflects the idea that we want to eat as much fat as we can get away with. I know it sounds hard to believe, but...

Yes, I know, your tastes change.

Exactly.

What about chemicals in our food and environment? Don't they cause a lot of disease?

Chemicals

Yes, but not compared to fat. I estimate chemicals in our food and environment as responsible for about one hundred thousand deaths per year. That is a rough estimate, but I believe it is in the right ballpark. That is a serious number, and I do believe it is worthwhile avoiding chemicals and additives in our food and pollution in our environment to the extent possible. But the approximately one million deaths (see chapter 15, "Ranking the Killers: How to Save a Million American Lives a Year") and related suffering caused by the excessive level of fat in our diet is a more serious issue by an order of magnitude.

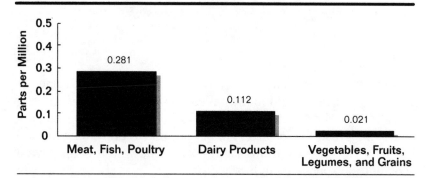

LEVELS OF PESTICIDES IN
VARIOUS CATEGORIES OF FOOD

Even though pesticides are originally applied to grains and vegetables, they end up being highly concentrated in meat.

Data from: P. E. Corneliussen, "Residues in Food and Feed," Pesticides Monitoring Journal 2 (March 1969): 140–52.

There are thousands of chemicals in our food and environment. How is it that fat, which is just one substance, or perhaps a few substances, causes so much more suffering?

I don't wish to downplay the importance of the pollution problem. It is a major health problem and the negative trends are of very serious concern. But to put the problems into perspective, our consumption of most chemicals is fairly small. For most food additives, we consume rather minute quantities. Fat, on the other hand, is consumed in relatively vast quantities by most Americans every few hours. The accumulated damage of this poisonous diet is comparably vast.

It is also interesting to note that many of the higher-fat foods also add relatively large quantities of pesticides and other chemicals to our diet. It takes 16 pounds of grain to produce 1 pound of meat.[7] Meat is, therefore, a concentrated source of pesticides, even though the pesticides are originally applied to the grains that the animals eat.

All right, suppose I'm game. How would I get started on making this life-style change?

For starters, you can read the rest of this book. Then, it is important to consult with your physician before starting any program of diet or exercise. In particular, if you have a condition, such as hypertension or diabetes, requiring medication or other medical attention, then careful medical supervision is important.

I thought a lot of doctors were not up on this stuff.

Doctors

Many doctors are not. Up until recently, preventive medicine and nutrition were not taught in most medical schools. But this is changing, although slowly. There is increasing recognition of the vital role nutrition plays in the formation of disease and in preventing disease. You have to consult with the right doctor, one who is supportive of good nutrition and who understands it.

It is also important to have the right attitude toward and relationship with your doctor. Think of him or her as your partner in health, not the fix-it person who repairs the machine when it breaks. A doctor I know tells his patients that their health is 85 percent their responsibility. They need to work on their health every day, then he'll take care of the other 15 percent. Physicians are marvelously trained to deal with a catastrophe when it happens, but they need your active participation to avoid disasters before they happen.

Having consulted with your physician and understanding the basic principles, you can give the 10% solution a try. We'll talk more about the process in a later chapter. The first few weeks will be ones of exploration. Think of it as an adventure. You'll be excited as you discover foods that you like that follow the guidelines. You need to devote enough time to look up the fat content of foods and keep track of the information.

You mean I have to write all this stuff down?

I don't recommend tracking everything. With regard to cholesterol and sodium, it is sufficient to learn the basic foods to avoid. But with regard to fat, I do recommend adding up fat grams, for at least the first few weeks. It is the only way to really learn the fat content of foods. Most people eat with little idea of the nutritional content of what they eat. Some people have a limited concept of caloric content, but are still relatively confused when it comes to fat content. Trying to manage your nutrition without writing it down (at least initially) can be compared to trying to manage your finances without balancing your checkbook, or even looking at price tags. If you shopped that way, you would be likely to get into trouble. Managing your nutritional balance is no different.

Ultimately, it will become second nature and you will know what you can eat. But initially, tracking fat content is the only way to improve your awareness of what has fat and what does not. Some of what you discover may surprise you.

So you wrote this book to provide a guide to making this life-style change?

That's one reason. But beyond explaining how to make the change, a more crucial purpose is to explain *why* the change is so important. People need to understand how their bodies work and the enormous influence we have on whether they work or not. In general, diseases don't just happen. We have far more impact on the development and prevention of disease than is widely recognized. Unfortunately, most people know more about how their car works than how their body works.

With these new high-tech cars, I'm not sure that's true anymore.

Misconceptions

Well, perhaps a lot of people are ignorant on both subjects. My other reason for writing this book is to address some of the common misconceptions that people have about nutrition and health, a number of which are fostered by the media in their oversimplified approach to this subject. There are a lot of books, articles, and other sources now available that address the subject of food and health. But I have not seen very many that clearly address these misconceptions.

Such as?

Perhaps the most important is the dramatic gains that can be achieved by a significant change in diet. The "moderate" approach provides only modest gains. The common wisdom that there is only so much you can gain from dietary change and exercise is only true if you limit yourself to these watered-down recommendations on the subject. Let people decide how much compromising they wish to do on their own after they have been educated on the subject.

Following the guidelines of the 10% solution can usually reduce the risk of these major diseases by 90 percent or more. If someone had a cure for cancer that was this effective, it would be a big story. But we're not used to an approach to disease that is not in the form of a pill, a shot, an operation, or some other medical procedure. I am not negative, in general, toward these traditional approaches to medicine. Antibiotics have greatly increased our life expectancy. Vaccines have wiped out some deadly diseases. There are many other examples. But there has been a prejudice against approaches to disease that involve nutrition and life-style, although that is now changing.

The incidence of atherosclerosis is not widely understood. The fact that about 90 percent of the adult population have some level of atherosclerosis and that most people will have high rates of it by middle age (in women, generally, after menopause) is not widely known.

Another misconception is that if this disease is so widespread, then it must not be a serious disease at all. People respond as if it were some existential condition like Kierkegaard's "illness unto death"— just one of those melancholy aspects of the human experience that we can't avoid.

But atherosclerosis is *not okay*. People should be as concerned about having atherosclerosis as they would be by having cancer, AIDS, or any other life-threatening and debilitating condition.

Are you trying to alarm people?

If there were nothing we could effectively do about it, then raising urgent concern would probably not be of much service. But we do have the knowledge to essentially eliminate this disease. And despite all the talk, all the articles, all the books, and all the advertisements, the only message that gets through is an extremely compromised, watered-down, and muddled one.

The fact is that the vast majority of heart attacks are avoidable. Just think about that next time you hear about someone having a heart attack. *It did not have to happen.* Coronary heart disease is not an inevitable and natural part of life and aging. And the one and a half million heart attacks and half million deaths from coronary heart disease are just the beginning in the tally of misfortune from the degenerative diseases caused by the high-fat, high-cholesterol, high-sodium, low-fiber, civilized diet. Beyond the death toll, much of the frailty and loss of bodily and sensory function associated with old age result from these conditions and their secondary effects.

I sometimes think of these guidelines as the natural laws of our bodies. Unfortunately, they are much more strictly enforced than the laws of society. In our society, we have executed about a hundred people over the past ten years for violating society's laws. But for violating the laws of our bodies, a hundred people are "executed" in our country every fifty minutes.

Well, we have other punishments for violating society's laws.

So do our bodies.

I suppose that's true.

There are other misconceptions concerning the source of the cholesterol in our blood and the mistakenly benign image of polyunsaturated fat. Finally, the palatability of this diet and life-style is a crucially important issue that I will want to return to. It is the only reason that people dismiss this approach. Most people who make statements doubting the palatability of the 10% solution are ignorant of how desirable and enjoyable this eating pattern can be, not to mention the immediate benefits to one's sense of well-being that result from improved circulation, improved oxygenation of the brain and other tissues, improved gastrointestinal functioning, and other improvements. But making it enjoyable does require some knowledge, and that is another reason for this book.

Okay, just one more question for this chapter.

Shoot.

Just who are you, anyway?

As I mentioned in the introduction, I'm not a doctor, although I have worked with a team of doctors on this material, and the book has been reviewed by this medical team to review its accuracy. I am a scientist who became interested in my own health and the health of those around me. I have been on something of a quest to understand the nature of both health and disease and what we might do to influence its course.

I found what I discovered in this quest to be rather unexpected. We really do have the means to eliminate almost all of the risk of diseases that account for at least two-thirds of all deaths and a comparable amount of the health-related suffering in our society. The point is not just to live longer, although avoiding the tragedy of premature death is certainly worthwhile, but to have the means to live a full and productive life as long as possible. I began to help many people around me by sharing with them the information on this topic that I had accumulated. I developed something of a reputation as a source of knowledge on the topic of nutrition and health and ended up in many conversations on the subject. I felt I needed to make a statement and share in an efficient way the insights I had gained through this interest. That's the genesis of this book.

And I have a question for you.

Yes.

Who, may I ask, are you?

Why, I'm the reader, of course.

You're a rather challenging reader.

Perhaps, but you have to understand that for most of us, this is a very new perspective on food and life-style.

Or a very old perspective.

Old for the human race, but new for most of us.

PART TWO

■

THE
10%
SOLUTION

5
■
Your Weight

Ideal Weight

Let's talk about how the principles of the 10% solution can be implemented in our daily lives.

I think that would be worthwhile. Why don't we start with how to lose weight.

That is a fine place to start. Attaining your optimal weight will contribute significantly to reducing your risk of all degenerative diseases, including heart disease, cancer, type II diabetes, and hypertension. You'll have more energy and will feel better in general.

I'll look better also.

Yes, you will. And perhaps because of that particular reason, losing weight has become a national preoccupation. At any one time, 50 million Americans are on a diet to lose weight. We spend $33 billion a year on diets and diet aids.[1] The sad fact is that 95 percent of the dieters will regain all of the weight they have lost or more.[2] The cycle of taking off weight and then putting it back on is actually worse for your health than never having lost it.[3]

Then maybe I shouldn't bother trying to lose weight in the first place.

The key is to change your attitude toward losing weight. Rather than thinking of a temporary period of deprivation, think instead of a lifelong commitment to a healthy pattern of eating.

You know, a lifetime of this seems like a lot longer than just a few months of dieting.

Yes, but you can skip the few months of dieting. You can make a commitment to a healthy life-style in just one day. While the weight won't come off in a day, you can start feeling better about yourself and your commitment immediately. And a lot of the immediate benefits of the 10% solution will become evident in only a couple of weeks.

I suppose I could make a commitment in a short period of time.

Unfortunately, it often takes the better part of a lifetime for people to wake up to the impact they can have on their longevity and well-being. You hear of people every day who never do.

Okay, so I make a quick commitment to a slow weight loss.

Yes, that is a good way to put it. The message is patience. Now, the first thing we need to determine is the amount of food you should be eating.

I'll take a large quantity, thank you.

We just may be able to accommodate you. But first we have to determine your ideal weight.

With better tailoring I could probably accommodate a bit more weight than otherwise.

Your clothes may, but you'll feel better to be at or near your ideal weight. There are two approaches to determining how much you should weigh. First, with a tape measure, measure the circumference of your wrist. Alternatively, use a piece of string and then mark it against a ruler. From table 1, use this measurement to determine your build. Then look up your height for the appropriate sex and build in table 2 to determine your optimal weight.

So if I have fat wrists, I can have a fatter body?

As it turns out, unless one is very obese, the wrists do not gain in size, and, thus, their circumference is a good indicator of one's inherent build size. A lot of overweight people assume they have large builds, whereas what they really have are medium or even small builds padded with a lot of extra girth.

TABLE 1

DETERMINING FRAME SIZE

	SMALL FRAME	MEDIUM FRAME	LARGE FRAME
Wrist measurement			
Adult males	less than $6\frac{1}{4}$ in.	$6\frac{1}{4}$–7 in.	more than 7 in.
Adult females	less than $5\frac{1}{4}$ in.	$5\frac{1}{4}$–6 in.	more than 6 in.

And the second method?

A more accurate approach involves body fat. Lean muscle mass is actually heavier than body fat. Thus, two people can be the same height, build, and weight and yet one may be healthier and slimmer than the other. The real objective in weight loss is to lose fat—not muscle, water, or temporary glycogen deposits. It is more important, therefore, to determine if you are at an ideal level of body fat than an ideal level of weight. Use the instructions in the section "Body Fat Charts" (see appendix 4) to determine your percentage of body fat.

We need some body fat, don't we?

Yes, for proper body composition, to cushion our bones, and as one form of energy storage, a certain amount of body fat is needed. It is not healthy to be significantly above or below this ideal of percent body fat, which is 15 percent for men and 24 percent for women.[4]

So women get to carry more body fat than men do?

Yes, something has to fill in those extra curves. These curves do have a biological purpose beyond their role as secondary sex characteristics, in terms of support for childbearing and nurturing.

The body fat tables tell you your current body fat percentage, but you cannot really tell what your ideal weight should be from these tables.

That's true. If you are over or under your ideal weight, then use tables 1 and 2 to get an approximate ideal weight. Then as your weight approaches your ideal weight, use the tables on body fat to confirm the more important issue of body fat.

All right, so I'm about 15 percent overweight. Now what?

Ideally, you should be within 5 percent of your ideal weight. Being 20 percent overweight triples your risk of hypertension and diabetes,

TABLE 2

DETERMINING ESTIMATED IDEAL WEIGHT RANGE

Weight in Pounds (in indoor clothing)

HEIGHT	MEN			WOMEN*		
	SMALL FRAME	MEDIUM FRAME	LARGE FRAME	SMALL FRAME	MEDIUM FRAME	LARGE FRAME
4 ft. 10 in.				96–104	101–13	109–25
4 ft. 11 in.				99–107	104–16	112–28
5 ft. 0 in.				102–10	107–19	115–31
1 in.	112–20	118–29	126–41	105–13	110–22	118–34
2 in.	115–23	121–33	129–44	108–16	113–26	121–38
3 in.	118–26	124–36	132–48	111–19	116–30	125–42
4 in.	121–29	127–39	135–52	114–23	120–35	129–46
5 in.	124–33	130–43	138–56	118–27	124–39	133–50
6 in.	128–37	134–47	142–61	122–31	128–43	137–54
7 in.	132–41	138–52	147–66	126–35	132–47	141–58
8 in.	136–45	142–56	151–70	130–40	136–51	145–63
9 in.	140–50	146–60	155–74	134–44	140–55	149–68
10 in.	144–54	150–65	159–79	138–48	144–59	153–73
11 in.	148–58	154–70	164–84			
6 ft. 0 in.	152–62	158–75	168–89			
1 in.	156–67	162–80	173–94			
2 in.	160–71	167–85	178–99			
3 in.	164–75	172–90	182–204			

COURTESY OF METROPOLITAN LIFE INSURANCE COMPANY.

*Women between 18 and 25 should subtract 1 pound for each year under 25.

doubles your risk of hypercholesterolemia (i.e., having a serum cholesterol level more than 250 mg/dl), and increases your risk of heart disease by 60 percent.[5]

Does it matter where on my body the fat resides?

Interestingly, recent evidence shows that it is the accumulation of visceral fat around one's middle that is particularly harmful. The "potbelly" appears to be the primary culprit in terms of health risk from obesity. For example, in a study published in the October 1991 issue of the *Journal of the American Medical Association*, researchers from the University of South Florida College of Medicine in Tampa showed that the risk of endometrial cancer was fifteen times higher in women with a high waist-to-hip ratio as compared to women with a low ratio.[6] Other studies have found strong links between obesity, particularly as it affects upper body weight (which resides primarily around the abdomen), to type II diabetes, hypertension, and heart disease.

Yes, I understand. So exactly what do I do?

Maintenance Calorie Level

The next step is to use table 3 to determine your maintenance calorie level, which is the number of calories you can eat to maintain your weight.

How much exercise do you recommend?

My recommendation is approximately 200 calories of exercise per day for a 100-pound person, 300 calories for a 150-pound person, 400 calories for a 200-pound person, and so on. We'll talk about how to compute the caloric value of exercise in chapter 7, "How to Exercise."

So table 3 gives me the amount I can eat to keep my weight the same?

Exactly, or should I say, approximately. Everyone's metabolism is a little different, so you will need to experiment a little to adjust this figure appropriately.

So to lose weight, I just eat less than this figure.

As far as calories are concerned, yes. There are 3,500 calories in a pound of body fat, so if you eat 500 calories per day less than your maintenance level, you will lose about a pound per week.

TABLE 3

MAINTENANCE CALORIE LEVEL

The table below provides an estimated maintenance calorie level based on your current weight and activity level. Use the following guidelines for activity level:

Sedentary: You sit most of the day (walking only occasionally), and do not have a regular exercise routine.

Moderately active: Your normal routine involves frequent walking or physical motion. Alternatively, your normal routine is sedentary but you have a regular exercise program equivalent to walking or running 20 or more miles per week.

Very active: Your normal routine involves continual vigorous physical activity (e.g., construction worker, mail carrier, gardener). Very active is equivalent to a sedentary life-style plus the equivalent of walking or running approximately 50 miles per week.

Note that your maintenance calorie level will change as your weight changes.

Since metabolic rates vary from individual to individual, this chart will provide only an approximate value, which you will need to adjust based on your own experience.

WEIGHT	SEDENTARY	MODERATELY ACTIVE	VERY ACTIVE
90	1,170	1,350	1,620
100	1,300	1,500	1,800
110	1,430	1,650	1,980
120	1,560	1,800	2,160
130	1,690	1,950	2,340
140	1,820	2,100	2,520
150	1,950	2,250	2,700
160	2,080	2,400	2,880
170	2,210	2,550	3,060
180	2,340	2,700	3,240
190	2,470	2,850	3,420
200	2,600	3,000	3,600

And if I eat 1,500 calories less than my maintenance level each day, I'll lose 3 pounds a week.

Not so fast. First, it is important to obtain adequate and balanced nutrition while you are losing weight. Second, the primary goal is to adjust to a new way of eating, that is, to change your tastes and attitudes toward food. You do not want to feel deprived and hungry during this process. That would defeat the entire purpose. While losing weight, you should eat at least 10 calories for each pound of your ideal weight, and in any event no less than 1,000 calories per day for a woman and 1,200 calories per day for a man, preferably more. I lost 40 pounds while eating more than 2,000 calories per day.

Conversely, to gain weight, you simply eat more than your exercise-adjusted maintenance level.

Not that I've had that problem, but wouldn't it be hard to gain weight eating very low fat foods?

Actually, no. There are many low-fat foods that have high caloric density. Eggless pasta, for example, is an ideal food, high in complex carbohydrates and low in fat, but you can go through calories pretty quickly. However, if someone is chronically underweight and finds that they are unable to gain weight with very low fat foods, then I would make weight gain a priority, and increase the fat level to some extent.

I have to keep track of every calorie I eat?

Keeping Track

It's not a bad idea, at least until you have established a pattern. But more important than tracking calories is tracking—

—fat level!

You're catching on. Counting fat grams is crucial, at least until you have developed an intuitive grasp of the subject. It is the best way, and the only effective way, to educate oneself on the fat content of foods. Many people concerned about their weight have a high level of awareness of calorie level, but few people have a comparable understanding of the fat content of foods.

Keeping track of fat is important for all the reasons we have cited. Furthermore, with regard to weight loss, it is indeed more important than calories. A 1988 study reported in the *American Journal of Clinical Nutrition* followed two groups of women who ate the *same* number of calories, but different levels of fat. The group that ate 40 percent of their calories from fat gained weight much more readily than the group eating only 20 percent of their calories from fat. A study at Stanford University had a similar result for men.[7]

Are there other advantages to a low-fat diet for losing weight?

Yes, it lowers your set-point, which is the weight your body tries to maintain.[8] It increases your maintenance calorie level. Substantially more of the weight you lose is body fat. A low-fat diet is also a far more satisfying way to lose weight. You eat a much larger quantity of food and are able to avoid hunger and feelings of deprivation. Following a low-calorie diet that is not low in fat is almost impossible for any sustained period of time. Most important, you are practicing new eating patterns that will enable you to sustain both your health and your weight loss long after the pounds have come off.

What about other approaches to weight loss?

Other Approaches

High-protein diets are a real disaster. They cause a potentially dangerous increase in uric acid level, which can leave your body in a very toxic state called ketosis.[9] It also results in increased atherosclerosis, fatigue, and nutrient deficiencies, and can cause kidney stones and other problems. A lot of the weight loss, particularly those early encouraging pounds, are just reductions in water content and glycogen stores, which are rapidly replaced when the diet stops.

Liquid diets work in the sense that you are reducing your caloric intake, so you do lose weight. But the recidivism rate for this approach is very discouraging. You are not losing weight by learning healthy new habits and changing your tastes, desires, and attitudes. You are, instead, temporarily living in a cocoon, eating in a very artificial way. People count the days until they are released from this gastronomic prison. They do not associate the benefit of the weight loss with proper eating habits, but rather with the artificial eating patterns that they are anxious to leave. Following a liquid diet is an exercise in deprivation, and there is little to encourage healthy habits once released. While most of these programs throw in some education on reducing fat and other guidelines, the only way to really learn healthy eating habits is to do it.

If you lose weight the 10% way, you are taking the really important step—changing your habits—while you lose the weight, and you will associate the positive feelings of losing weight with your new habits. By the time the weight is lost, keeping it up (that is, keeping your weight down) is easy because your habits have already changed. Once you have achieved your ideal weight level, you simply change the quantity of food to your maintenance level, but you do not change the type of food you eat.

Exercise is also very important in terms of burning calories and increasing your metabolic level (that is, your rate of burning off calories), even while you are not exercising and lowering your set-point.

Any other tips for losing weight?

Your Goal

Yes, don't make losing weight your primary goal. If your goal is the development of a healthy life-style, you are more likely to succeed, with regard to both your health and permanent weight loss. Don't be too anxious to drop pounds. Enjoying the experience is crucial. You want to associate the experience of attaining a healthy weight with the experience of healthy eating. It may take a few months longer, but you'll never have to lose weight again.

Exercise is also crucial for both health and weight loss. It will accelerate the weight loss and will keep your body composition in optimal form as your body changes shape.

I could certainly benefit from firming up this fat around my middle.

You can't firm up fat. You have to lose the fat, but exercise will help you to do that. Then you can firm up the muscles that remain.

What about weight plateaus?

Weight Plateaus

They are a major reason that people get discouraged and drop out of weight-loss programs. Keep in mind that your weight is a function of many diverse processes in your body. There are some desirable processes that will actually increase your weight. Gained muscle mass and vascular expansion from exercise may temporarily cause a small gain in weight, but these constitute very desirable phenomena. Muscle tissue weighs more than fat tissue, so you can lose body fat and inches without necessarily losing weight. Increasing your intake of complex carbohydrates may cause an increase in glycogen stores, which is perfectly healthy. Changes in medication, menstruation, constipation, water retention, and other phenomena may all cause a slowing down or even a temporary reversal of weight loss. Keep in mind that your real goal is the loss of body fat. None of these factors causes an increase in body fat, so do not be discouraged by minor shifts of weight in the wrong direction.

Most important, be patient.

6
∎
How to Eat

Fat

So how do I keep to 10 percent calories from fat?

Since a gram of fat has 9 calories, you can eat about 1.1 grams of fat per 100 calories. Now some items will be less than this, and some will be more, but that is the nominal goal.

Having determined the number of calories you intend to eat, multiply that figure by 1.1 percent (or .011) to determine your goal for fat grams (or use table 4). For example, at 2,000 calories per day, your goal is 22 grams of fat.

There's a lot of computation involved here.

Yes, you do have to calculate a few numbers, and you do have to keep track of a few things, but it's the only way to learn.

Do I have to keep track of cholesterol also?

Cholesterol

You should be mindful of it, but you don't really have to track it as carefully. Avoiding fat will keep you out of trouble with regard to cholesterol in most instances. As we discussed earlier, the primary exceptions are egg yolks and organ meats. Lobster, shrimp, and crab have moderate amounts of cholesterol, so they should be eaten in moderation. If you cut out egg yolks and organ meats and eat limited amounts of lobster, shrimp, and crab, you will generally be okay on cholesterol, as long as you keep your fat level to 10 percent of calories.

Iron will take care of itself?

Iron

Avoiding sources of fat and cholesterol, particularly meat and other foods of animal origin, will automatically avoid concentrated sources of iron. Red meat is very high in iron. Liver is especially high. It would also be a good idea to avoid supplements which include iron (unless you have a significant iron deficiency) and foods "fortified" with iron.

How about sodium?

Sodium

If you are not suffering from hypertension, then again I feel that mindfulness is sufficient. As a rule of thumb, you want to keep to about 1 mg of sodium per calorie, so avoid foods that significantly exceed this ratio. For example, a 100-calorie portion should have on the order of 100 milligrams of sodium (on average). Note that one

TABLE 4

RECOMMENDED FAT CONSUMPTION

DAILY CALORIC INTAKE	NUMBER OF GRAMS OF FAT TO ACHIEVE 10 PERCENT CALORIES FROM FAT
1,000	11
1,200	13
1,400	16
1,600	18
1,800	20
2,000	22
2,200	24
2,400	27
2,600	29
2,800	31
3,000	33

teaspoon of salt has 2,300 milligrams of sodium. If you do have hypertension or even a tendency to hypertension, then sodium is a far more serious issue. Then I would count sodium—again until the issue becomes second nature.

Just how do I track these things, anyway?

Many products are now labeled with their caloric, fat, cholesterol, and sodium levels, and that is of enormous help in becoming nutritionally aware. Become label conscious. Read labels both for the ingredients in the products you eat, as well as their nutritional breakdown. For other items, you will need a guide that provides the nutritional breakdown of foods. A brief guide is provided in appendix 2, "Nutritional Content of Food," in this book, which should be adequate to get started. If you would like a more comprehensive listing of foods, I recommend *Food Values of Portions Commonly Used,* by Jean A. T. Pennington and Helen Nichols Church. It is a wonderfully complete and accurate guide—a real bible of nutrition. I find it quite interesting just to read different sections to see how different foods compare.

Sounds fascinating.

Now you're being sarcastic.

Well, how many people really want to read a book of foods and their nutritional breakdown?

Okay, you don't have to read it, but it is an invaluable reference guide.

Now, what about more complex foods, such as prepared foods either from a can or a restaurant?

You'll have to use your judgment. Compare it to foods that you do know the nutritional content of. As you have more experience, you will become better at estimating. Do the best you can; your estimates will be more accurate than you think.

Let's review exactly what I am supposed to eat.

Grains

The heart and soul of this diet are grains in forms as natural and unprocessed as possible. Grains can be cooked and eaten directly; they can be cooked with vegetables in casseroles; they can be eaten in salads and in many other ways. Grains are also the primary ingredient in a variety of other desirable foods, such as breads, cereals, and pastas. Grains are a relatively complete food. They are primarily complex carbohydrates but also include protein, fiber, small amounts of essential fatty acids, vitamins, minerals, and other nutrients.

There are three considerations that are worth mentioning with regard to grains. First, eat a variety of grains. Don't get all of your grain calories from a single grain, such as wheat. In addition to wheat, which is ubiquitous in the United States, there are oats, rice, rye, barley, triticale, buckwheat, millet, and many others. Each grain has a different balance of vitamins, minerals, amino acids, and fatty acids, so distributing your intake among different grains is important. Second, try to avoid breads, cereals, pastas, and other grain-based products that are high in fat, eggs, salt, and sugar. Again, read your food labels. A slice of bread with 70 to 100 calories should not exceed 2 grams of fat, preferably 1. It is desirable not to have eggs listed as an ingredient. Sugar (or its synonyms, such as glucose, sucrose, dextrose, honey, molasses, maple syrup) should not be among the first several ingredients on the ingredients list. Finally, try to eat grains in as unprocessed a state as possible. Processing and refining tend to strip away the valuable fiber, vitamins, minerals, and other essential nutrients.

What else can I eat besides grains?

Legumes and Vegetables

Next to grains, legumes such as beans (including soybeans), peas, and lentils are excellent sources of complex carbohydrates, soluble fiber, protein, essential fatty acids, and other nutrients. They also make nutritious and tasty casseroles when cooked with various grains.

Next, we move to vegetables, all of which are excellent sources of complex carbohydrates, fiber, and other nutrients. You can eat all vegetables except—

—olives and avocados.

Fruit and Dairy

You're really catching on now. Fruits and fruit juices are fine, and provide a blend of complex and simple carbohydrates, along with other nutrients. Eat as much in whole-fruit form as possible to get the optimal amount of fiber.

Another important category are dairy products made with skim milk. One percent (fat by weight) milk is acceptable, although 2 percent milk is much too high in fat. Skim and very low fat (1 percent) milk provide a broad variety of products: milk, yogurt, cottage cheese, non-fat frozen yogurt (instead of ice cream), and a variety of very low fat cheeses. These are sometimes hard to find, but it is worth seeking them out to provide greater variety in your diet. Milk products are excellent sources of protein, iron, and calcium.

Egg whites are low in fat but provide protein and other nutrients and are quite useful as egg substitutes in recipes.

Meat and Fish

Finally, we come to very lean meat and fish. This is an acceptable category, but you have to limit the quantity. As I discussed earlier, I recommend limiting lean meat or fish to around 4 ounces per day, although it is possible to stay under 10 percent calories from fat while eating as much as 8 ounces of lean meat or fish. Meat is limited to very lean grades of beef or pork, or white meat chicken or turkey cooked without the skin. The skin is nearly 100 percent fat. If you leave the skin on while cooking, the skin bastes the meat with saturated fat. Also, avoid self-basting chickens and turkeys, as the basting liquid that is injected in the bird is nearly 100 percent fat. Very lean grades of beef, such as flank and round steak, are acceptable.

Preferable to meat is fish. While fish also contains relatively high levels of fat, the fat is rich in omega-3 fats, which in many individuals is beneficial in thinning the blood and possibly reducing cholesterol and triglyceride levels. It is important that the preparation process not add fats or oils. Meat and fish can be baked in a tomato-based sauce, steamed, poached, grilled, or broiled in wine, defatted chicken stock, or low-sodium soy sauce. Also acceptable are clams, oysters, mussels, and scallops. Shrimp and lobster contain moderate amounts of cholesterol and should be eaten in limited amounts.

Perhaps the most important point is to eat a broad variety of foods. This will avoid taste fatigue and will provide all of the proteins, essential fatty acids, vitamins, minerals, and other nutrients you need. By eating a variety of foods, you will not need vitamin or mineral supplements, with the exception of calcium for certain individuals. It is far preferable to obtain your vitamins and minerals from food rather than from a pill or capsule. Vitamins and minerals in food tend to be in the right proportions and are in a form that is easily absorbed and utilized by the body.

Do I have to throw out all of our recipes and start over?

Recipe Conversion

In general, recipe conversion is relatively straightforward. In the recipe conversion guide in chapter 13, "How to Eat Revisited," I have provided a number of substitutions that, on the whole, work quite well. You will have to experiment, since some of these substitutions may require minor adjustments in preparation and cooking. As a rule of thumb, try to convert recipes that already contain some healthy ingredients. If you have to substitute every ingredient in the recipe, it may be an interesting experiment, but it probably will not be successful. In addition to converting your existing recipes, a number of recipes are contained at the end of this book. Chapter 14, "Quick-and-Lean Cuisine from the Kurzweil Kitchen," also contains a list of cookbooks that follow the guidelines of the 10% solution.

Okay, now what about restaurants.

Restaurants

The most important resources you will need in restaurants are a little common sense and patience. With a little practice, you should have no difficulty staying very close to these guidelines. In general, the better the restaurant the more willing they will be to accommodate your needs. Joe's Hamburger Heaven and your local greasy spoon may be less willing to modify their cuisine. For the most part, American restaurants are not unfamiliar with patrons asking for low-fat, low-cholesterol items. You may find greater resistance and ignorance on these subjects in a number of European countries. Asian cuisine (as served in Asia), however, is often close to ideal, although Japanese food is very high in salt.

Explain your needs in a patient way to your waiter or waitress. Ask that foods be baked, grilled, or broiled in wine, low-fat chicken stock, water, or even dry. Ask them to hold the oil, butter, margarine, mayonnaise, cream and cream-based sauces, egg yolks, and cheese. You may need some persistence. Most waiters have relatively little knowledge of nutrition, and they may not be familiar with the ingredients or nutritional content of their menu. Nondescript sauces are suspect—they will often contain cream, oil, or butter. See the guide for dining out in chapter 13, "How to Eat Revisited," for suggestions of items you can order in different types of continental and ethnic restaurants.

Keep your priorities in mind. Fat and cholesterol are the primary substances to avoid unless you are hypertensive, in which case sodium should have equal priority. In general, your first dietary concern should be fat and cholesterol, then sodium, and then sugar.

You know, it's not easy to hold a lengthy negotiation with a waiter, especially if you are with other people.

It usually does not need to be lengthy. By selecting your items carefully and using a few well-chosen words, you should be able to communicate your needs without much difficulty. In your hometown, as well as places that you travel to frequently, try to find particular restaurants that you know can follow the guidelines. Ultimately, it should require very little negotiation once the restaurants become familiar with your needs. But being responsive to the social aspects of dining is one reason that it is important to keep your priorities in mind when dining out.

Any other situations worth being aware of?

Parties

If you are invited to a party, it makes sense to discuss your dietary needs with the host or hostess. Explain that you do not wish to put them to any significant trouble. Usually, some minor adjustments will enable you to eat many of the items being prepared. These may include such accommodations as putting your potatoes or vegetables aside before they are doused with a cheese- or cream-based sauce. It is better to discuss this issue in advance rather than frustrate both the host and yourself by eating little of what is served.

Functions such as luncheons and planned dinners are relatively straightforward. Call ahead and explain your needs. When traveling, call your airline at least twenty-four hours ahead and order a "low-fat, low-cholesterol" meal. I have also had success ordering a meal that is "vegetarian, no egg or dairy." You can specify this when you order your tickets. Taking some condiments with you when you travel to a foreign country, such as non-fat milk powder and no-oil salad dressings, is also a good idea.

What about other family members?

Family Members

I'm glad you mentioned that, because a supportive and cooperative environment is very important to successfully changing your habits. Ideally, your family will follow the same diet. As I explained earlier, children may eat a somewhat higher level of fat than 10 percent (I recommend 20 to 25 percent), but there is no reason why they cannot eat the same foods that are prepared for you. If everyone in your household eats a similar diet, then preparation is greatly simplified, and you will feel supported in your efforts.

What if I can't get my spouse to adopt the same approach?

Hopefully your spouse will at least support your own efforts, if not actually adopt the diet. While it is easier and more enjoyable to approach this as a mutual effort, you have to take responsibility yourself for your own health and well-being. Keep in mind that it's your body and your job to keep it healthy.

It is not a good idea to be too aggressive in promoting your dietary approach with others, even your own family. You can explain what you are doing, why it makes sense, and how it has become an enjoyable way to eat and live. People will notice that you look and feel good and that you are enthusiastic about your life-style.

You could also write a book on the subject.

Hey, that's a great idea.

7

How to Exercise

Aerobic versus Anaerobic

In addition to a healthy diet, the other important requirement I recall you mentioning is exercise.

Yes, that is the other primary consideration.

If I jog a few times a week, is that good enough?

Jogging is certainly a satisfactory form of exercise. It is not the ideal exercise to start out with, for reasons I will discuss in a moment.

What form of exercise do you recommend?

First, it is important to distinguish between aerobic exercise, which literally means "with oxygen," and anaerobic exercise, which involves a high-intensity activity that can only be sustained in short bursts. Examples of aerobic exercise are walking, swimming, cycling, rowing, and cross-country skiing. Any aerobic exercise is very beneficial in terms of significantly lowering the risk of cardiovascular disease, cancer, and other diseases, as well as providing immediate benefits in terms of weight loss, reduced hypertension, improved sleep, and better mood. Regular aerobic exercise can also reduce elevated triglyceride levels and can boost the levels of HDL, the good cholesterol.[1]

Examples of anaerobic exercise include sprinting, forms of calisthenics, weight lifting, basketball, and tennis.

Tennis is not aerobic exercise?

No, not really. There is some cardiac benefit from the significant exertion involved in a sport like tennis, but it is not an optimal form of aerobic exercise. I would consider these types of sports more as supplements to a regular aerobic exercise program, not the primary component of one.

Aerobic exercise is activity which requires movement of the large upper or lower body muscles continuously in a regular rhythm for at least twenty minutes. Aerobic exercise increases your heart rate and your demand for oxygen but is sustainable for an extended period of time. During aerobic exercise, you should be at your training heart rate.

Training heart rate?

Training Heart Rate

The training heart-rate range is between 65 and 85 percent of your maximum heart rate, which you can estimate as 220 less your age.[2] So, for example, if you are 40 years of age, your theoretical maximum heart rate is 180, and your training heart-rate range would be between 117 and 153 beats per minute.

How do I determine my heart rate?

The best way is to obtain a sports watch that provides a pulse readout. Then you do not need to stop your exercise to determine your heart rate. Otherwise, you need to briefly interrupt your exercise and count your pulse for fifteen seconds, then multiply this figure by four. It is important to take your pulse as soon as you stop exercising, because your heart rate will slow down immediately. Once you have estimated your heart rate, continue your exercise routine.

So what's the best form of aerobic exercise?

Walking

The ideal aerobic exercise is walking. It's simple. Virtually everyone knows how to do it. You can do it most anywhere. You should have

MAXIMUM HEART RATE
AND TRAINING HEART RANGE

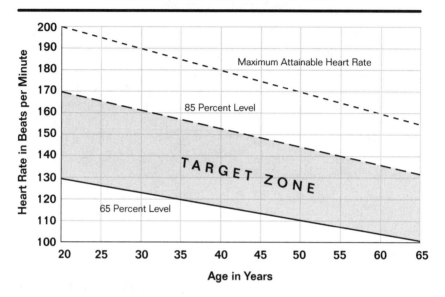

The Maximum Heart Rate shows the peak heart rate for average individuals. Any individual may vary from these averages, which apply to about two-thirds of the population. Shown below the maximum heart rate are the corresponding training heart-rate ranges for each age.

little difficulty elevating your heart rate into your training range on a sustained basis. It does not put undue strain on any of your joints. It is an excellent form of low-impact aerobic exercise.

Is that all there is to it—you just walk?

There is nothing unusual about the style or technique of walking required. There are, however, some considerations we should discuss in establishing a safe and effective exercise program.

First, you should consult your physician before starting any regular exercise program. Your doctor can advise you on any special considerations with regard to your physical condition and health. This is essential if you have indications of heart disease or other serious illness.

Exercise Stress Test

In addition, the American College of Sports Medicine recommends that certain people undergo an exercise stress test before starting an exercise program as one way of screening for heart disorders, including advanced atherosclerosis.[3] They recommend a stress test prior to starting an exercise program if you are (1) age 45 or over, or (2) between 35 and 44 and have at least one risk factor for coronary artery disease (such as an immediate family member who developed coronary artery disease before age 50, if you are obese, if you smoke, have high blood pressure, or a high cholesterol level), or (3) at any age and have cardiovascular disease, lung disease, diabetes, or hyperthyroidism. If you are under 45, appear to be in good health, and do not have any of these risk factors for coronary artery disease, then you do not need this test, according to the American College of Sports Medicine.

What is an exercise stress test?

It is an electrocardiogram (ECG) administered for ten to fifteen minutes while you exercise on a treadmill or stationary bicycle. Your blood pressure and pulse are also continually monitored. The difficulty of the exercise is progressively increased during the test. The test is stopped when you are too tired to continue, or if any symptoms are noted, such as an abnormally high blood pressure reading, abnormal pulse rate, shortness of breath, chest pain or other discomfort, or an abnormality in the ECG. There is some risk in a stress test, although this is minimal if administered properly by a trained health professional.

The test is far from perfect. About 10 to 20 percent of stress tests give false positives (incorrectly indicating a heart or artery abnormality) and 20 percent to 40 percent yield false negatives. Thus, the exercise stress test will not capture all instances of artery blockage, and any positive indications that it does provide need to be confirmed by further medical tests. Nonetheless, it can be a useful screening procedure that your doctor or fitness instructor may request you undergo before starting an exercise program.

All right, let's say I'm ready to go. Now what?

The next step is to start. Begin slowly. The objective is to exercise on a regular basis, to build this activity into a predictable routine.

Endurance and the ability to perform more quickly and for longer periods of time will come naturally as your fitness improves.

It is important not to overdo it. You should feel like you are exerting yourself, but if you feel pain in your legs (shinsplints, for example), then slow down and rest. If you ever feel pain in your chest, then stop

THE BENEFITS OF EXERCISE

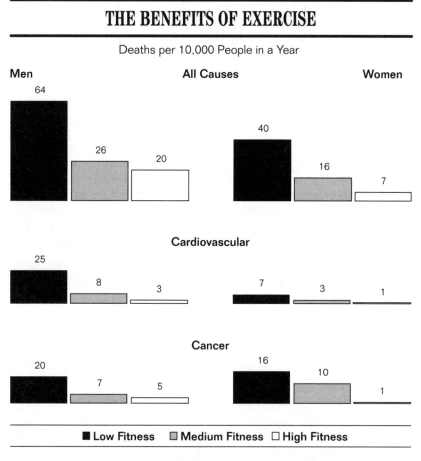

Deaths per 10,000 People in a Year

■ Low Fitness   ▨ Medium Fitness   ☐ High Fitness

The results of an 8-year 13,344-subject study conducted by the Institute for Aerobics Research reported in November 1989 in the <u>Journal of the American Medical Association</u> demonstrate the dramatic impact of even moderate exercise on mortality. The subjects in group 1 were sedentary and of low fitness. Those in groups 2 and 3 walked 30 to 60 minutes per day, 4 to 5 times per week, and were of medium fitness. Groups 4 and 5 walked or ran 20 to 30 miles per week or more and were of high fitness.

immediately and consult your doctor, because you may be experiencing angina pain indicative of advanced atherosclerosis. (If the pain persists, you could be having a heart attack.)

It is also important to have the right walking shoes. Do not use ordinary sneakers or even running shoes. Obtain a good-quality pair of shoes designed specifically for walking.

How much do I need to do?

Benefits

The results of an 8-year study reported in 1989 in the *Journal of the American Medical Association* are instructive in answering this question.[4] The study divided the 13,344 participants into 5 fitness categories. Individuals in category 1 were sedentary and had no regular exercise program. Individuals in categories 2 and 3 were of medium fitness, which was achieved by walking 30 to 60 minutes per day, 4 to 5 times per week. Individuals in categories 4 and 5 were of high fitness and walked or ran 20 to 30 miles per week or more.

The results were unexpectedly dramatic, and there were significant gains between low and medium fitness, and again between medium and high fitness. The most significant gains were between low and medium fitness, indicating that even moderate regular exercise is of immense benefit. Overall death rates for the medium-fitness group were 60 percent less than those of the low-fitness group. Death from cardiovascular disease for men was down by more than two-thirds. There was further benefit for both men and women in the high-fitness category, particularly with regard to cardiovascular disease.

Amount of Exercise

I would recommend the equivalent of walking 3 miles per day or more, 5 or more days per week, although even 4 days per week of regular aerobic exercise is of significant benefit. Once you gain some experience and fitness, this will require about 45 to 50 minutes for each session. Again, it is important to build up to these levels. If you are very out of shape, even walking 1 mile may be strenuous. So build up gradually, doing a bit more each day. Making a real and permanent commitment to a regular and predictable program is the most important step you can take.

TARGET EXERCISE PATTERN

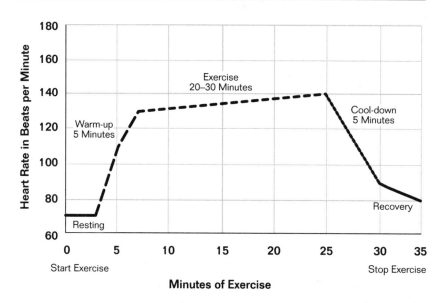

The diagram shows a desirable pattern of heart rate for an aerobic exercise session.

So I just walk, building up to 15 or more miles per week.

The Five Phases of Exercise

It is a little more complicated than that. You should **start out** with a few minutes of stretching, which will help to reduce injuries, improve coordination and range of motion, and help to relax the body. The most important target of stretching are the hamstrings, lower back, quadriceps, shins, calves, and Achilles tendons.

The **second phase** is warm-up, which involves walking at an easy pace, about 3 miles per hour, for a few minutes. This allows you to build momentum, thereby gradually reducing the stress on your muscles and on your heart.

The **third phase,** which should be the bulk of your exercise routine, is the aerobic phase in which you exercise sufficiently rigorously

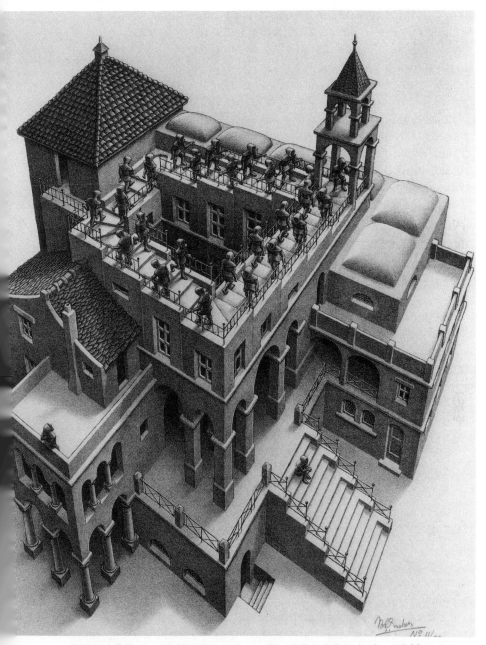

Only in an Escher drawing can you walk uphill indefinitely. In real life, you can achieve this effect only with a treadmill or a stair-climbing machine. (© 1960 M. C. Escher/Cordon Art-Baarn-Holland.)

to bring your heart rate into your training range. This should last at least 20 minutes to obtain a training effect on your heart. In order to cover at least 15 miles per week (once you are sufficiently fit to do this), you will probably want to walk in your training range for 30 to 40 minutes each session. In general, you will need to walk at least 4 miles per hour in order to achieve your training heart-rate range.

Following the aerobic phase is the **fourth phase**, cool-down, which is similar to warm-up. This allows your heart rate to return to normal gradually and prevents a pooling of blood in your legs and feet. Then the **fifth and final phase** is another several minutes of stretching to maintain limber joints, muscles, and tendons.

If I have difficulty getting into my training heart-rate range by walking, are there any ways to make walking more intense?

Varieties of Low-Impact Aerobic Exercise

Yes, there are a variety of ways. You can vigorously swing your arms, which will increase your heart rate and also boost your calorie consumption by 5 to 10 percent. You can do what is called interval walking, which is alternating several minutes of very brisk striding with several minutes of a more moderate pace. This also increases your heart rate and makes the activity more interesting. You can walk on sand if that is available to you, which can increase the calories expended by as much as 30 percent.

You can walk uphill. At a 10 percent incline, you nearly double your expenditure of calories. Of course, it is only in an Escher drawing that you can walk uphill indefinitely without ever going down. To achieve this in real life, I would suggest using a treadmill. The ultimate in walking uphill is stair climbing. You should be careful, however. Walking up metal or concrete stairs carries a high risk of serious injury. I would suggest one of the stair-climbing machines, which have become quite popular. By walking two steps per second, a 150-pound person can burn more than 1,000 calories per hour.

A very effective way to increase both heart rate and calorie consumption is by carrying hand weights. You should not use hand weights if you have heart disease, hypertension, or back problems of any kind. Use one- or two-pound weights and a controlled pattern of arm movements. Do not swing the weights wildly.

TABLE 5

CALORIE EXPENDITURE PER HOUR FROM WALKING

Calories Burned per Hour

WEIGHT (LBS)	MILES PER HOUR				
	3.0	3.5	4.0	4.5	5.0
100	162	181	201	306	413
120	195	218	241	367	496
140	228	254	281	429	578
160	260	291	322	490	661
180	293	327	362	552	744
200	326	364	402	613	827

The calories burned per hour by walking on a level surface without hand weights.

TABLE 6

CALORIE EXPENDITURE PER HOUR FROM WALKING ON A 5 AND 10 PERCENT INCLINE

Calories Burned per Hour

WEIGHT (LBS)	FLAT SURFACE	5 PERCENT INCLINE	10 PERCENT INCLINE
100	162	229	296
110	179	252	326
120	195	275	355
130	212	298	385
140	228	321	414
150	244	345	445
160	260	367	474
170	276	389	503
180	293	413	533
190	309	435	562
200	326	459	593

The calories burned per hour by walking 3 miles per hour nearly doubles on a 10 percent incline.

Okay, now what about running or jogging? Isn't that an intense form of walking?

Essentially, yes. Running is definitely aerobic and is more intense than walking. While I would never discourage someone who runs on a regular basis from continuing this excellent form of aerobic activity, I do think it is worthwhile to point out some of the disadvantages to those considering what form of exercise to start with. Jogging or running is, in essence, a series of jumps, each of which conveys a load to your feet and legs equal to three times your weight or more. The force on your feet is even greater, up to 30 times the force of gravity. This sends a shock wave through your body at 200 miles per hour, which is absorbed by your bones and soft tissues. All of this puts cumulative stress on your body, particularly the feet, ankles, lower legs, and knees. Over time, this can cause shinsplints, tendinitis, stress fractures, orthopedic difficulties, and other problems. A large fraction of runners develop injuries, some of which can be serious. To some extent, the potential for injury has been ameliorated by the development of well-designed running shoes. I strongly recommend that you obtain appropriate footwear designed specifically for running if you wish to consider this form of exercise. It is also desirable to find a relatively soft surface to run on, such as dirt, grass, or a running track, as opposed to concrete. There is no question, however, that you can obtain intense aerobic benefits from running, and it certainly is efficient.

What other forms of exercise do you recommend?

There are a variety of low-impact aerobic exercise activities that are ideal for increasing cardiovascular endurance and strengthening the pulmonary system. Swimming is low impact, although it is important to use proper form. One advantage of swimming is that it is easier to move one's limbs in the water because of the significant reduction in one's apparent weight. For this reason, swimming and water aerobics (aerobic exercise in the water using a flotation ring) are ideal forms of exercise for anyone, especially the elderly, and others who suffer from muscle or joint infirmities and injuries. Also, swimming is excellent for active people who, due to injury, cannot continue their usual aerobic activity. Because swimming is a non–weight-bearing form of aerobic activity, it is significantly less stressful on the body than other forms of exercise.

Aerobic classes can be ideal, although I would emphasize the low-impact variety. A competent instructor will guide you through the appropriate stages of stretching, warm-up, aerobic exercise, and cool-down. Aerobic dancing is also enjoyable. Any movement to music can help keep up both momentum and motivation.

Bicycling is both aerobic and low impact if the proper form is used. One disadvantage of bicycling is the rapid change from high intensity to low. Experienced cyclists are able to maintain a fairly even expenditure of energy through appropriate gear changes, although this takes practice. Continuous aerobic exercise is easy to achieve on

TABLE 7

THE CALORIC VALUE OF DIFFERENT FORMS OF EXERCISE

(PER HOUR)

ACTIVITY	120-POUND PERSON	150-POUND PERSON	170-POUND PERSON	190-POUND PERSON
Skiing, cross-country, uphill	897	1,121	1,270	1,420
Squash	694	867	983	1,099
Running, 6.7 miles per hour	632	790	895	1,000
Jumping rope, 80 per minute	537	671	760	850
Swimming, crawl, fast	511	638	723	808
Basketball	452	565	640	715
Aerobic dancing, intense	442	552	626	700
Walking, climbing hills with 11-pound load	422	528	598	668
Skiing, cross-country, moderate	389	487	552	617
Tennis	357	446	505	565
Aerobic dancing, medium	337	421	478	534
Cycling, 9.4 miles per hour	327	409	464	518
Walking, normal pace	262	327	371	415
Canoeing, leisure	144	180	204	228
Writing (sitting)	95	119	134	150
Standing	88	110	125	140
Eating (sitting)	75	94	107	119
Resting (lying down)	72	90	102	114

Data from: W. D. McArdle, F. I. Katch, and V. L. Katch, Exercise Physiology: Energy Nutrition and Human Performance 3d ed. (Philadelphia: Lea and Febiger, 1991).

indoor stationary bikes. When cycling outdoors, be sure to use a safety helmet and try to avoid roads with heavy traffic.

An ideal form of exercise is cross-country skiing. This activity provides a workout for muscle groups in both the upper and lower body. It is vigorous and invigorating, particularly in an attractive setting. The only disadvantage is that it is not always available. Another exercise that uses both the upper and lower body is rowing (in a boat or on a machine). Here again, proper form is essential to avoid lower back injury.

Tips

It isn't always possible to exercise outdoors, given the vagaries of the weather.

That is a very good point. Since it is desirable to exercise almost every day, depending on the weather is not a good strategy for people in most places in the world. One solution is membership in a health club with appropriate facilities. This has the added benefit of supervision, which can be both instructive and motivational.

It is also very desirable to have some facilities in your home. For many people, this is the most efficient way to make exercise a regular part of their day. Although not inexpensive, the one piece of equipment that I would strongly recommend is a treadmill. If your primary aerobic activity is walking, having your own treadmill is an ideal way to assure a continuous program. Without your own treadmill, maintaining a regular program of walking may be impossible unless the weather in your area is predictably accommodating. Most people find that a treadmill is a much more satisfactory way to exercise at home than a stationary bicycle, which can become tedious.

I'm glad you mentioned tedium, because any of these exercises can become tedious if you do it every day.

I'm not sure I agree with that. If you find the right exercise for you, it can be an enjoyable part of your routine. Walking outside can be a refreshing way to tour your neighborhood.

Assuming your neighborhood is one you want to walk around in.

Yes, that certainly is a consideration. Other ways to avoid tedium include exercising with friends, listening to music, or watching television. Or the exercise period can be a time of reflection, an opportunity to let your thoughts wander. Physical exertion combined with mental relaxation is an ideal combination to reduce stress.

You may also wish to vary your exercise routine—walk one day, bicycle another—as a way of adding interest. What is most important is that you develop an exercise routine that is enjoyable to you and that you can look forward to. Many people report that once you become accustomed to an exercise routine, it feels awful to stop.

Any recommendations on when to exercise?

I would strongly suggest picking a time of day to exercise that can become a normal part of your routine. It is not a good idea to exercise within thirty to forty-five minutes after eating. Therefore, many people find it convenient to exercise right before a meal, in the morning before breakfast, before lunch, or before dinner. It is also not ideal to exercise late at night right before going to sleep, particularly if you have any difficulty sleeping.

How am I supposed to find the time for this? There are so many things that are crucial for me to do: spend time with my family, eat right, exercise, not to mention all the demands of work.

I can't solve that problem for you. You have to set priorities. But it is important to note that exercise will pay for itself. The dramatic improvements in your energy level, ability to sleep, and sense of well-being mean that you are not really "losing" time. It turns out that the busiest and most successful business executives are frequently the most diligent about their exercise routines.

I guess people like that are diligent about everything they do.

Perhaps they are. But the most important thing about exercise is not any of the fine points of technique and form, rather just the fact that you do it on a regular basis.

As they say, no pain, no gain.

Actually, I should point out that exercise should definitely not be painful. There is no harm in breaking a sweat. In fact, it is difficult to achieve one's training heart-rate range without sweating. But you should avoid pain. Pain is certainly demoralizing, and, depending on the source, can be an indication of injury, angina, or other condition that should not be tolerated. A good test to see if you are overexerting yourself is the talk test. If you are too fatigued to carry on a conversation, then you are working too hard and should slow down.

As with weight loss, it is important to get on the right track and make a commitment to stay on it. Do not be overly anxious about your progress.

So I should not be concerned with the progress of my exercise program?

You should not be *overly* concerned. But I do recommend that you keep a written record of your progress, because if you keep up the program you cannot help but advance each week in your endurance and fitness. Seeing a record of your progress will be a positive motivation to keep going.

So this is something else I have to keep track of now?

This does not need to be onerous. If you are walking, you can just write down how far you went and how long it took. You can even do this just once a week to see how your capability improves over time.

Sometimes I have to travel. It's kind of difficult keeping up an exercise routine on the road.

It shouldn't be. That's one reason I recommend walking as a mainstay of any exercise program. It is not always possible to find a bicycle or a swimming pool, let alone a facility for cross-country skiing. But walking is usually quite feasible. Also, with the increasing interest in fitness, many hotels provide exercise facilities, and you can make this a criterion in your selection of a place to stay. As for finding time, it just comes down to priorities.

How about if I am not feeling well?

Use common sense. Do not exercise if you are ill, particularly if you have a fever. If you miss a week or more of your exercise routine, then restart your program cautiously once you are well. You lose fitness twice as quickly as you develop it, so do not be discouraged if it takes time to get back to the level of fitness you reached prior to the illness.

Well, I shouldn't be getting ill if I follow the 10% solution, isn't that right?

I'm afraid I can't give you that guarantee. You will certainly dramatically reduce your risk of heart disease, cancer, and other major diseases and strengthen your immune system, which helps in fighting any disease. You are likely to have minor illnesses a lot less frequently by avoiding the poisonous diet that our society consumes and by keeping your body fit. But we cannot say that you are assured of avoiding all illness.

How about calisthenics? Aren't they good for turning fat into muscle?

First of all, you can't turn fat into muscle, nor can you firm up fat. You have to lose the fat through a weight-loss program aimed at reduction of body fat. That is achieved by a low-fat diet, calorie control, and exercise. At the same time that you are losing your excess fat, you can develop your muscles through exercise. Calisthenics will firm and tone your muscles, and there is nothing wrong with that. But for cardiovascular fitness as well as for weight loss, you need aerobic exercise, and calisthenics is not aerobic.

Any other tips?

Take advantage of every opportunity to use your body rather than the array of labor-saving devices that surround us. Use the stairs as opposed to the elevator. Walk or bicycle to your destination instead of hopping into the car for short trips. These are not substitutes for your regular exercise routine, but this is a useful attitude to develop.

Anything else?

Yes, a reminder that exercise alone is not sufficient. Exercise will not reduce levels of LDL, the bad cholesterol in your blood. There is a myth that you can eat whatever you want if you just exercise. But the long list of marathon runners who have had sudden and often fatal heart attacks due to advanced atherosclerosis is a clear indication that exercise alone is not an antidote for the devastating effects of a diet high in fat, cholesterol, and sodium.[5] The dietary and exercise recommendations of the 10% solution go hand in hand. They work together synergistically. The benefits of applying both principles is greater than the sum of the benefits of either one alone.

8
∎
The Mind-Body Connection

Stress

I understand that stress plays an important role in the development of disease.

It is an important issue, although not a simple one.

None of these issues is simple.

The dietary principles—10 percent calories from fat and similar guidelines for cholesterol, sodium, and other nutrients—are reasonably simple, although the scientific evidence justifying them and the means of implementing them in our lives are more complicated. Articulating the essential role of stress in our health and well-being is more difficult.

Perhaps that just reflects the state of our knowledge in this area. Nutrition can also seem confusing if you are lacking the right road map.

That is very well put. The difficulty is that we cannot simply say that stress is bad for you. In certain circumstances, some forms of stress can be very damaging to one's health. In other situations, circumstances that we would consider very stressful may not be damaging or can even be energizing. Consider the example I cited in chapter 1: the experience of the European populations during World War II—populations hiding in subway tunnels while their homes were firebombed, other populations fleeing their homes when caught between opposing armies. Yet the rate of heart disease did not increase during those terrible years. The only impact that has been noted was the dramatic *decrease* in heart disease in those countries in which food rationing was imposed during the exact period of time in which rationing was in effect. And we know that the principal consequence of the rationing was the limitation of precisely those foods that are high in fat and cholesterol: meat, eggs, cheese, butter, milk, cream, and cooking oils.

On the other hand, there are many examples of life situations, and perhaps most important, our reactions to them, that appear to have a profound effect on our ability to resist or overcome disease. Many studies have shown that certain types of chronic stress can contribute to disease. Conversely, studies have shown the ability of the mind to assist in both resisting and overcoming disease through such methods as meditation and other relaxation techniques.

Just what is stress?

Essentially, stress is the arousal of the body and mind to demands and challenges that present themselves.

That doesn't sound like a bad thing.

Stress is not necessarily harmful. We need a certain amount of challenge to avoid apathy and boredom. Even positive changes in our lives represent stress. The term *eustress* refers to our reaction to constructive change: a job promotion, an award, getting married, even going on a vacation. The type of stress that appears to be harmful to our health is the excessive activation of our fight-or-flight response.

Fight or flight?

Fight or Flight

That refers to the primitive origins of this mechanism. When our paleolithic ancestors confronted a menacing foe, whether animal or human, they had the choice of confronting the danger or fleeing; thus the term *fight or flight*. The process starts with our pattern recognition and cognitive faculties perceiving danger. Once that judgment is made, the rest is automatic. A perception of danger triggers a chain reaction of neural and hormonal changes that puts the body into a state of readiness for action. The hypothalamus signals the pituitary gland, which produces a hormone, which in turn stimulates the adrenal cortex to produce cortisol. Cortisol is carried in the bloodstream and causes a dramatic but temporary increase in metabolism. A spinal reflex signals the adrenal glands to produce adrenaline and noradrenaline, also known as epinephrine and norepinephrine. These hormones have a dramatic effect on the body, including nearly halting the digestive process and increasing blood pressure, blood sugar, cholesterol levels, and breathing and heart rates. Other effects include dilation of the pupils, the activation of blood-clotting mechanisms to prepare for the possibility of injury, and the mobilization of internal energy stores for the possibility of extreme physical exertion.[1]

I take it that these changes are harmful.

Not necessarily. We need the fight-or-flight mechanism to survive, otherwise we would not have the capacity to respond appropriately to danger. A problem arises when this mechanism is overutilized. It is *chronic* stress that is harmful. It's as if your body is in a constant state of emergency. Then the temporary effects, such as increased blood pressure and cholesterol and decreased blood flow to the liver and digestive organs, can become permanent.

Does this have to do with the type A personality?

The Type A Personality Revisited

The so-called type A personality gained publicity in the mid-1970s and is described as a person who is hard driving, overly ambitious, impatient, competitive, aggressive, always working to a deadline, and generally possessing the traits of a workaholic. In contrast, type B personalities are described as relaxed, easygoing, accepting, and complacent. These early studies suggested that having a type A personality was a risk factor for the development of heart disease. More recent studies have cast doubt on the type A personality as a risk factor, at least as it was originally defined. The contemporary research indicates that of all the aspects that make up the classic type A pattern, the only ones that appear to be related to an increased risk of heart disease, are those involving anger, cynicism, and hostility.[2] People with hot tempers and/or suspicious, angry, hostile natures are more likely to die from heart disease. Other type A characteristics, such as competitiveness, ambition, even workaholism, were not found to be risk factors.

For example, a long-term study was conducted on a group of 118 lawyers who had taken the Minnesota Multiphasic Personality Inventory, a standard personality test, 25 years earlier, while in law school.[3] Those who had higher scores for hostility had a death rate from heart disease that was more than four times higher over the subsequent 25-year period than those with low scores for hostility.

Another dramatic study was a 25-year follow-up study of 255 physicians.[4] Here the hostile physicians were 6 times more likely to die than the group who scored low on the hostility characteristic.

THE DANGER OF BEING HOSTILE

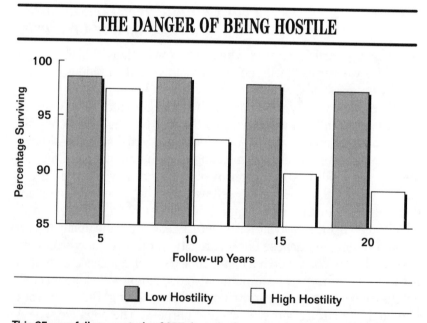

This 25-year follow-up study of 255 doctors shows the progressive risk of the hostile personality trait.

Data from: J. Barefoot, G. Dahlstrom, and R. B. Williams, "Hostility, CHD Incidence, and Total Mortality: A 25-Year Follow-up Study of 255 Physicians," Psychosomatic Medicine 45 (March 1983): 59–63.

Hostility and anger. Are those the only personality traits linked to disease?

Researchers have discovered a similar link between "suspicious" personalities and increased mortality rate, although suspiciousness is linked to hostility and anger. A study reported in 1987 at Duke University followed 500 men and women with an average starting age of 59 for a period of 15 years.[5] Men who were characterized as having a suspicious personality were twice as likely to die as their more trusting peers. The suspicious women were 29 percent more likely to die than their more trustful peers. There are other studies that demonstrate the healthful benefits of a positive and trusting outlook on life.

So the original idea of the type A personality was not accurate.

The Four Cs: Challenge, Commitment, Curiosity, and Creativity

It was only partially correct. The health implications of having characteristics we associate with being competitive and ambitious depend on why the person has those characteristics. There are, after all, constructive reasons why a person might be eager to achieve a set of goals. These can be characterized by the four Cs: challenge, commitment, curiosity, and creativity. A challenge is a goal that, while difficult to achieve, is worthwhile and meaningful to that individual. Commitment is the ability to place an overriding priority on attaining a challenging goal, to see progress toward a goal as more important than sacrifices that may be required. Curiosity is a desire for knowledge and an openness to life's wonders. Creativity is the ability to create knowledge, to harness one's curiosity to discover new wonders. People who are characterized by the four Cs often appear to be type A in that their high level of commitment and willingness to take on challenges cause them to appear driven and hardworking. But their work is rooted in a strong sense of self and purpose. The negative type A pattern is driven by something different—by cynicism, anger, and hostility, by a persistent sense of being treated unfairly and a need to be aggressive to get what is due.

Meyer Friedman, a cardiologist and one of the originators of the type A concept, has spent the past thirty years studying the research on the link between behavior and personality and heart disease. Friedman describes the negative type A as a one-dimensional personality, someone with a profound absence of spiritual life.

You have to be religious to avoid heart disease?

By spiritual life, Friedman is not referring specifically to a life with strong religious beliefs, but rather a life that has meaning, that attaches importance to human relationships and to other social and cultural concerns that enrich our lives.[6] If the hard work and apparent impatience of the type A person emerges from concerns and beliefs that are deeply rooted in their own structure of values, then this commitment to achievement is supportive of cardiac health. If the pattern is the result of the "erosion of personality" that results from chronic suspiciousness, then it is destructive. You might say it has to do with whether or not our energy is directed out toward the world in a constructive fashion or directed inward in a destructive fashion.

This perspective sheds light on why the years of World War II, as stressful as they may appear, did not cause an increase in heart disease. The populations in these wars were not passive bystanders. In previous centuries, war was an activity engaged in primarily by professional armies. But in this century, war has been a struggle of entire societies. The first two Cs, challenge and commitment, certainly characterized the attitude of these populations in that circumstance. And since we might regard war as the father of invention and a major impetus to the creation of technology, we can include creativity as well.

Still, it is hard to avoid stress in our society.

The Stress Scale

True, stressful change is a part of life, particularly in the rapidly changing technology-oriented society we live in. Researchers Thomas Holmes and Richard Rahe studied five thousand individuals—the events in their lives and their reactions to them. They developed a stress scale ranking various events ranging from Christmas to the death of a spouse. They found that the higher your total stress score in any particular year, the more likely you were to become ill.

Based on what you said earlier, it would seem that different people would experience different levels of stress when faced with these events.

TABLE 9

STRESSFUL EVENTS AND HOW THEY RATE

Death of a spouse	100	Death of close friend	37
Divorce	73	Change in work	29
Death of an immediate family		Children leave home	29
member	63	Outstanding achievement	28
Personal injury	53	Trouble with boss	23
Personal illness	53	Vacation	13
Marriage	50	Christmas	12
Fired from job	47	Minor law violations	11
Retirement	45		
Change in health of immediate			
family member	44		

Data from: T. H. Holmes and R. H. Rahe, "The Social Readjustment Rating Scale," Journal of Psychosomatic Research 11 (1967): 213–18, esp. 216.

These ratings represent average stress levels, which Holmes and Rahe were able to statistically associate with levels of disease. But it is certainly true that we each have different capacities to cope with stressful change. Stress is inherently an *internal* phenomenon. How we experience events depends on our outlook, perspective, and personality.

It would seem that the easygoing type B personality might have an easier time accepting change than the type A.

Not necessarily. The passivity of some type Bs may enable them to cope with change. On the other hand, a secure and well-grounded type A person may see change as a challenge and use his or her creativity to effect a positive result from an otherwise difficult situation.

How can you tell if you are not dealing constructively with stress?

The Symptoms of Stress

Physical symptoms can include high blood pressure, headaches, rapid heartbeat, aches and pains, muscle tension, and gastrointestinal discomfort. Behavioral indications would include difficulty sleeping; compulsive behavior, including compulsive use of food, drugs, alcohol, sex, or gambling; problems in concentration; accident proneness; and social withdrawal. Emotional signs include nightmares, crying spells, feelings of worthlessness, excessive or compulsive worrying, mood swings, restlessness, and anxiety. Spiritual signals include a sense of emptiness, loss of life's meaning, excessive confusion, and doubt about one's direction in life.

Those are all pretty general symptoms.

Yes, there is no simple test to determine how well you are dealing with the stress in your life; it is a matter of judgment. But it is a crucial judgment because the link between our health and our ability to deal constructively with our lives is now strongly supported by a growing corpus of scientific literature. Most of us can benefit from improving the balance of our lives and our ability to cope with life's challenges.

Just what can I do to relieve stress?

False Stress Relievers

Let's talk first about what not to do.

Don't eat a high-fat diet?

Food

I'm not sure I would have listed a high-fat diet first on a list of false tension relievers, but it certainly should be included. Compulsive eating in general is not an effective way to reduce stress. Even if the foods you overeat are healthy ones, this habit will contribute to excess weight and will stress your gastrointestinal system. Moreover, the foods that people eat when combating tension and anxiety tend to be high in fat, cholesterol, sodium, sugar, and calories. Finally, it just doesn't work. You may feel some temporary satisfaction while you are eating, but when you're done you are likely just to have added the feeling of being stuffed and the associated feelings of guilt to your original anxiety.

So what is first on your list of false stress relievers?

First, second, and third on the list are the three drugs most abused in American and most other advanced societies: tobacco, alcohol, and caffeine.

Tobacco

Nicotine appears to ease anxiety and promote a sense of alertness by stimulating the production of a variety of hormones, including adrenaline. Smoking also provides an oral gratification linked to our earliest feelings of satisfaction from sucking. Yet cigarette smoking is linked to more than 350,000 American deaths a year from heart disease; lung, larynx, and other cancers; emphysema; and other respiratory and circulatory problems.[7] Even putting these devastating diseases aside, smoking substantially reduces the oxygen available to the body's tissues, and the constant assault of carbon monoxide, nicotine, tar, and dozens of other poisonous gases dramatically reduces one's sense of well-being. This deterioration of virtually all of the body's systems clearly adds to the overall level of stress.

Alcohol

Alcohol is a close second to tobacco as our most abused drug, accounting for more than 100,000 deaths per year. Alcohol abuse is a major risk factor in heart disease; can cause severe liver damage, hypertension, gastrointestinal disorders, and brain damage; and contributes to a variety of cancers.[8]

I thought moderate use of alcohol was found to be beneficial to one's heart.

This issue has not been resolved. A variety of studies on alcohol and its effects on health discovered what is called a J curve (sometimes called a U curve).[9] The incidence of heart disease was found to be lowest in those individuals who consumed a moderate amount of alcohol. Those who did not drink at all were found to have a somewhat higher rate of heart disease. Those who drank heavily, that is, more than the equivalent of two glasses of wine or beer a day, also had higher rates of heart disease, with the rates dramatically increasing with increasing usage. Thus, the disease-incidence curves looked like the letter J (or U).

That sort of makes sense. People who don't drink at all must be a bit uptight.

Perhaps, but a group of English researchers began to suspect the data. They began to think about what types of individuals would abstain completely from alcohol. They reasoned that there must be two very different groups: one that has always abstained and another that is presently abstaining for health reasons because they are recovering alcohol abusers or have heart or other problems and thus need to reduce or eliminate alcohol consumption. This latter group clearly includes individuals whose health has already been damaged (from alcohol abuse or otherwise). They reran the data, removing the men with previously existing cardiovascular-related conditions from consideration, and the curve flattened out. Having corrected this methodological flaw, no benefit was seen for moderate use of alcohol.[10]

A more recent study, which followed fifty thousand men for two years, claims to have controlled for any bias caused by preexisting disease in the participants. This major study, conducted at the Harvard School of Public Health and reported in the August 1991 issue of the British journal *Lancet*, again reported a protective effect from moderate use of alcohol.[11] Those who drank the equivalent of one or two glasses of wine a day had a 26 percent reduction in the risk of heart disease compared with those who drank no alcohol. The researchers attributed this benefit to the ability of alcohol, when it is metabolized in the liver, to cause an increase in levels of HDL (the good cholesterol) in the blood, as well as to cause a possible blood-thinning effect that would reduce the likelihood of a blood clot causing a coronary event. At higher levels of consumption, the researchers found the usual harmful effects of alcohol seen in cirrhosis of the liver, high blood pressure, and behavioral problems.

The methodology of this study can also be criticized, however. Because the researchers eliminated anyone with any signs of preexisting disease from the group of drinkers, they may have eliminated from this group precisely those people for whom the alcohol had been harmful, leaving only those who were not negatively affected by many years of moderate drinking. Thus, this attempt to control the composition of the group for preexisting disease may have made the group of moderate drinkers look healthier than they otherwise would have been. Eliminating those with preexisting disease from the group of nondrinkers may not have helped the apparent health of this group as significantly (as the group of moderate drinkers) because the nondrinking group probably had fewer people negatively affected by alcohol to begin with. Also, former alcohol abusers were not explicitly excluded from the teetotaling group. This was presumably controlled for by excluding those with evident disease, but former alcohol abusers with incipient disease would not necessarily be excluded. Finally, the study looked at short-term effects, not long-term potential problems resulting from liver damage or cancer.

A 1987 study found that women who consumed the equivalent of even a single drink per day had a significantly higher risk of breast cancer.[12] Other studies show increased risk of hypertension and stroke from moderate consumption of alcohol. So I would say that the impact of moderate use of alcohol on health has still not been clarified, although it may be the case that there is a marginal positive impact on the risk of heart disease for those who eat the "normal" high-fat diet. For those who follow the 10% solution, I don't see any positive effect.

So you don't recommend any use of alcohol.

No, I wouldn't say that, and I do consume alcohol in small quantities. Excessive consumption of alcohol always made me fall asleep anyway, so I was never prone to abusing it. My recommendation is to limit alcohol to no more than two drinks (6-ounce glasses of wine or beer or mixed drinks) per day, with less preferable. Keep in mind that alcohol does contain calories and the calories have no nutritional value.

Although occasional use can provide a feeling of relaxation and euphoria, it should be noted that alcohol is basically a depressant. It is not an answer for chronic feelings of stress and tension. Any attempt to use it for this purpose will only deepen one's feelings of anxiety and depression. Beyond the long-term damage to one's health, alcohol abuse is noted for damage to one's ability to maintain relationships and has well-known behavioral consequences.

What about coffee?

Caffeine

Caffeine—found in coffee, tea, colas and other soft drinks, chocolate, and other foods—is probably our most commonly abused drug. Virtually the entire adult population uses it, and tens of millions of Americans abuse it (more than 22 million Americans drink five or more cups of coffee per day). It is commonly used to combat chronic sleep deprivation, although ironically it is a major contributor to sleeplessness. Caffeine appears to improve alertness, but it really just creates a jumpy, yet still tired, person. It can cause headaches, a sense of restlessness, digestive problems, heart arrhythmias, and hypertension. Even a single cup of coffee can significantly elevate blood pressure and adrenaline for more than two hours, adding significantly to the effects of stress.

Caffeine is surprisingly addictive, more so than most people realize. Even very small amounts can contribute significantly to problems of chronic anxiety and panic disorders.[13] One psychiatrist who specializes in panic disorders indicated that at least half his patients were able to eliminate their symptoms by completely eliminating caffeine from their diet. He also found that even a single cup of coffee or one caffeinated soft drink could reactivate panic disorders and sleeplessness. It is fair to say that people suffering from chronic anxiety, panic disorders, and sleeplessness should at least test the impact of eliminating caffeine from their diet.

Are there any other drugs on your list of false stress relievers?

Benzodiazepines (Tranquilizers and Sleeping Pills)

Perhaps the quintessential class of drugs that appear to relieve anxiety in the short term, but can create a chronic pattern of heightened anxiety and drug dependence in the long term, are tranquilizers and the closely related class of sleeping pills. In both cases, the most widely prescribed drugs are the benzodiazepines. In 1986, approximately 86 percent of the pills prescribed as tranquilizers or antianxiety medication were benzodiazepines, such as Valium (diazepam), Librium (chlordiazepoxide), and Tranxene (clorazepate). About 75 percent of the sleeping pills were also benzodiazepines, particularly Dalmane (flurazepam) and Halcion (triazolam).[14] While these drugs may have some value in assisting someone through a brief period of acute stress, sustained use can be both ineffective and dangerous. First of all, benzodiazepines rapidly lose their effectiveness as sleep-inducing agents. They actually often result in persistent insomnia, thus turning an acute problem into a chronic one. Other common effects include restless or fragmented sleep, nightmares, lethargy, and daytime fatigue.[15] Perhaps most serious, these drugs are addictive and can cause chronic depression. They can start a cycle of drug dependency.

A particularly dangerous benzodiazepine is Halcion (triazolam). Because of its rapid withdrawal from the body, it can cause acute problems of disorientation, panic, aggravated nightmares, severe feelings of depression, and even suicide. Oddly, it is the most widely prescribed sleeping medication in the United States, although it is banned in a number of European countries.[16]

Are there other sleep and anxiety medications other than benzo-diazepines?

Yes, examples include barbiturates such as phenobarbital and meprobamates such as Miltown. Each such drug has its pros and cons, but there is widespread agreement in the medical community that a safe and effective sleeping or antianxiety medication simply does not exist. These drugs should be used with extreme caution in acute situations.

So why are these drugs so widely used?

That tells you something about our society. We expect quick and immediate cures for whatever troubles us. We tend not to want to struggle with problems.

There are situations where certain psychotropic drugs work when nothing else does. One important example is lithium, which is used for manic-depressive disorders.

You haven't mentioned any illegal drugs.

Cocaine and Heroin

I have discussed abuse of legally available drugs first because they are the biggest problem in terms of health. Probably because illegal drugs are illegal, their use and abuse is somewhat less frequent. However, I do not mean to minimize the problem of illegal drugs, particularly cocaine. Cocaine upsets the regulation of dopamine, norepinephrine, and other neurotransmitters in the brain, which are vital for one's ability to think as well as for one's sense of well-being. Early use causes a surge of dopamine, which is experienced essentially as a strong sense of pleasure. This high is followed by a reduction in dopamine and other neurotransmitter levels, which is unpleasant. This cycle can lead rather quickly to dependency. Ultimately, extensive repeated usage can diminish and possibly deplete the brain's supply of dopamine. At this stage, a person requires a large dose of the drug just to achieve neurotransmitter levels that are merely not agonizing. The situation of the cocaine addict is quite desperate; his or her regulation of dopamine and other neurotransmitters is out of control. Regaining that control is, unfortunately, very difficult.[17]

The social urgency of the problem stems from the psychological and behavioral impact of cocaine addiction. Unlike heroin, which produces a relatively withdrawn state (at least for those four-hour periods during which a heroin addict's need for heroin is satisfied), cocaine produces a state of paranoia, irritability, and aggressiveness. This can be a dangerous state of mind, particularly when combined with one other attribute of cocaine-induced psychosis, which is a loss of certain inhibitions, such as those concerning interpersonal violence. Crime related to heroin addiction is typically economic: The heroin addict is desperate for his or her next fix. But the potential violence of a cocaine addict is worse: He or she is dangerous with or without the drug.

So which problem is worse, legal or illegal drugs?

In terms of lives lost and sheer impact on health and well-being, one would have to say legal drugs. Fifty million Americans smoke, and any regular use of tobacco would have to be considered abuse. There are about 20 million Americans who abuse alcohol. More than 20 million Americans abuse caffeine. About 20 million abuse prescription drugs, with some estimates running much higher. There is, of course, a great deal of overlap in these numbers, in that the average number of drugs abused by abusers of drugs is approximately two. Nonetheless, the number of Americans that abuse one or more legal drugs is approximately 75 million, or nearly half the adult population!

There are about 6 million "drug addicts," individuals addicted to cocaine, heroin, and other "hard" illegal drugs. About 20 million Americans make some regular use of cocaine. So the health implications are comparably smaller. But when assessing the problems of illegal drugs, you have to add the compounding social dislocation, crime, and violence.

I don't think it is useful to try to rank these two aspects of our drug problem. The more important perspective is to see the abuse of drugs, both legal and illegal, as part of the same problem, rooted in the same quest, however misguided, for a sense of well-being. Our society is awash in drugs. Any discussion of the "drug problem" that ignores the abuse of legal drugs is bound to be ineffectual, not to mention hypocritical. One observer compared our national "war on drugs," which largely ignores the overarching problems of tobacco and alcohol addiction, to a naval strategy that ignored the Atlantic and Pacific oceans.

Okay, I think we all understand what not to do. Just what do you recommend as sources of relief from our often stressful and harried lives?

I'm glad you asked that question. I have a ten-point program for effectively managing stress.

Okay, let me guess, your **first guideline** *is to eat a diet that is low in fat, cholesterol, sodium, sugar...*

Diet

That is certainly a reasonable place to start. Ending the assault of a poisonous diet on one's body and mind will end an enormous source of stress. The greater sense of well-being and the reality of health that results will go a long way in reducing stress. You will sleep better. Your brain and other tissues will be better oxygenated. Blood pressure and atherosclerotic plaque development will all be greatly alleviated. These and the many other benefits we have discussed all have a bearing on one's level of stress.

Following the nutritional guidelines of the 10% solution will also enable you to maintain an ideal weight. Avoiding excess weight will eliminate another chronic source of stress.

Worrying a lot less about heart disease, cancer, stroke, and these other diseases should also reduce one's level of stress.

Good point; it certainly does so for me.

Drugs

The **second guideline**, closely related to the first, is to ingest a "diet" that is also low in tobacco, alcohol, caffeine, benzodiazepines, cocaine, and other drugs. For most of these drugs, particularly tobacco and cocaine, "low" means none.

Okay, what's next?

Aerobic Exercise

The **third guideline** is the other cornerstone of my recommendations in the 10% solution: aerobic exercise. Aerobic exercise will directly and immediately provide tangible benefits in reducing stress and promoting relaxation. The natural release of endorphins from continuous exertion is a healthy alternative to artificial stimulants and depressants. Exercise also promotes a natural cycle of sleep. Anyone with difficulty sleeping should stop ingesting caffeine and boost their aerobic exercise. I do not recommend exercising just before retiring, however.

Sleep

The **fourth guideline** is to sleep.

Sleep?

Yes, make sure you get adequate sleep.

But isn't it stress that may cause an inability to sleep in the first place?

Yes, I understand that, and the other guidelines will help you to attain a natural and healthy sleep cycle. My point here is that you should allow enough time for an adequate amount of sleep—to give a high priority to obtaining a healthy quantity and quality of sleep. If you have not slept adequately, even minor problems feel quite stressful and your entire outlook is colored negatively. Researchers have estimated that more than a third of the population is chronically sleep deprived. And consuming a lot of caffeine in the morning will only aggravate the inherent stressfulness of inadequate sleep.

How much sleep is enough?

That varies from individual to individual, although seven to eight hours a night is typical. If you stop consuming a toxic diet and get in touch with your body and its feelings, you will know when you have obtained adequate rest.

Balance

The **fifth guideline** is to achieve to balance in your life. Stress is not an isolated issue that you can deal with once a week. Dealing with stress effectively is a matter of dealing with your life effectively. That is why these recommendations cut across fundamental issues of life-style. By balance, I am referring to work, family/friends, and self, and the need to keep these three poles of one's life in balance. The balance will differ from person to person, and there is great overlap, to be sure. If one's work, for example, is raising one's children, then the poles of work and family overlap, but there is still a distinction to be made between the work of child raising and the opportunity to experience moments of love and sharing. Freud said the two great issues in life are work and love, which are the first two of the three poles I have mentioned. The third pole—one's self—refers to the importance of integrating one's life into a pattern that is satisfying and meaningful, of taking the time to assess one's values and goals, to understand one's own needs and to give them priority.

One obvious form of imbalance is represented by the workaholic, but excessive dependence on social forms of gratification (family/

friends) or excessive concern with one's own needs and desires (self) to the exclusion of others can also represent a lack of balance. This guideline is perhaps different from many of the others in this book, in that it is impossible to quantify, but it is important nonetheless to consider the importance of balance and to assess this issue for oneself periodically.

Fair enough.

Vacations

The **sixth guideline** is to take a vacation.

Terrific—too bad I don't work for you.

The point is to take time periodically to change your routine. A vacation does not need to involve lying in the sun, although that may be what you enjoy doing. It could involve taking a week to work in your yard, paint your garage, take a course. It could even involve sorting out old files. Just do something different from your usual routine.

Talking

The **seventh guideline** is to talk with someone.

You mean like we're doing now.

Not exactly. I mean, talk about your true feelings, share on a regular basis your fears, your worries, your hopes, what delights you, and what scares you. It is important to have someone you can really talk to without worrying about being embarrassed, making a good impression, or appearing silly.

So just who might that be?

Good question. It is not always obvious who can fulfill that role. Sometimes it is a relative, although family members are often the ones creating the feelings that you need to talk about and may not provide the kind of nonjudgmental attitude called for. A good friend, perhaps, can provide the necessary trust and confidence. A spouse or lover can provide the requisite intimacy, and it is certainly desirable that you talk about your feelings in such a relationship. As with a relative, however, you may still need someone you can talk to about your spouse/lover. Other possibilities include one's pastor or teacher, maybe even your boss.

No, I don't think my boss would be high on my list for this purpose.

Very often, this role can be filled by a therapist, psychiatrist, psychologist, social worker, or counselor, who is trained to provide exactly this kind of supportive and understanding relationship. Unfortunately, the idea of talking to a therapist has negative associations for many persons. It is a common perspective that there has to be something wrong with you to have regular sessions with a therapist. It must mean that you are mentally ill, or at least neurotic. Yet, for most of us, our lives are sufficiently complex and demanding that having a professionally trained person, capable of being objective, to share our feelings and important life decisions is bound to be helpful. We don't hesitate to hire professionals to assist us with our taxes, legal problems, house selection, money management, and many similar issues, so why not professional consultation on the most important issues facing us: dealing with our own emotions. Our internal life is at least as complex as our tax returns and even more confusing. My own feeling is that most everyone can benefit from a relationship of this type.

That's not inexpensive, you realize.

This is true, although some therapists will provide a sliding scale based on need and ability to pay, and some clinics provide these services on a reasonable basis.

But regardless of who can fill this role for you, everyone has the need to share their most intimate feelings. Just the act of articulating one's feelings—fears, hopes, desires—to another human being has an enormously beneficial impact, provided, of course, that the person you are talking to is truly listening. It helps put difficult issues into perspective. Even painful subjects can begin to be seen in a constructive context once you articulate them. One's perspective can become increasingly distorted if this type of intimate sharing is routinely ignored in one's life.

Okay, what's next?

Listening

The opposite of the seventh, the **eighth guideline** is to listen. It is very therapeutic to listen, to truly listen, to what others have to say. And when people feel that you are really listening, they will start to open up and share their inner feelings. It's just a natural human response and need. Don't be so enamored with what you have to say that you fail to listen to others. They say a wise man can learn more from a fool than the other way around.

Being a good listener is more difficult than it may appear. The first challenge is to simply allow the other person to talk, by not interrupting and by paying close attention. The more important challenge, however, concerns what you do with the information you receive. You need to keep an open mind, to try to perceive the world from the other person's perspective. Even if you don't agree with everything that is being said, provide feedback that lets the other person know you understand what he or she is saying and feeling and the derivation of his or her thoughts. The most critical aspect of creative listening is empathy.

Time Management

The **ninth guideline** is to give some explicit thought to your own time management. How you spend your time reflects your priorities. As an exercise, write down your priorities, in terms of work, family, friends, exercise, sports, relaxation, and so on. Then, for the following week, write down how you actually spend your time. How does your allocation of time match your intended priorities? In terms of the fifth guideline, above, how well does your time management reflect an optimal and comfortable balance between work, family/friends, and self? With all of the pressures of modern life, it is easy for your allocation of time to stray substantially from what you desire, and also from what is healthy. If you find a discrepancy, consider how you would like your time commitments to change and then develop a strategy for making the change. On the one hand, it is often not possible to make significant changes overnight. After all, we have responsibilities and obligations that cannot just be dropped. On the other hand, given a well thought-out plan, most people have a greater ability to control their destiny, not to mention their daily schedule, than they realize.

It is a worthwhile exercise to try to develop a schedule that will accommodate the various objectives you have. This is particularly important if you are attempting to make a change—adding a regular aerobic exercise program, for example. In terms of avoiding unnecessary sources of stress, try not to overschedule and overcommit. Projects and commitments often take more time than initially anticipated. Also, it is desirable to leave time free for problems and opportunities that arise. An overscheduled life does not leave time for spontaneity.

The value of a schedule is that you avoid procrastination that will only exacerbate stressful situations. You have the opportunity to establish your priorities. You decide what responsibilities you need or want to accommodate. You also learn when and how to say no. After all, you can't please everyone.

Often I can't even please myself.

That shouldn't necessarily be your last priority.

I'll keep that in mind. So, what's the last guideline?

The Relaxation Response

The **tenth guideline** is to evoke the relaxation response.

You'll have to explain that further.

I was planning to. The relaxation response was discovered when Dr. Herbert Benson, then the director of the hypertension section of Boston's Beth Israel Hospital and now at New England Deaconess Hospital in Boston, and other researchers at the Harvard Medical School and Boston's Beth Israel Hospital studied the physical and mental effects of a variety of methods of evoking a calm state, including yoga and several forms of meditation. They discovered a hypothalamic response that was the converse of the fight-or-flight response: reduced levels of epinephrine and norepinephrine and, in turn, lowered levels of blood pressure and blood sugar and breathing and heart rates.[18] Moreover, they discovered that regular use of these techniques and regular elicitation of this response were able to produce permanently lowered blood pressure levels, improved sleep patterns, improved gastrointestinal functioning, improved blood flow, and other benefits.[19] A recent study of the elderly found that regular use of a meditation technique that elicited the relaxation response resulted in a dramatic reduction in deaths during the three-year period of the study, as well as substantially improved mental acuity and mental outlook.[20]

How do you achieve this relaxation response?

Research directed by Benson has cataloged a number of techniques that demonstrably and reliably produce the relaxation response. One such class of techniques is yoga, which combines meditation with stretching exercises and breathing control. Benson has also documented the health benefits of people experiencing the relaxation response on a regular basis.[21]

I understand that yoga is not easy to learn.

Yoga, Biofeedback, and Visualization

Yoga involves an extensive body of knowledge and skill, and one can certainly devote many years of study and practice to mastering this school of thought. Indeed, there are several different schools of yoga which comprise this ancient tradition. However, to simply evoke the relaxation response does not require becoming a master of these techniques. A beginner can learn enough in a relatively short period of time to begin to achieve some of the benefits of the relaxation response.

Another technique is biofeedback, which involves the use of equipment to provide visual or auditory feedback reflecting internal states of tension, such as blood pressure and heartbeat. Usually performed at a clinic, biofeedback techniques have been shown to be effective in treating hypertension, headaches, and other stress disorders.[22]

Another method is called visualization, which involves using all of the senses to imagine a desired result. This is often used by athletes to improve performance. When used as a method for treating anxiety, the desired result one visualizes is a situation that is peaceful and serene.

It sounds as if all of these techniques require professional guidance and instruction.

In general, that's true. Learning yoga, biofeedback, or visualization techniques from a book is certainly not as effective as obtaining the guidance of a skilled practitioner. However, I will describe here one technique that Dr. Benson has extensively studied. It is a simple method that Dr. Benson derived from transcendental meditation and other sources, with a concentration on its applicability as a treatment for stress.[23] Dr. Benson and his colleagues at the Harvard Medical School have spent more than twenty years studying the physiological changes produced by this and other relaxation techniques and the health benefits of experiencing the *relaxation response*, a term that Benson popularized, on a regular basis. By studying the practices of both Eastern and Western religions and other lay practices that produce the relaxation response, Benson sought to find and describe a simple method that would capture the essential components necessary to produce the physiological changes of the response.[24]

Okay, I'm game, let's hear it.

Meditation

The technique involves the following elements:

First, find a quiet and comfortable environment, preferably one in which you feel safe and in which you enjoy being. It is also desirable that you not be disturbed by other persons, the phone, or other distractions.

Second, sit comfortably and close your eyes.

Relax your muscles, starting with your feet and working up to your face.

Now become aware of your breathing. As you breathe out, say a particular word or sound to yourself. This is the heart of the technique, so this aspect bears some discussion. Most any sound that you like will do, although I suggest a one- or two-syllable sound that contains no hard consonants (such as b, d, g, k, p, q, t, x). A suitable sound would be "oh one" or "ah one." Another possibility, which Benson himself recommends, is simply the word "one." When you say the word to yourself, do not actually say it aloud, just think it. Let the sound say itself. Just start the sound off in your mind and let it repeat itself with your breath. It is important to let your mind feel free to wander where it may, so you do not want repeating this sound to be difficult. Once you start it up, it should just repeat itself naturally. If, after a while, you notice that it has stopped, gently start it up again. Do not force the sound to repeat itself. Just let it happen.

A vital aspect of the method is a passive attitude. The technique used here is essentially the opposite of a mental discipline. This technique is considered nonconcentrative as opposed to concentrative. For people who are used to disciplining themselves both physically and mentally, this can be confusing. Don't worry about how well you are doing. Let thoughts come and go. Some will be pleasant; some may be distressing. Both will pass and will lead to other thoughts. The repetition of the sound with your breathing should also not be a discipline; just let it happen, and when you notice that it is not happening, just gently start imagining the sound again repeating itself with your breath.

As you gain experience meditating, the sound (sometimes called a "mantra," although, technically, a mantra is a Sanskrit word from a specific tradition) will become more subtle and less clearly articulated. This is desirable—eventually the sound will become just a feeling of the sound. To assist with this process of the sound becoming more subtle, it is desirable not to say the word(s) out loud (even when not meditating).

If you find certain thoughts to be disturbing, let them pass. If that fails, try returning to the sound that is repeating itself with your breath. If you really want to stop, then stop the sound, wait a few seconds, and end the meditation by gradually opening your eyes.

Continue this process for fifteen to thirty minutes. You can open your eyes briefly to check the time if you wish, but do not use an alarm. When you are done, stop the sound and just sit quietly with your eyes closed for a couple of minutes. Then open your eyes gradually and sit with your eyes open for a few minutes. Then gradually stand up. If you are tired, you may find yourself falling asleep. While the purpose of meditating is not to get additional sleep, if you do find yourself nodding off, that is okay.

To obtain a health benefit, the technique should be practiced once or twice a day. In general, avoid a period of two hours after each meal, since the digestive process may interfere with your ability to elicit the desired response. It makes sense, therefore, to practice this meditation technique prior to a meal.

The key to the technique is the passive attitude. This includes not worrying about how well you are doing and letting thoughts, positive or negative, wash over you.

Benson's research has uncovered a wide range of subjective experiences that occur during meditation, although a feeling of peacefulness and tranquility is not uncommon. However, because the method specifically does not include trying to elicit peaceful thoughts or feelings, your experience may vary from session to session and from minute to minute. The research has demonstrated that the physiological changes associated with the relaxation response are elicited regardless of the subjective experience, whether it be tranquil or otherwise.

This method contrasts with other mental techniques that involve disciplining the mind to concentrate, whether it be on a particular sound or even on the idea of relaxation. In the reference notes, I provide information on where you can receive training in this type of meditation.

Wouldn't I do just as well to use these twenty minutes to get some extra sleep? Isn't sleep a relaxation technique?

As we discussed, getting an adequate quantity and quality of sleep is very important as one element of a life-style that deals effectively with stress. Not sleeping adequately is indeed very stressful. Both sleep and the relaxation response involve significant and measurable physiological changes, which have been extensively studied. They are not the same, however. And while sleep is necessary, getting additional sleep will not achieve the beneficial endocrine changes that are achieved through regular elicitation of the relaxation response.

The only problem I have here is that, between following the nutritional guidelines, exercising, spending time with my family, getting adequate sleep, and now practicing relaxation techniques, when I am supposed to find the time to do anything else, like earn a living?

That's a reasonable challenge. Let's take these issues one at a time. The nutritional guidelines may take some time at first, in terms of learning the fat content of foods and exploring the world of foods that comply with the guidelines and that you enjoy. But I can share with you from my own experience and that of many others that after a period of learning and adjustment, following the guidelines does not involve a time investment on an ongoing basis. Spending time with your family or friends is, presumably, something you want to do. If you really believe you have no desire or need for this type of interaction with others, then you need to examine that in yourself. As for sleep, this is also something you need, and it is counterproductive to try to cut back on it. Similarly, I have found that exercise more than pays for itself in terms of greater energy, better sleep patterns (meaning you will get more sleep without spending more time in bed), and a more positive attitude about each day's challenges.

Relaxation techniques offer the same promise. The time spent on them will repay itself in terms of demonstrable physiological, mental, and emotional benefits, seen in greater effectiveness in other spheres and an enhanced sense of well-being. That is why I emphasized time management earlier. You would be surprised at how much you can accomplish and how many things you have time for, if you carefully consider the management of your time. Most people waste enormous amounts of time and personal energy in ways that are both unproductive and that do not contribute to the sense of well-being that everyone seeks. The different elements of the program I have outlined—diet, exercise, balance, relaxation—work synergistically. Rather than interfering with your life, a healthy and well-balanced life-style will make you more effective in achieving your personal goals and enhancing your life. There is really no alternative.

9
■

The Kurzweil Challenge: Ten Easy Steps

The Challenge

Suppose I would like to give this life-style a try, but am not quite sure that I'm ready to make a lifetime commitment. What do I do?

I would suggest taking the Kurzweil Challenge. Trying a diet that follows the guidelines of the 10% solution for a single meal, or a day, or even a week, does not represent a fair trial. If you have grown up on the Western "civilized" diet, then you need to allow sufficient time for your tastes to change. Otherwise, you will gain a false impression of what this life-style feels like.

Or tastes like.

The same can be said for exercise. If you're out of shape and begin a walking or other aerobic exercise regimen, you may find it exhausting and feel some discomfort in your legs. But once you're in shape, the experience of regular aerobic exercise is quite different. It is invigorating and certainly not uncomfortable.

So how long is a fair trial?

Two months, which is enough time to experience at least some of the phenomenon of having your tastes change. It is also sufficient time to experience many of the immediate benefits, as well as to obtain significant progress in weight reduction, if that is an issue, and improvement in blood lipid levels.

Drug Dependencies

The **first step** in the Kurzweil Challenge is to deal with any drug abuse or dependency problems that you may have. This includes alcohol abuse, any use of cigarettes or any tobacco product, abuse of caffeine, any use of illegal drugs, and abuse of prescription drugs. It would be difficult to make progress in improving the healthfulness of one's life-style while continuing a destructive habit or pattern of this type.

Do you mean that there is little value in improving one's diet if you have a drug dependency problem?

There is unquestionable value in replacing the toxic American diet with a healthful diet under any circumstances. At the same time, it would not make sense to ignore a habit as destructive to health as smoking or abusing alcohol or other drugs. In many of these circumstances, it would also be difficult to establish the necessary discipline to make a life-style change without also dealing with a substance dependency problem.

How do you suggest solving problems of this sort?

That is a complex issue and not the primary focus of this book. For many of these substances, overcoming a pattern of abuse can be far more difficult than making the change in eating patterns that I've discussed. In general, one needs the assistance of trained professionals, particularly in the case of abuse of alcohol and other drugs. For alcohol, Alcoholics Anonymous has an impressive record. There are also numerous clinics and treatment centers that specialize in problems of alcohol and drug dependency. Many hospitals offer smoking cessation programs. There are many commercial products that purport to assist one in ending the use of cigarettes, although the effectiveness of many of these products is questionable. In general, the assistance of another person or organization who has the appropriate training and experience is key to making this type of change.

All right, what's step two?

Consult Your Physician

Step two is to have a full physical with your physician and to discuss the program you are embarking on, including the exercise. He or she will bring to your attention any special health problems you may have that you may need to take into consideration. In particular, if you have heart disease or angina pain, your exercise program needs to be carefully monitored; otherwise it could be dangerous. Exercise is still very important to improve your health in this situation, but it will require careful, professional supervision. If you are taking medication for diabetes or hypertension, this program of diet and exercise is likely to enable you to cut down substantially or eliminate these medications. But this has to be done gradually, as the underlying diabetes or hypertension improves as the result of these life-style changes. Any changes in medication need to be supervised by a doctor.

Note on your baseline record any special health problems that you have.

What if my doctor is not supportive of this type of life-style change?

If your doctor has specific concerns regarding any special health issues that you have, then these certainly need to be taken into consideration. If your physician is cool to this type of dietary and life-style program because of ignorance on his or her part, then that is another matter. Although doctors have, up until recently, received relatively little, if any, training in nutrition, there is a rapidly growing awareness in the medical community of the crucial role of nutrition and other life-style factors in the formation of disease. It is important that you have a doctor who is aware of these issues and who is willing to discuss them with you. There are a growing number of doctors with enlightened attitudes on these issues. If you are not satisfied with your physician's understanding of these matters and willingness to discuss them with you in a constructive fashion, then you could consider finding a doctor that is informed on these crucial issues. It is your responsibility to select your physician and it is an important decision that deserves thought and attention on your part.

Baseline Measurement

The **third step** is to establish a baseline. Use a copy of the Baseline Chart in appendix 3, "Charts for the Kurzweil Challenge," to record your current blood levels, physical measurements, and feelings. Three months from now, you will write down the same figures and observations and compare.

To fill out this chart, first have your doctor measure your total serum cholesterol, HDL level, triglycerides, and glucose. Also get the standard biomedical battery of blood tests to screen for kidney, liver, and thyroid problems. It is important that you obtain an HDL reading, which is not always measured with total serum cholesterol. Also note your blood pressure. Have your doctor give you all of these figures, as opposed to just telling you that "it's okay."

Next, measure your weight and compute your percentage of body fat, using the tables in appendix 4 of this book. You may also wish to record your chest, hips, and waist measurements.

Write down all of these figures. Also, write down how you feel. How well do you sleep? Do you have any aches, pains, discomforts of a minor or major nature? Describe the state of your gastrointestinal system. Try to characterize your mood and outlook. These are admittedly subjective issues which are difficult to describe. They are, nonetheless, quite relevant, and it is worth recording these observations as best you can. If your outlook or sense of well-being changes, it will be gradual, and you may not remember how you felt when you began this process.

I thought you said two months.

We're going to be making a one-month gradual transition. Then there will be a full two-month trial.

Monitoring Current Life-style

For **step four**, we are going to spend about a week just monitoring your current life-style, while you learn about the issues we have been discussing. Each day, write down your calories and fat grams consumed and calories expended in exercise. Use a copy of the Weekly Chart in appendix 3, "Charts for the Kurzweil Challenge." Review the material in this book and begin to increase your consciousness of the nutritional composition of the food you are eating, particularly its fat content. Note which foods are high in fat and which are low. Note to yourself foods low in fat and cholesterol that you enjoy. Mark a date on your calendar that is about a week after the day you start tracking your food and exercise. That is the date you will start making a change.

So I change my diet and exercise pattern on that day.

Gradual Transition

Yes, but gradually. **Step five** begins on the day you have marked. We now begin a three-week period of gradual change from your current pattern to the 10% solution. Begin by eliminating high-fat foods that are easy to do without. For example, you can replace ice cream with non-fat frozen yogurt or sorbet. Start to emphasize those low-fat foods that you normally eat. Look around for foods that you enjoy that comply with the guidelines. You will be surprised to discover that this is easier than you may expect. Many people have reported to me that making this change was easier than they had anticipated. Indeed, that was my experience.

Similarly, gradually increase your aerobic exercise until you are exercising four to seven times per week for forty-five minutes or more per session (as long as your doctor feels this is appropriate for your condition). Don't strain yourself; your capacity will grow naturally.

If you are overweight, then reduce calories to at least 500 below your maintenance level (see tables 1, 2, and 3 in chapter 5), but don't go overboard on calorie restriction or you will find the experience too difficult. Our primary goal here is to change your diet in a way that you find rewarding and satisfying. Weight loss will occur naturally and gradually. It is difficult to remain overweight if you are eating a diet that is very low in fat. Do not make weight control your primary goal, but it will happen anyway.

Try to do better each week in terms of reducing fat, cholesterol, and sodium and increasing complex carbohydrates and fiber. It is important to continue to write down food calories, fat grams, and calories expended in exercise each day so that you can monitor your progress. While you are making this gradual transition, you are continuing to explore and learn the wonderful world of low-fat foods.

Step six, I assume, is to make the full change to the 10% solution.

Two-Month Trial

Yes, after the three-week transition in step five, above, you now begin the two-month period in which you follow the guidelines strictly. You have spent about a month exploring different foods and gradually changing your eating and exercise patterns. Now you are going to give the program a fair two-month trial. I will note that it is possible to skip step five and make a sudden transition. Some people prefer to make the change quickly and then get used to it gradually. Personally, I adopted this way of eating in one day and have never looked back. But most people prefer to have a period of gradual transition. Use copies of the Weekly Chart during this period to monitor your progress and to be sure that you are following the guidelines until it becomes second nature.

What about exceptions? If I blow it, do I have to start over?

The issue of backsliding is a crucial one. Unfortunately, we live in a society that reinforces its unhealthy way of eating with a continual stream of powerful messages. You probably don't have to walk more than a few dozen yards to find some reinforcement of the American way of eating. Once your new habits are established, you will not find this a difficult life-style to maintain, because the way you feel will be self-reinforcing. But at this stage, you are indeed vulnerable to backsliding.

A firm commitment to at least giving this a fair trial is important to succeeding. If your attitude is that you are going to allow yourself occasional exceptions (e.g., "I'll just have rich desserts on the weekend"), you will actually make it more difficult for yourself, not less. You will continue a mind-set that indicates that what is really good is the type of food you are trying to get away from, and that this new approach is just an extended period of deprivation. Most important, your tastes will never change. It is like someone who is trying to stop the use of cigarettes by smoking only a few cigarettes every weekend. That is just not a fruitful approach to changing one's habits. If you are strict about this for a period of time, your tastes will change, but you have to give them a chance. That is, after all, why you are embarking on this two-month trial, to test my assertion that this phenomenon really does occur.

And if I do backslide nonetheless?

Just carry on. You don't have to start over. Your daily record will indicate how well you are doing. If you are really not achieving 10 percent calories from fat, then you may want to extend the two-month period so that you do achieve two months reasonably close to this goal.

Remember that the number of grams of fat you can eat should be about 1.1 percent of the number of calories you eat. For example, at 2,000 calories per day, 1.1 percent equals 22 grams of fat, which represents 10 percent calories from fat.

At this point, we've made the change, so what's next?

Progress Measurement

After two months of reasonably careful compliance with the guidelines of the 10% solution, you move to **step seven,** where you make another assessment. Write down again (using the Progress Chart in appendix 3) all of the measurements as well as the subjective issues that you recorded in your baseline record. This means having your doctor measure again your total serum cholesterol, HDL cholesterol, triglycerides, glucose, other blood levels, and blood pressure. Record your weight, compute and record your body fat percentage. Note again how you feel—changes in sleep patterns, aches and pains, the state of your gastrointestinal system, and so on.

Note improvements by comparing the baseline chart to the progress chart. Have you lost weight? Have your cholesterol levels improved? Blood pressure? Are you sleeping better? Do you feel better? If you had significant health issues such as angina pain, type II diabetes, or hypertension, have you and your doctor noted improvements in these conditions?

Do you perceive improvements in alertness from the increase in oxygenation of the brain that a lower-fat diet provides? Is your gastrointestinal tract happier? Are you more regular? Has your complexion improved?

How do you feel about the fact that this type of diet dramatically reduces the risk of heart disease, stroke, and the most common forms of cancer?

How have your tastes changed? Two months is not enough time to fully experience this phenomenon, but some of your tastes and attitudes toward food will have altered in this time period. Have you found foods that you enjoy? Is the diet satisfying? Are you ever hungry?

I cannot fill out this chart for you. But if you are like most people who have given this approach to diet and exercise a legitimate chance, you are likely to have noted dramatic improvements in many of these areas. But you make the assessment.

Permanent Commitment

Step eight is to consider a permanent commitment. You have already taken the most difficult step, which is to actually change your pattern of diet and exercise. But you have not yet taken the most important step, which is a lifetime commitment to the 10% solution. You should have experienced enough of the benefits by this time to assess its beneficial impact on your life. But two months is not long enough to firmly establish new habits. The benefits you have experienced will rapidly vanish if you revert to an unhealthy pattern. They will be permanent only if the change is permanent.

Another Assessment

Assuming you make this commitment, the **ninth step** is to to make another assessment after another nine months. Use a copy of the Progress Chart in appendix 3, "Charts for the Kurzweil Challenge." The improvements that you probably noted in your cholesterol levels and in other manifestations of your dramatically healthier patterns of eating and living are not fully reflected after a two-month period. For example, we have substantial cholesterol stores throughout the body which take time to draw down. You are likely to experience further improvements in your overall health after this additional period of time.

That's only nine points. What is the tenth point?

Write the Author

The final step is to write the author.

That's you.

Yes. I would be delighted to hear about your experience and add it to my growing file of people who have dramatically improved many aspects of their health and well-being. If you are comfortable sharing your baseline, two-month, and nine-month charts, that will add to my knowledge base. I will keep the information in confidence and use it only for statistical analysis. Any additional comments will also be appreciated. Please send the material to Raymond Kurzweil, care of Crown Publishers, Inc., 201 East 50th Street, New York, New York 10022. Note that I will not be able to respond personally to each of you.

What would you say is the key to your ten-point program?

The key is commitment. If your resolve is strong, it is easy. Otherwise, it is very difficult. There is just too much continual external reinforcement in American society of the wrong way to eat, not to mention the subtle though powerful media campaigns encouraging smoking and drinking. The reinforcement to maintain a healthy life-style has to be *internal*. You are likely to gain this motivation if you give the program a chance. Then it becomes self-sustaining. That is why I structured an approach incorporating a two-month trial. That is enough time to begin tapping the internal reinforcement you need to sustain this program.

And that is also why I have written this book, to provide the perspective on how profound a contribution we can all make to our own health and well-being.

10

■

The Second Fountain

Caloric Restriction

There is one issue I would like to discuss separately, which is calorie restriction. There is a recent body of research that strongly suggests we have the ability to slow down aging—to extend both life and youthfulness—through calorie reduction.

Why do you separate this discussion from the chapters that discuss nutritional issues?

Because the evidence for this school of thought is still preliminary, and I want to contrast this with the other issues for which the evidence is overwhelming. The evidence for the health benefits of a diet that is low in fat, cholesterol, and sodium and for the benefits of regular aerobic exercise is a rich mosaic that includes extensive human studies. The evidence for the benefits of restricting calories is based on animal studies. The animal studies are dramatic and have been totally consistent across many different species, so I feel they are worth discussing.[1] On the other hand, I do want to contrast the primary guidelines of the 10% solution (low fat, etc.), for which we have conclusive evidence, from this somewhat more speculative issue.

Fair enough. First of all, what is the calorie restriction program suggested here?

The Animal Experiments

Let me describe the rat experiments that have been conducted. The control group was fed a normal diet and lived a maximum normal life span, of approximately one thousand days. Typically, the control rats died from the deterioration of their hearts, kidney disease, or cancer. The experimental group had a restricted diet, which consisted of about one-third fewer calories than the control group's diet but otherwise contained adequate nutrients, including vitamins, minerals, protein, essential fatty acids, and so on. They lived for about 1,500 days, or 50 percent longer.[2] I have to stress that this is a very dramatic and unusual finding. It has been consistent over many studies.

Of at least equal significance was the slowing of the aging process. Not only did the low-calorie rats live longer, but they largely avoided the feebleness, poor health, sluggishness, and grizzled appearance that accompanied the old age of the normal-eating group, even toward the end of the extended lives of these low-calorie rats. For example, the coats of the normal-eating rodents, which are smooth and white early in life, typically turn gray and oily by 24 months of age. The low-calorie rodents, in contrast, kept their fur white and shiny for 40 months or more. Maze experiments showed that the low-calorie rats were significantly more successful at running mazes than normal-eating rats of the same age. Rates of diabetes and cataracts and the strength of the immune system were all dramatically better in the low-calorie rodents. Long after the normal-eating rats had died, the low-calorie rats continued to have shiny coats, very low rates of cancer and other diseases, and the higher levels of energy and responsiveness associated with youth. When these low-calorie rats did die, they often appeared to do so of no obvious cause. According to Dr. Edward Masoro, a physiologist at the University of Texas Health Science Center in San Antonio, "When we look inside them, they're completely clean."[3]

Other experiments have tried exposing both groups to high levels of carcinogens. The low-calorie rats have shown significant resistance to the introduced cancer-causing chemicals, whereas the normal-eating rodents easily succumb.[4] Even strains of rats that are specially bred to be prone to cancer, autoimmune conditions, and other diseases gain significant protection from a low-calorie diet. Dr. Richard Weindruch, a gerontologist at the National Institute on Aging in Bethesda, Maryland, comments that "any kind of screwed-up animal seems to benefit from caloric restriction."[5]

There have been many experiments conducted on rats and on a wide range of other animals, all with consistent results. The low-calorie animals live significantly longer, generally about 50 percent longer, they age more slowly, and are generally much freer of disease even toward the end of their lengthened life spans.

Why does this work? I mean, what is going on here?

The Mechanisms

That is a very good question. The evidence provides some important pieces of the puzzle, but no one has a complete picture yet. One issue is the level of glucose in the blood. The low-calorie animals have significantly lower levels.[6] This results from the fact that the low-calorie animals burn glucose for fuel at the same rate as the normal-eating animals, but with less caloric intake there is less unnecessary glucose left over. It is well known that free-floating glucose can have a variety of harmful interactions with essential proteins and enzymes. It is generally accepted that a lower serum glucose level is beneficial.

Another important issue are the so-called free-radicals, highly reactive oxygen molecules that are a by-product of the metabolism of food. These molecules cause a gradual deterioration of body tissues, particularly fragile cell membranes. Many researchers on aging attribute many or even most of the aging processes to the gradual deteriorating effect of oxygen free-radicals floating in the bloodstream.[7] The low-calorie animals have substantially lower levels of oxygen free-radicals (which result from less food metabolism) and correspondingly less oxygen damage to cell membranes. Researchers have also discovered that the levels of a liver enzyme that detoxifies free-radicals are about 60 percent higher in the low-calorie animals.[8]

Other researchers have discovered that the low-calorie animals have more robust DNA-repairing enzymes. Deterioration in the DNA code causes cancer and accelerates other aging processes, so the greater effectiveness of these enzymes would account for the slower aging and lower rate of tumors in these animals.[9]

It has also been noted that the low-calorie animals have slightly lower temperatures, indicating a lower rate of metabolism.[10] It is, after all, the "fires" of metabolism that raise the body's temperature. Metabolism clearly causes gradual damage, so a lower rate of metabolism will cause a lower rate of such damage.

It certainly makes sense that a lower rate of calorie consumption will result in a lower rate of food metabolism.

The Number of Calories in a Lifetime

Yes, that does makes sense. And it is interesting to note that the total lifetime quantity of food eaten by the low-calorie animals and the normal-eating animals was roughly the same. The low-calorie animals ate approximately two-thirds as much food per day and lived 50 percent longer, so the total amount of food eaten over the life span was about the same as that of the normal-eating animals.

That would suggest that there is a certain number of calories allocated per lifetime, and if these calories are eaten more slowly, the result is a longer life.

That is the suggestion, which is intriguing to say the least. To look at it another way, the indication is that the clock of the aging process is not governed by the passage of time, per se. That is, we do not age with the passing of each minute, but rather with the consumption of each calorie. This is consistent with the view of living cells as heat engines. Another way to view this is to say that it is our "mileage" that causes aging and deterioration rather than the number of months lived, where mileage in this instance refers to the consumption of fuel.

So if an animal were to eat, say, one-third as many calories as another animal, it would live three times as long as the other?

No, there is a limit to this approach because of the other requirement I mentioned, that of obtaining sufficient nutrients. Without adequate vitamins, minerals, protein, and other nutrients, a human or other animal will become ill and ultimately die if the deficiency is not reversed. It appears that at least in the case of animals such as rats, the optimal level of calories for longevity is about two-thirds that of what the animals will eat if they are eating freely. Below that, it is difficult or impossible to obtain adequate nutrition.

There have not been any human studies?

There have not been any human intervention studies. Unlike the issues of lowering fat and cholesterol and increasing aerobic exercise, the issue of lowering caloric intake has not yet had extensive human experimentation. However, the animal studies have been remarkably consistent across experiments and across species. There is a strong suggestion that the effect will remain consistent up the evolutionary ladder. We know from other scientific studies that effects that are this dramatic in rats and this consistent across other animal species do generally extrapolate to humans. That is why we rely on rat studies when it comes to testing carcinogens. We routinely ban carcinogens that cause cancer in rats without ever conducting human studies.

There have been some human population studies. For example, the people living in the Okinawa region of Japan have forty times the number of centenarians (people 100 years of age or older) than the northeastern prefectures.[11] Furthermore, they have very little serious disease before the age of 60. Okinawans remain active much longer than their peers in other regions of Japan. The primary difference in their diet appears to be a lower caloric intake.

So what would the impact on humans be?

If we extrapolate the animal studies to humans, some researchers have estimated that the maximum life span of humans might be extended from 110 years to 150 or more.[12]

But very few of us live to 110 as it is.

This is true. These estimates refer to a theoretical maximum potential life span. Perhaps of greater significance, however, is the implication that by eating a diet that is low in calories and otherwise healthy, we are more likely to live out whatever potential we do have.

Are there any disadvantages to caloric restriction?

A Cautionary Note

There is one cautionary note I would like to make. There is evidence from the animal studies, and also preliminary research with humans, that excessive restriction of calories can cause a preoccupation with eating. This can trigger an eating disorder or other neurotic behavior.

I imagine people or animals significantly curtailing their eating must be hungry.

Yes, exactly. And hunger is a condition that you definitely want to avoid. Avoiding feelings of deprivation is both a goal and a guideline of the 10% solution. It is a goal because we desire a life-style that is satisfying and fulfilling. It is a guideline because the program will not be self-sustaining if you are hungry all the time.

As it turns out, there is synergy between the low-fat orientation of the 10% solution and caloric restriction. Eating foods that are low in fat and high in fiber allows you to reach a state of satiety with far fewer calories than eating the foods that make up the normal American diet. But I am strongly opposed to reducing calories below the point at which you have satisfied your feelings of hunger.

You seem to be giving me a mixed message here.

That is a fair statement, and probably another reason why this chapter is not located in the front of the book. The mixed message is the following. There is considerable evidence that calories do count. Eating excessive calories has a negative impact in terms of both decreasing longevity and speeding up the aging process. Conversely, restricting calories up to a certain point appears to slow down the aging process.

On the other hand, any program that requires continual deprivation will ultimately fail and is likely to have negative behavioral consequences. Even when you are losing weight, I recommend that you eat a sufficient number of lower-fat calories so that you are never hungry.

So just what do you suggest?

The Guideline

Again, the evidence for the wide-ranging benefits of eating a diet that is 10 percent calories from fat and low in cholesterol and sodium, obtaining regular aerobic exercise, and following the other guidelines I have called the 10% solution are overwhelming, and I strongly recommend them to optimize health and well-being. The evidence for caloric restriction is not yet as extensive. However, it may take a long time before we have a comparable level of evidence. After all, the evidence for a low-fat, low-cholesterol diet has been accumulating since World War II, which is almost half a century. You may not want to wait that long before considering this issue. On the other hand, keep in mind the strong proviso that you must obtain adequate nutrition, and there is a real danger that a long-term program of caloric restriction may lead to a nutritional deficiency. There is also the issue of avoiding feelings of hunger that I discussed earlier. There are, of course, many poor areas in the world where people eat a low-calorie diet because that is all they can afford. In general, these people are not obtaining all the nutrients they need. Needless to say, the poverty causes other problems, in that the food the people have available tends to be high in pathogens, and there is generally very inadequate health care, if any.

Having said all that, what I would recommend, and what I am doing personally, is reducing caloric consumption to a level that enables me to maintain a weight that is approximately 95 percent of my ideal weight. My wrist measures 7 inches, so according to table 1 in chapter 5, "Your Weight," I have a medium frame but am at the top end of that range. Since I am 5 feet, 6 inches tall, my ideal weight according to table 2 is 147 pounds. I maintain my weight at 95 percent of this figure (140 pounds) by eating about 2,100 calories per day and exercising an average of 350 calories per day.

Now you're talking about controlling weight; I thought we were talking about restricting calories.

They are essentially equivalent. Each calorie level corresponds to a maintenance level for a particular weight. For example, when I weighed 188 pounds, my maintenance level was approximately 2,900 calories per day. Now, at 140 pounds, my maintenance level is about 2,150 calories. If I were to eat 2,900 calories per day, my weight would rise and eventually stabilize back at 188 pounds. At 2,150 calories, my weight has stabilized at 140 pounds. Not surprisingly, one's maintenance level at a particular weight is roughly proportional to that weight (i.e., as your weight goes down, your maintenance calorie level goes down, too, by roughly the same percentage).

Thus, stabilizing your weight and stabilizing your food consumption (and exercise routine) are essentially equivalent.

And you follow the other recommendations of your 10% solution?

Of course.

So what are you trying to do, live to be 150 years of age?

First of all, the research suggests that the benefits of caloric restriction on aging start when you start the caloric restriction, so there is a difference between starting at age 40 and starting much earlier in life.

But I am less concerned with how many years I will live than with the quality of those years of life.

So how exactly would you state this guideline?

I would recommend maintaining your weight at approximately 95 percent of your ideal weight indicated by tables 1 and 2 in chapter 5. You can estimate what your maintenance level of calories should be for this level by table 3 in chapter 5, but keep in mind that everyone's metabolism is different, so you will have to adjust this figure from experience. That is why I have stated the guideline in terms of weight rather than calories. Expressing the guideline in this way automatically takes into consideration your rate of metabolism. Also, you should have little difficulty avoiding feelings of hunger with this guideline. I strongly recommend, however, that you *do not allow your weight to fall appreciably below 95 percent of your ideal weight (as indicated by table 2).*

The content of the diet should obviously follow the guidelines of the 10% solution. Blood glucose levels and the level of oxygen free-radicals are also reduced by eating a diet that is low in fat and high in fiber. Eating a diet high in natural grains, vegetables, and fruits will also assure you that you are obtaining adequate nutrition. It is important to eat a varied diet to make sure that you are getting all of the vitamins and minerals you need.

There is only one problem I have with this guideline.

What's that?

While eating a diet that is low in fat, cholesterol, and sodium may appear at first glance to involve a sacrifice in palatability, you have strenuously pointed out that this is ultimately not the case. You have repeatedly indicated that once you discover the variety of foods that do comply with these guidelines and once your tastes adjust, the 10% solution represents an enjoyable and satisfying way to eat. So there is no real sacrifice involved.

Yes, that's true.

But with this guideline there is a sacrifice. You have to eat less.

But consider that if aging is indeed governed by metabolism, which is to say that we have a certain number of calories to eat in our lifetime, and assuming that our life is not cut short by an accident or other unpredictable event, then it would make sense to eat somewhat less each day and thereby enjoy a longer life. After all, there are many other enjoyable things to do in life besides eat.

Eating is right up there, I have to tell you.

I'll grant you that. I have always loved to eat and still do. I would make two points here. First, the potential is not just to extend your life in terms of number of years, but to make those years healthier. All of the guidelines of the 10% solution, including this one, are intended to make those years more fulfilling. Second, I still eat a reasonably large quantity of food. While 2,150 calories may seem limited on a "normal" high-fat diet, on a diet that is only 10 percent calories from fat it is a rather significant quantity. As I pointed out earlier, low-fat food goes a lot further in terms of quantity for the same number of calories. I am never hungry and eat three satisfying meals a day.

Do you want to explain the title of this chapter?

The first "fountain of youth," if you will, is the set of other guidelines we have been discussing: 10 percent calories from fat and so on. The evidence that such a life-style will delay or even eliminate most of the diseases and other conditions that are normally associated with aging has been growing substantially for half a century. The issue of caloric restriction is now the second major approach to extending mortality and delaying morbidity that has gained some level of scientific corroboration.

So spend your calories wisely.

Yes, indeed.

11

■

The Kurzweil Challenge
to Society

The Challenge

It would be useful if our society externally reinforced healthy habits rather than destructive ones.

Yes it would, and I have some ideas along those lines.

Yes, I'll bet you do. Another ten-point program?

I thought you'd never ask. Indeed, I have a ten-point Kurzweil Challenge to Society.

Okay, let's hear it.

The Medical Community

The **first challenge** is to the medical community. More than any other constituency in society, physicians need to take a leadership role in these issues. People look to their doctors for guidance. There are many doctors who have indeed provided substantial leadership in changing the views of society on the role of nutrition in health and whose pioneering research has provided the rich mosaic of scientific evidence we have today. On the other hand, most doctors in their day-to-day practice do not provide this perspective to their patients. Even those patients who are in great need of this knowledge—persons with heart disease, angina pain, advanced atherosclerosis, hypertension, type II diabetes, cancer—generally receive a very watered-down set of recommendations. As I discussed in part I of this book, the public-health recommendations are precompromised at 30 percent calories from fat rather than the optimal level of 10 percent. I have had numerous discussions with physicians who acknowledge that 10 percent calories from fat is the optimal level, but then they go on to say something along the lines of, "My patients would never accept ..." So the optimal health recommendations are severely compromised before the patient ever hears them. And then the patient is told that if he or she follows these (watered-down) recommendations, it will be helpful, but only partially so, because the genetic impact is so much greater than the impact of life-style. And of course, if one follows these highly compromised public-health recommendations on the fat and cholesterol content of food, then it is true that one had better have benevolent genes. The fact that almost everyone (with only rare exceptions) can reduce their risk of contracting these diseases by 90 percent or more is just not revealed. Indeed, most doctors are not aware of this.

The reason for this situation is that most doctors know very little about nutrition. Very little of substance is taught in medical school about this vital subject, and the vital link between what we eat and these diseases of affluence is generally not appreciated or understood.

My recommendations to the medical community are to take these nutritional issues seriously, to learn about them, and then not to pre-compromise this knowledge before disseminating it to your patients. People are quite capable of compromising on their own, if that is their proclivity.

It seems that medical schools should give this issue a higher priority.

Medical Schools

That brings me to **point two**, which concerns our medical schools. A survey conducted in 1984 by the Joint Liaison Committee on Medical Education of the American Medical Association and the Association of American Medical Colleges reported that only 27 percent of American medical schools offered even a single separate course in nutrition. A 1985 survey by the Committee on Nutrition in Medical Education of the Food and Nutrition Board of the National Research Council indicated that the majority of medical schools teach less than twenty hours of material related to nutrition during the four years of medical education. This results not only in the widespread ignorance of this subject that we see in the medical profession, but in the underlying message that nutrition is but an incidental health issue. This is changing in some quarters, but the surface has only been scratched.

My challenge to medical schools is to teach an orientation to medicine that emphasizes prevention through life-style alteration, where the doctor is a partner in health maintenance, not just the fix-it person that quickly repairs the "machine" when it breaks down. This would include providing an extensive and thorough background in the nutritional roots of disease and disease prevention.

The Health Insurance Industry

My **third challenge** is to the health insurance industry, which includes several major government programs such as Medicare and Medicaid. Having explored with numerous doctors, as well as with industry leaders and policymakers, the issue of developing a consensus on preventive medicine through nutritional and life-style counseling, I have come to realize that our entire system of third-party reimbursement for medical care makes it self-defeating for physicians to attempt to take this approach to health care seriously. It is difficult for a physician to recommend a nutritional approach to treating a disease without having some means of providing that education to his patients efficiently. Yet, third-party payers will generally not provide reimbursement for nutritional counseling or education. When you consider that a change in diet is an ideal form of treatment for a type II diabetic or someone suffering from advanced atherosclerosis, this is a remarkable state of affairs, yet is almost universally the case. Given that the adage "an ounce of prevention is worth a pound of cure" certainly applies in this instance, it would make economic sense to encourage this approach to health maintenance. Indeed, the health insurance industry would find it in its economic interest to aggressively promote illness prevention through life-style alteration.

It would seem that society needs to understand what is already known about nutrition to a much greater degree.

Nutritionists

Yes, and that brings me to my **fourth challenge**, which is to the nutritionists. In general, there is greater awareness of these issues among this group than in the medical community.

That is hardly surprising.

One would expect nutritionists to have a greater interest in and knowledge of nutrition. But even here, there is the same issue of a quick willingness to precompromise the message. Of course, many nutritionists just pass on the public-health recommendations without a thought as to where they come from or whether or not they are truly optimal. But I know nutritionists who do understand these issues and who, themselves, follow a diet of 10 percent calories from fat yet have so little confidence in the ability of their clients to accept an optimal position on these matters that they do not share this perspective outside their profession. My challenge to this group is to provide the leadership on nutritional issues that is rightfully yours and, again, to not precompromise the truth.

Most people have little contact with nutritionists.

The Food Industry

That says something in and of itself about our society's priorities. Most of the public's education on nutritional issues comes from food advertisements, which brings me to my **fifth challenge**—to the food industry. On the positive side, food advertisements do deserve credit for popularizing and encouraging the public's interest in reducing fat, cholesterol, and sodium in the diet. On the other hand, many of the ads are quite misleading. For example, consider all of the foods that loudly proclaim that they are "cholesterol free," yet are high in fat, which as we have discussed is the most important factor in determining blood cholesterol levels. We see ads promoting margarine as a health food, despite the fact that it is 100 percent fat, most of which is polyunsaturated, which damages health in a variety of ways.

My challenge to the food industry is twofold. First, continue the process of developing low-fat, low-cholesterol, low-sodium foods that appeal to the American palate. Second is to avoid misleading health claims that only perpetuate common misconceptions.

That's easy for you to say, but it seems to me unavoidable that advertisers are going to put the best possible face on their products. If there is even some partial health benefit, they will tout it, and if there is a health danger, you can hardly expect advertisers to go out of their way to point that out.

The Media

Good point, which brings me to my **sixth challenge**—to perhaps the most influential group of all, and in many ways the sector of society in the best position to educate the American people: the *media*. On the program side, the news media have the opportunity to present these issues in a powerful way that is convincing and informative. The media, more than government or even the educational sector, have the ability to set the agenda of change and to focus attention on dramatic problems. One can certainly imagine some powerful documentaries on the specter of the American people eating themselves to death. On the advertising side, there is, again, a highly leveraged opportunity for influence, constructive or otherwise. Madison Avenue has mastered the means, not only to convey knowledge, but to effect deeply rooted longings and fears.

But in terms of advertising, the media promotes what it is paid to promote.

For starters, there is public-service advertising, and while there are many worthwhile messages promoted in this way, the message that we can save a million lives a year through nutrition and other life-style factors has a deplorably low priority. I also feel that both the media, itself, and the advertising agencies that create advertisements could take a stand against some of the more egregious examples of misleading advertising.

Such as?

The most obvious example is cigarette advertising, which links the act of smoking to virility, social acceptance, good times, an almost innocent form of pleasure. But smoking poisons virtually every system in the body, and there is nothing virile, ingenuous, or fun about the health impact, short or long term.

But my primary challenge to the media is to deliver the message of the overwhelming impact of life-style on health and well-being in a way that is effective. It is difficult to deliver a message in a way that truly gets through. It is not a matter of people receiving the message and then rejecting it. It is more a matter of it simply bouncing off most people. We are so used to being bombarded with many hundreds of messages every day, that people do not even bother to evaluate most of them. But the media has the techniques and the power to change

American attitudes in a fundamental way if they put their collective minds to the task.

Isn't that the purpose of this book?

Yes, and a book is part of the media. But it will take more than one book to change society.

A book can be very influential.

We shall see.

What is your seventh challenge?

Government

Challenge seven is directed at government, which also has enormous capacity to provide leadership on vital issues of health. Look at the government-led program against smoking.

As you point out, 50 million Americans still smoke.

True, but more than 100 million American adults do not smoke, which is a far better ratio than in Europe or Japan. So government leadership can make a difference.

The public enthusiasm for physical fitness started with President Kennedy's call for Americans to shape up, a prime example of presidential leadership which required no legislation. The government can also improve food labeling and encourage research to further document the benefits of a healthy diet and life-style. Most of all, the government can play the kind of leadership role on the issue of diet that it has in other areas of substance abuse.

Doesn't there need to be a public consensus first?

In a democracy the priorities of government cannot stray too far from public attitudes. On the other hand, responsible officials from the president to the surgeon general, as well as authoritative government bodies with their own influence and reputation, such as the National Institutes of Health, can help shape that consensus.

As one effective approach, I would advocate health-risk warnings on foods that are high in fat and/or cholesterol.

You mean the kind of warnings we now have on cigarettes, but for ice cream, for example?

Exactly, ice cream should lose its innocence.

Schools

Speaking of ice cream, **challenge eight** is directed at our schools. We should start with school lunches, which are prime examples of poor nutrition. A recent study estimated American school lunches at about 40 percent calories from fat. We do not necessarily need to go down to 10 percent calories from fat, but could still teach good nutrition by example through a more healthful lunch program.

Schools should also teach nutrition, which is, after all, a vital subject for health and happiness. If nutrition is discussed at all in today's schools, it is usually a simpleminded and misleading rendition of the four food groups.

Children are sometimes difficult to influence.

Parents

Yes and no. Children are also very impressionable and soak up their culture almost effortlessly. Perhaps of the greatest influence on children are their parents, to whom I address my **ninth challenge**. Education on nutrition, which is a somewhat personal and intimate aspect of life-style, is often the province of the home. Parents need to impress on their children the power and importance of what they put in their bodies. Of course, the best way to teach a subject like this is to set a good example.

And the last challenge?

Everyone

My **tenth challenge** is directed at everyone. As I mentioned before, the medical community is a service-providing institution that in many ways reflects the priorities of its constituency. While our medical delivery system does not constitute a perfect market, it is nonetheless difficult for doctors, hospitals, and other medical institutions to provide an orientation to health care at variance with what the public is demanding. And if people demand quick and easy solutions that do not require us to reflect on our own contribution to our health and well-being, then that is what the medical system will try to provide. The reality is that, while our medical technology can be brilliant in acute situations, true healthfulness can only be achieved and sustained through a healthful life-style.

So take the Kurzweil Challenge.

PART THREE

■

GUIDES
TO
THE
10%
SOLUTION

12
■
The Ten-Minute Guide to the 10% Solution

This chapter gathers together in a single concise guide all of the principles of the 10% solution. While much of this material has been presented earlier in this book, it is organized here for the purpose of providing a brief yet thorough reference.

1. What It Is
The 10% solution is a nutrition, exercise, and life-style program designed to maximize both the enjoyment of life and longevity. Through extensive medical and health research, the dietary and health principles have been shown to dramatically reduce the likelihood of developing major diseases that account for at least two-thirds of all deaths in the United States and other Western societies. The 10% solution also addresses the principal health risks of the Japanese diet and life-style. Other benefits include an immediate beneficial impact on health and well-being.

The words *ten percent* refer to the most important guideline: limiting fat consumption to 10 percent of caloric intake. This guideline is emphasized both because of its central importance and because it is the least well understood of the principles. Other guidelines concerning the intake of cholesterol and salt, moderation of alcohol consumption, restriction of smoking and other forms of drug abuse, exercise, and stress management are more widely understood. While some level of fat consumption is necessary to maintain health, the level of fat consumed in Western societies is far in excess of what the human species evolved to tolerate. The major thesis of this book is the central contribution of the vastly excessive consumption of fat in the diet to the development of the principal degenerative diseases of the Western world, including heart disease, stroke, hypertension, diabetes, and cancer. The 10% solution refers, however, not just to the fat guideline, but to the entire program of dietary and lifestyle modification.

2. Benefits
In most individuals following the 10% solution, **atherosclerosis** is halted and even reversed. Since atherosclerosis is the principal cause of virtually all heart attacks, the risk of developing **coronary heart disease** is dramatically reduced. The risks for contracting other diseases and life-threatening conditions caused by atherosclerosis are also dramatically reduced—including **thrombotic** and **embolic strokes** (the most common forms of stroke in the United States), **claudication** (blockage of blood to the legs), **impotence** in men, **aneurysms**, and other conditions.

The 10% solution is an ideal program for controlling **hypertension** without medication (many of these medications have been shown to increase the risk of heart disease) and, thus, for avoiding **intracerebral hemorrhage** (another principal form of stroke). It also has been shown to be effective in controlling or preventing **type II diabetes** (usually without medication) and **hypoglycemia**.

Studies of societies that eat a diet following these principles, as well as studies of American populations, have shown these dietary and lifestyle principles lead to dramatically reduced incidences of **breast cancer, ovarian cancer, colon-rectal cancer, uterine cancer, prostate cancer, lung cancer**, and other cancers.

The 10% solution also significantly reduces the risk of **glaucoma, cataracts, hearing loss, arthritis, gallstones**, and **gout.** `

It strengthens the immune system, which is effective in combating diseases ranging from cancer to **minor viral infections**.

High-fat diets clog the capillaries within hours of a typical high-fat meal as a result of **red blood cell aggregation**. The 10% solution prevents this condition, thus **improving capillary circulation,** which **improves energy level, alertness**, and **sleep patterns**.

The 10% solution is the ideal program for sustained and permanent **weight loss**. It also prevents the cycle of **food cravings** that result from the common high-fat, high-sugar diet.

The high-fiber content of the 10% solution encourages better **digestion** and **regularity** in elimination. A low-fat diet also significantly improves **complexion** problems.

Overall, it improves the sense of **well-being**.

3. Who This Is For
The 10% solution is for **all adults** except for pregnant women and those who are chronically too thin and have great difficulty maintaining adequate weight. See section 6, below, for the guideline exceptions for pregnant women, chronically thin adults, and children.

4. Nutritional Principles
The most important principle is to reduce **fat** intake to **10 percent of calories**, as opposed to the 35 to 40 percent (or more) that is typical of the Western diet. In addition to avoiding **saturated fat**, it is important to dramatically reduce the intake of **polyunsaturated fat**. Consumption of polyunsaturated fat reduces HDL levels (the good cholesterol), increases the risk of cancer (even more than saturated fat), suppresses the immune system, and increases red blood cell aggregation which blocks the capillaries. While **monounsaturated fat** (found in most vegetables) and **omega-3 fat** (found in fish such as salmon and swordfish) are regarded as "less bad" fats, they should nonetheless be included in the fat total. If a person eats 2,000 calories per day, then 22 grams of fat would represent 10 percent of calories.

Cholesterol intake is to be reduced to 100 milligrams a day or less, compared to the 500 milligrams or more consumed in the typical Western diet.

Studies have suggested that an average or higher blood **iron** level is a risk factor for heart disease, particularly when combined with an elevated level of LDL cholesterol. The source of iron in the blood is iron in the diet. Avoiding sources of fat and cholesterol in the diet, particularly meat and other foods of animal origin, will automatically avoid concentrated sources of iron. It would also be a good idea to avoid iron supplements (unless you have a significant deficiency), vitamin and mineral supplements that include iron, and "fortified" foods.

Menstruating or giving three units of blood per year will also significantly lower blood iron levels and may help lower the risk of atherosclerosis and heart disease.

Protein is to be limited to less than 15 percent of calories per day. The Western diet is typically excessive in protein as well.

Complex carbohydrates (vegetables, grains, legumes, cereals, pastas, breads) are encouraged as the primary constituent of the diet. They should comprise 70 to 80 percent of the calories consumed. Fruits, which contain both complex and simple carbohydrates, are also encouraged.

Sugar is seen as empty calories, and excessive sugar consumption can lead to high insulin–low blood sugar cycles. However, minimal inclusion of sugar and its equivalents (glucose, sucrose, dextrose, molasses, maple syrup, honey, etc.) is not particularly harmful.

Sodium, found principally in salt, is to be restricted to less than 2,000 milligrams per day. This is particularly important for anyone with increased risk of hypertension. Sodium consumption in the Western diet is typically more than 6,000 milligrams per day, with the Japanese diet being 10,000 to 15,000 milligrams per day or more. This is a principal factor in the Japanese tendency toward hypertension and intracerebral hemorrhage (one of the leading causes of death in Japan).

A diet high in complex carbohydrates will necessarily be high in **fiber**, which aids in digestion and the healthy functioning of the gastrointestinal tract. Fiber should be 40 grams per day or more, compared to less than one-third that amount in the typical Western diet. Soluble fiber, found in beans and peas, is particularly desirable and may reduce cholesterol. Insoluble fiber found in most fruits and vegetables is the most effective in inhibiting the promotion, or growth, phase of cancer.

It is important to eat a **variety** of foods to obtain necessary **vitamins** and **minerals**. If the diet is sufficiently varied, then vitamin and mineral supplements are not necessary. Adequate **calcium** to prevent osteoporosis can be obtained from non-fat milk products, although women may wish to consider calcium supplements.

5. Caloric Restriction

There is a recent body of evidence that indicates the potential for a significant extension of longevity and delay of morbidity through caloric restriction. Animal experiments have found an extension of life span by approximately 50 percent as a result of reducing caloric intake by 33 percent. Interestingly, the normal-eating animals and the low-calorie animals ate the same number of calories in their lifetimes. The low-calorie animals not only extended their life spans by approximately 50 percent, but also extended youthfulness and avoided the feebleness, poor health, sluggishness, and grizzled appearance of old age, even as they neared the end of their extended lives. Some of the mechanisms identified that can account for the extended longevity include a lower blood glucose level, significantly reduced levels of oxygen free-radicals, and improved levels of free-radical detoxifying enzymes and DNA-repairing enzymes. The key to this approach is obtaining an adequate intake of nutrients (vitamins, minerals, protein, essential fatty acids) when reducing calories.

The evidence for the other guidelines of the 10% solution (10 percent calories from fat, low cholesterol and sodium, aerobic exercise, etc.) represent a rich mosaic of evidence gathered for more than fifty years. It includes conclusive and extensive human intervention and population studies. The evidence for the benefits of caloric restriction are more preliminary and are based on extensive animal studies but no human studies to date. However, the animal studies are consistent across experimenters and across species.

Because of the lack of human studies, the importance of obtaining adequate levels of all nutrients, and the importance of avoiding feelings of hunger, it is suggested that a more moderate guideline be followed than has been suggested by the animal studies. One's weight should be maintained at approximately 95 percent of the ideal weight specified by tables 1 and 2 of chapter 5, "Your Weight," *but not significantly lower than this level.* Caloric intake should be at the level necessary to maintain this weight.

6. Exceptions

Chronically thin adults may wish to increase the percentage of calories from fat to 20 or 25 percent. Otherwise, 10 percent is strongly recommended.

The guidelines are also appropriate for **children**, except here, also, a higher percentage of calories from fat is recommended, again for greater caloric density to allow for optimal growth. The recommended guideline for children is 20 to 25 percent calories from fat, which is still considerably lower than the 40 to 50 percent typical of Western societies. There should be no restriction on fat intake for children under 2 years of age.

Pregnant women should take care to eat sufficient calories, protein, iron, and calcium. Skim milk and 1 percent fat milk products are good sources of all of these nutritional categories. Pregnant women may also wish to increase somewhat their intake of lean meat and fish to obtain sufficient calories and protein. I recommend that pregnant women increase their fat intake to around 20 percent of calories to help avoid nutritional deficiencies.

A woman should gain approximately 10 pounds of weight during the second trimester of pregnancy and 24 to 30 pounds overall to avoid the risk of low birth weight in her newborn.

Persons without any major risk factors:
- Who do not have diabetes or hypertension
- Who have never had coronary heart disease, cardiovascular diseases (such as stroke), angina, cancer, or indications of these diseases
- Who have no immediate (nuclear) family members who have had these diseases
- Whose total serum cholesterol level is less than 160
- Whose cholesterol-to-HDL ratio (on their higher-fat diet) is less than 3.5
- Whose weight is less than 105 percent of their ideal weight
- Who exercise regularly
- Who do not smoke, or abuse alcohol or other drugs

and who would prefer to eat 15 percent calories from fat rather than 10 percent, may do so.

Persons without any indication of hypertension and who have never had diabetes, hypertension, coronary heart disease, cardiovascular diseases, or angina may eat 3,000 milligrams of sodium a day.

7. Other Substances

Smoking is damaging to one's health, dramatically increasing the risks for atherosclerosis, heart disease, hypertension and stroke, cancer, emphysema, and other diseases. People should not smoke and should avoid cigarette smoke in the air.

Low to moderate **alcohol** usage (preferably less than two glasses of wine, beer, or spirits per day) is acceptable, although the calories are "empty." Excessive use of alcohol is damaging to one's health and behavior. Moderate alcohol usage may provide a modest protective effect against heart disease for those who eat the "normal" high-fat diet, although the evidence is still not entirely clear. Moderate use of alcohol may, however, increase the likelihood of certain cancers. For persons following the guidelines of the 10% solution, there is no benefit in moderate use of alcohol, although moderate use is not restricted.

Caffeine is to be avoided. It increases the risk of heart disease and hypertension. Anyone who suffers from anxiety or panic disorders or has difficulty sleeping should not consume any caffeine.

Abuse of any **drugs**, legal or illegal, is to be avoided.

Additives and **chemicals** in food are to be avoided to the extent possible. Some may be safe, but many are found not to be.

8. Exercise

Aerobic exercise has been found to lower the risk for heart disease, cancer, and other diseases. Together with a low-fat diet, it is a necessary component of any weight-loss program. It is effective in lowering high blood pressure. It improves one's mood and sense of well-being. The dietary recommendations, above, and regular aerobic exercise work synergistically to provide the maximum health benefit.

Aerobic exercise is any exercise that increases the heart rate into the training heart-rate range for a sustained period of time (at least twenty to forty minutes). Ideal is **walking** or **cycling**. **Running** is effective aerobic exercise, but does have a high risk of injury. **Swimming, rowing,** and **cross-country skiing** are other forms of aerobic exercise. Stop-and-go activities such as tennis are not ideal, although they do provide some aerobic benefit. The **training heart-rate range** is 65 percent to 85 percent of one's maximum heart rate, which is roughly computed as 220 less one's age.

Exercise should proceed in five phases: a few minutes of **stretching** (to prepare one's muscles for exertion), a few minutes of **warm-up** (start slow), **aerobic exercise** (at least thirty to forty minutes), a few minutes of **cool-down** (slow down again), and, finally, a few more minutes of **stretching**.

An exercise period of at least forty-five minutes four to seven times per week is recommended.

People starting an exercise program should consult their doctor. Persons (1) 45 years of age or older, or (2) between 35 and 44 who have at least one risk factor for coronary artery disease (such as an immediate family member who developed coronary artery disease before age 50, obesity, smoking, high blood pressure, or high cholesterol level), or (3) at any age who have cardiovascular disease, lung disease, diabetes, or hyperthyroidism, should have an exercise stress test (an electrocardiagram test administered while exercising on a treadmill or stationary bike) before starting a regular exercise program.

9. Stress

Chronic stress can aggravate existing conditions. In particular, it can accelerate atherosclerosis and lead to coronary heart disease. If one's atherosclerosis is already in the 70 percent-plus (percentage of blockage of the coronary arteries) danger zone, then a stressful event can trigger the coup de grace of a complete blockage by a blood clot (a heart attack, stroke, aneurysm, or other incident).

The behavior of the so-called type A individual (hard driving, relentlessly committed to work) is detrimental to health if the behavior pattern includes chronic hostility and anger. Negative chronic stress is distinguished from more constructive forms of sustained effort which are characterized by the four Cs: commitment, challenge, curiosity, and creativity.

Chronic stress can be managed short term through relaxation techniques and long term by reassessment of life and work patterns.

Stress is characterized by activation of the fight-or-flight mechanism, a chain reaction of neuronal and hormonal changes, which include the sudden production of epinephrine (adrenaline) and norepinephrine (noradrenaline) by the adrenal glands, the disruption of the digestive process, and increases in blood pressure, blood sugar levels, cholesterol levels, and breathing and heart rates. It is also manifested in the dilation of the pupils, the activation of blood-clotting mechanisms, and the mobilization of internal energy stores. The fight-or-flight mechanism is necessary for survival because it provides the capacity to respond appropriately to danger. *Chronic stress is characterized by excessive activation of this mechanism,* which can result in permanently raised levels of blood pressure and cholesterol and other changes that are detrimental to physical and mental health.

Physical symptoms of chronic stress can include high blood pressure, headaches, rapid heartbeat, aches and pains, muscle tension, and gastrointestinal discomfort. Behavioral indications include difficulty sleeping, compulsive use of food, drugs, alcohol, sex, or gambling, or any other compulsive behavior; problems in concentration; accident proneness, and social withdrawal. Emotional signs include nightmares, crying spells, feelings of worthlessness, excessive or compulsive worrying, mood swings, restlessness, and anxiety. Spiritual signals would include a sense of emptiness, loss of life's meaning, excessive confusion, and doubt about one's direction in life.

False stress relievers are substances or behaviors that appear to relieve stress in the short term but lead to greater levels of chronic stress and anxiety in the long term and are dangerous to one's health and well-being. These include abuse of tobacco, alcohol, caffeine, benzodiazepines (which comprise the bulk of prescription tranquilizers and sleeping pills), cocaine, heroin, and other legal and illegal substances. Abuse of food and other compulsive behaviors can also be regarded as false stress relievers.

A ten-point program for effectively managing stress:

1. Follow the nutritional guidelines of the 10% solution.
2. Do not use tobacco. Do not use cocaine and other illegal drugs. Consume as little alcohol as possible, not to exceed the equivalent of one or two glasses of wine or beer a day. Consume as little caffeine as possible. Persons with anxiety or panic or sleep disorders should avoid caffeine completely.
3. Follow the guidelines of the 10% solution for aerobic exercise.
4. Give a high priority to obtaining a sufficient quantity and quality of sleep.
5. Balance the three poles of life: work, family/friends, and self.
6. Take periodic time off from your regular routine (i.e., take vacations).
7. Share your innermost feelings (fears, worries, hopes, delights) with someone on a regular basis.
8. Listen empathetically to others.
9. Manage your time. Set an approximate schedule so that you consciously set your priorities. Learn when to say no to commitments. Do not overschedule; allow sufficient time for problems, opportunities, and spontaneity.
10. Evoke the relaxation response—a physiological mechanism that is essentially the opposite of the stress (fight-or-flight) mechanism. It can be evoked through techniques such as yoga, biofeedback, and certain forms of meditation. A meditation technique that has been thoroughly researched at Boston's Beth Israel Hospital is described in chapter 8.

10. Target Weight and Serum Lipid and Glucose Levels
Weight should be within 5 percent of ideal weight. See tables 1 and 2 in chapter 5, "Your Weight," to determine ideal weight.

Total **serum (blood) cholesterol** should not exceed 160 mg/dl. Ideally, it should be 150 or less.

There have been misleading reports of correlations between very low serum cholesterol levels and the incidence of cancer, alcoholism, and other conditions. A very low serum cholesterol level does not cause cancer or alcoholism. Rather, the casuality runs in the opposite direction. Certain cancers (including preclinical cancer) and in some cases abuse of alcohol can cause very low cholesterol levels. Abuse of alcohol in turn is linked to a variety of other conditions including increased rates of suicide. A low serum cholesterol level that results from eating a low-fat, low-cholesterol diet is not a risk factor for these conditions.

The **ratio of total cholesterol to HDL** (the good cholesterol) should be less than 4, ideally as close to 2.5 as possible. However, if your total serum cholesterol level is 150 mg/dl or less, then the level of HDL and the ratio of total cholesterol to HDL are less important.

Triglycerides should be 100 or less.

Fasting (i.e., before breakfast) **glucose** should be less than 120. An elevated glucose may indicate diabetes.

11. Weight Loss

The nutrition and exercise guidelines of the 10% solution are ideal for weight loss. While losing weight, daily calorie consumption should equal at least ten times your ideal weight. This will provide steady and sustainable weight loss. Once the weight is lost, continue all of the guidelines, but increase the calorie level until weight is sustained. Eating less then 1,000 calories per day for a female or 1,200 calories per day for a male is not recommended, as it may lead to nutritional insufficiencies.

12. Review of Foods

Foods to Emphasize

- Breads made without added oils, butter, and margarine. Breads made from natural unprocessed grains are preferable.
- Pastas made without oil or eggs. Whole-wheat pastas are ideal.
- Cereals without added fats, salt, and sugar.
- Any whole grains or grain products.
- All vegetables except avocados and olives (which are high in fat).
- All fruits and fruit juices.
- Legumes such as peas, beans, lentils, etc., are ideal and good sources of soluble fiber.
- The only nuts encouraged are chestnuts, which are low in fat.
- Air-popped popcorn.
- All dairy products that are non-fat (i.e., made from skim milk),

including skim milk, non-fat yogurt, skim-milk cheese. Cottage cheese made from 1 percent fat milk is acceptable.
- Soybean products, including tofu, while relatively high in fat, are acceptable in moderation.
- Egg whites.
- Up to 4 ounces per day of fish or lean white meat of chicken or turkey (cooked without the skin), although it is possible to eat up to 8 ounces if necessary. Very lean red meat (flank steak or round steak) is also acceptable, although fish or lean fowl is preferable.
- Clams, oysters, mussels, and scallops are acceptable (up to the total of 4 to 8 ounces per day for fish or lean meat).

Foods That Can Be Eaten Occasionally

- Sugar and its equivalent (sucrose, glucose, dextrose, honey, maple syrup, corn syrup, molasses, brown sugar, etc.).
- Grain products (breads, cereals) made with small amounts of added fat (such as oil).
- Pastas made with small amounts of egg.
- Avocados and olives are high in monounsaturated fat and should only be eaten in moderation (but count the fat grams toward your limit).
- Mild (low-sodium) soy sauce.
- Alcohol, up to one or two drinks per day (preferably less).
- Low-fat milk products (1 percent milk fat).
- If you must use an oil, use olive oil or canola oil, which are high in monounsaturated fat, but use very limited amounts, if any.
- Coffee and caffeinated teas should be avoided, but if you must consume caffeine, limit yourself to one or two cups of coffee (or the equivalent) per day or drink decaffeinated coffee or tea.
- Lobster, crab, and shrimp contain moderate amounts of cholesterol (although low in fat) and may be eaten in moderation.
- Smoked foods and charbroiled foods contain a powerful carcinogen, which is largely responsible for the high rate of stomach cancer in Japan, and should be eaten in very limited quantities.

Foods You Should Never Eat

- Any meat that is not very low in fat. Avoid chicken or turkey cooked with the skin. The skin itself is 100 percent fat and should never be eaten. Most forms of red meat are very high in fat and should not be eaten. Organ meats are very high in cholesterol and should never be eaten. Deli meats are usually very high in fat and sodium as well and should not be eaten.

- Animal fats, butter, hydrogenated vegetable oils, lard, margarine.
- Coconut oil and palm oil, which are high in saturated fat.
- Mayonnaise (avoid all salads made with mayonnaise, such as tuna salad, etc.), unless it is non-fat.
- Oils high in polyunsaturated fat, such as corn oil and most vegetable oils.
- Whole dairy products, including milk, cream, sour cream, whole milk yogurt, ice cream, cream cheese, all cheeses (unless made with skim milk). Cheeses made from partially skimmed milk are still too high in fat.
- Nuts (except chestnuts).
- Never use the salt shaker.
- Egg yolks.
- All fried foods.
- Non-dairy creamers.
- Highly salted foods.

13. Tips
- Eat a variety of foods. This will assure you of getting adequate levels of all nutrients, including vitamins and minerals. This will also avoid taste fatigue.
- When you start out, count your fat grams. This is more important than counting calories. The fat content of foods is not always intuitive, until you get some experience. Counting fat grams is the best way to learn the implications of the most important guideline. For example, if you are eating 2,000 calories per day, then limit yourself to 22 grams of fat per day. Count all sources, even small ones, as they add up. Even an apple has half a gram of fat.

  You can determine fat grams in several ways. The easiest is to look them up on the nutritional labels, found on many food products. Appendix 2 of this book, "Nutritional Content of Food," has additional information on the fat content of different foods.
- Eat at least three meals a day. Do not skip breakfast or lunch.
- Use spices rather than salt to flavor foods.
- Never fry foods. Steaming and poaching are useful cooking techniques. You can sauté foods (but not in oil!) using wine, defatted chicken stock, mild (low-sodium) soy sauce, or water. If you sauté in wine, 85 percent of the calories and all of the alcohol are gone within one minute.
- Another alternative is to broil foods. I recommend use of stove-top grills.

- Plan ahead.
- When traveling by airplane, call ahead (at least twenty-four hours) and order a low-fat, low-cholesterol meal.
- If you travel to Europe or another place where low-fat milk products may not be readily available, take non-fat milk powder with you. You can carry it in a small container and then use it (with bottled water) to make skim milk for your cereal or as a beverage.
- If you are invited to a function, call ahead and explain your dietary needs; they will usually be readily accommodated.
- If you are invited to a party by a friend, call ahead and explain your dietary needs to the host or hostess. Usually, they can be accommodated easily without requiring a lot of effort. For example, your hosts may put your baked potato aside before filling it with a cheese filling or put your vegetables aside before putting on a butter sauce. This is preferable (both for you and your host or hostess) to not eating most of what is served.
- It is important to have a good source for low-fat foods and cooking condiments. A good health-food store is ideal. Not everything in a health-food store is low in fat, but these stores do tend to be good sources of low-fat products. They are also excellent sources of organic and whole-grain products that are hard to find in a regular supermarket.
- Look for the increasing variety of no-fat and low-fat (as well as low-sodium) foods that are becoming commercially available due to increasing public demand.
- Be wary of "low cholesterol" or "no cholesterol" labels. While reducing cholesterol intake is certainly important, it is not sufficient. Many of these products are very high in fat.
- Read food labels. The ingredients list will tell you if there are added fats, such as oil. The nutritional breakdown will tell you the amount of fat, cholesterol, sodium, and (sometimes) fiber. If a product has 1 or 2 grams of fat per 100 calories, then it is okay from a fat standpoint (but count the grams because they add up). If a product has 5 or 6 grams of fat (per 100 calories), then you immediately know it's not for you.
- Be wary of labels such as "low in fat" without reading just what that means. For example, "2 percent low-fat milk" has 5 grams of fat per serving, which is too high and represents 38 percent calories from fat. One percent low-fat milk has 2 grams of fat per serving and is acceptable, although skim milk is better.

- The essential fatty acids come primarily from whole grains, beans, vegetables, fruits, and fish. Meat is not a good source of essential fatty acids, so there is no danger of any deficiency in essential fatty acids from eliminating or restricting meat from the diet. There is no RDA (Recommended Daily Allowance) of essential fatty acids, but experts suggest that at least 3 percent of calories come from essential fatty acids. The diet described here will provide in excess of that amount.
- Intestinal gas and flatulence are common when people make significant changes in their diet. Some intestinal gas is normal and a natural consequence of changing your diet, as well as of the high-fiber content of a diet that is high in complex carbohydrates. People vary in their reactions, but most people will find that this experience diminishes as your digestive tract adjusts to the dietary change. If you are troubled by flatulence, then limit bran, legumes, and other foods particularly high in fiber. Also choose cooked vegetables over raw vegetables.
- Have your cholesterol tested. Make sure it is a "fasting" test (a test taken in the morning before you have had anything to eat). Make sure they measure your HDL, triglycerides, and glucose levels. These are not automatically tested for. Very often a cholesterol test will measure only total serum cholesterol. Everyone should know their serum cholesterol, HDL, triglyceride, and glucose levels.
- Keep in mind that your tastes will change. High-fat foods that may appeal to you before making this type of modification are likely to appear greasy and unappealing once you have become used to the nutritional principles of the 10% solution. Conversely, foods that may initially seem bland will become quite tasty as you get used to a diet in which foods are not drenched in fat, salt, and sugar.
- Occasionally you may backslide and make an exception to the 10% solution. You shouldn't let that discourage you. On the other hand, making regular exceptions, even once or twice a week, will prevent the process of your tastes changing. Then the 10% solution will remain a discipline forever, which ultimately will cause it to fail. Being strict about these changes initially is important for the phenomenon of taste change to occur. The first month requires discipline, the second is easier, then your desires are likely to become consistent with the principles of the diet.
- Most important, keep an open mind!

13

■

How to Eat Revisited

WHAT'S FOR BREAKFAST

The best way to become nutritionally conscious is to read food labels when available. In addition, appendix 2 provides the nutritional content of common foods.

There are many breakfast foods that are consistent with the 10% solution. Here is a sample.

1. COLD CEREALS

The cereals below are low in fat, cholesterol, sugar, and sodium. Some of the cereals have more fiber content than others.

All Bran
Basic 4
Bran Buds
Bran flakes
Cheerios
CommonSense Oat Bran
Cornflakes
Cracklin' Oat Bran
Crispix
Crunchy Corn Bran

Fruitful Bran
Grape-Nuts
Grape-Nuts Flakes
Just Right
Kenmei Rice Bran
Multi Grain Cheerios
Nutri-Grain
Nutty Rice
Oat bran
Oat squares

100% bran
Product 19
Puffed kasha
Puffed millet
Puffed rice
Puffed wheat
Raisin bran

Rice Chex
Shredded Wheat 'n Bran
Shredded wheat
Special K
Total
Wheaties

2. HOT CEREALS

Cream of Rice
Cream of Wheat
Farina
Grits (without butter)

Oat bran
Oatmeal
Wheatena

The following **grains** can be cooked for a healthy hot cereal: barley, buckwheat groats (kasha), bulgur, cornmeal, hominy grits, rice, rye.

3. SKIM OR 1 PERCENT MILK

4. BAGELS, ENGLISH MUFFINS, BAGUETTES, BREADS, RICE CAKES

5. OMELETTES made from egg whites or low-fat (or non-fat) egg substitutes

6. FAT-FREE EGG OMELETTE (see recipe for omelette in chapter 14)

7. FRENCH TOAST made with egg substitutes

8. LOW-FAT CREPES (see recipe for Fruit Crepes in chapter 14)

9. PANCAKES made with egg substitute and pancake mix (check the grams of fat; some pancake mixes are higher in fat than others)

10. CHEESE BLINTZES made with low-fat cottage cheese, skim milk, and egg whites

11. FRESH FRUIT

Apples	Grapes	Papayas	Plums
Apricots	Honeydew melons	Passion fruit	Raisins
Bananas	Kiwifruit	Peaches	Raspberries
Blackberries	Kumquats	Pears	Starfruit
Blueberries	Mangos	Persimmons	Strawberries
Cantaloupes	Nectarines	Pineapples	Tangerines
Cherries	Oranges	Plantains	Watermelons
Grapefruits			

12. FRUIT JAMS, JELLIES, PRESERVES

13. VERY LOW FAT CHEESE

Hoop cheese
Havarti low-fat cheese
Cabot low-fat cheese
Jarlsberg "lite"
Tasty-lo dill

Cottage cheese, low-fat
  (1 percent) or non-fat
Fromage blanc
Alpine Lace fat-free cheese

Check your store for other low-fat cheeses.

LET'S HAVE LUNCH

The following is a sample of lunch foods that comply with the 10% solution. There is an increasing variety of non-fat and very low fat items available in your supermarket, so keep an eye out for healthy alternatives.

1. SALADS

GREENS	FILLINGS	SALAD DRESSINGS
Boston	Onions	Lemon juice and sugar
Green leaf	Carrots	Balsamic vinegar
Red leaf	Eggplant	Low-fat or non-fat salad
Iceberg	Cauliflower	dressings:
Romaine	Green beans	Seven Seas
Spinach	Broccoli	Kraft
Watercress	Snow peas	Cain's
Swiss chard	Corn	Tomato sauce
	Summer squash	Non-fat or low-fat sour cream

FILLINGS	SALAD DRESSINGS
Red, green, yellow bell peppers	Low-fat or non-fat mayonnaise dressing:
Zucchini	Miracle Whip
Mushrooms	Cain's
Lima beans	Kraft
Sugar snap peas	Cucumber and low-fat yogurt
Garbanzo beans	dressing
Tomatoes	Low-fat or non-fat cottage
Kidney beans	cheese
Cucumbers	
Asparagus	
Green beans	
Yellow wax beans	
Alfalfa sprouts	

2. SANDWICHES

MAIN INGREDIENT

Skinless white-meat chicken
Skinless white-meat turkey
Tuna (canned in water)
Fish, baked, grilled, or poached:
  catfish
  cod
  haddock
  striped bass
  rainbow trout
  salmon
swordfish
tuna
shellfish
Vegetarian sandwich (mixed vegetables)
Baked eggplant
Small portions of red meat: round, flank, or eye round
Tabbouleh (made without oil or a small amount of olive oil)

MIXED WITH

Cranberry sauce	Tomatoes	Cucumbers
Apple sauce	Lettuce	Peppers
Onions	Celery	Alfalfa sprouts

BREAD

Rye	Sourdough	Tortillas (corn)
Whole wheat	Milano	Bagel
Bran	Vienna	Whole-wheat
Oatmeal	Pita bread	English muffin
Pumpernickel		

CONDIMENTS

Mustard
Low-fat or non-fat mayonnaise
Low-fat or non-fat salad dressings
Horseradish

Catsup
Worcestershire sauce (no salt)
Balsamic vinegar

3. STEAMED VEGETABLES with potato or with low-fat (1 percent) cottage cheese

4. PASTA (prepared without butter, margarine, or oil) with a low-fat tomato or marinara sauce)

5. FRUIT PLATE

6. SOUP

Bean soup
Chicken soup
Cucumber soup
Gazpacho
Manhattan clam chowder
Melon soup

Noodle soup (with eggless
   noodles in chicken base)
Salsa chowder
Tomato soup
Vegetable soup
Vegetarian chili
Zucchini soup

7. THE SALAD BAR: low-fat or high-fat?

Salad bars contain nutritious vegetables, fruits, and grains, but **avoid** the following high-fat items:

Bacon bits
Butter, margarine
Cream-based soups
Croutons
Cheese and processed meats
Muffins
Nuts and seeds
Tuna, chicken, egg, potato, pasta salads smothered in high-fat oil,
   salad dressing, or mayonnaise
Whole, hard-boiled eggs

IT'S TIME FOR DINNER

A small sampling of what you can eat.

1. MEAT

Fish prepared without oil
Lean beef: round, flank, or
  eye round
Lean white-meat chicken

Lean white-meat turkey
Shellfish: clams, mussels, oysters,
  scallops, shrimp, lobster

2. VEGETABLES (also see salad list for "Let's Have Lunch," above)

Asparagus
Artichokes
Beets
Bok choy
Brussels sprouts
Cabbage
Collards
Eggplant
Endive
Kale
Kohlrabi
Okra
Parsnips
Turnips
Pumpkins
Yams

LEGUMES

Beans
Azuki
Black
Cranberry
Fava
Kidney
Lima
Pinto
Marrow
Mung
Navy
Pea
Soy (tofu)

Peas
Black-eyed peas
Chick-peas/garbanzo beans
Cow
Field
Split
Lentils

3. GRAINS

Alfalfa
Barley
Bulgur

Cracked-wheat bran
Corn
Millet

Oats
Rice

4. ANY FRUIT

5. PASTA

Bow ties
Capellini

Chow mein noodles
Couscous

Fettuccine
Linguine

Macaroni	Ravioli	Spaghetti
Malfatti	Rigatoni	Tortellini
Manicotti	Rotini	Vermicelli
Mostaccioli	Shells	Ziti

6. SALADS (see "Let's Have Lunch")

7. BREADS

8. SAUCES

Béarnaise sauce (made with no vegetable oil, butter, margarine, or egg yolks)
Barbecue sauce
Fruit sauce
Herb sauces

Low-fat sour cream
Low-fat yogurt sauce
Madeira sauce (made with chicken broth and cornstarch)
Marinara sauce
Salsa

SNACKIN' IT

Many low-fat snack items are appearing on supermarket shelves. Here is a small sample of nutritionally sound snack alternatives.

Air-popped popcorn
Angel-food cake
Applesauce
Baked apples or pears
Corn tortillas (not fried)
Cut-up fruit and skim milk or low-fat cottage cheese
Cut-up vegetables
Fruit gazpacho
Ice milk or low-fat/non-fat yogurt
Jell-O
Low-fat cakes and cookies
Low-fat desserts found in the frozen-foods section of the supermarket (see "Frozen Foods," below, for examples)

Low-fat sponge cake
Low-salt pretzels
Matzo
Non-fat milk shake (skim milk, flavor extracts, and fruit mixed in a blender)
Rice cakes (there are now many flavors in the supermarket)
Wheat-bread sticks
Wheat or raisin toast with jelly or jam (no butter or margarine)

FROZEN FOODS

There is an increasing selection of low-fat items available in the frozen-foods section of your supermarket. Remember to always check the number of fat grams because the words "low fat" on the package do not always guarantee that the product will comply with the 10% solution. Remember also to consider serving sizes. Some manufacturers will use artificially small serving sizes to make their products appear more nutritionally sound than they are. For example, if a package contains 6 servings, and you eat half the package, then you need to multiply all of the nutritional quantities (calories, fat, sodium, etc.) by 3 (servings).

It is also important to check on sodium content. Some low-fat products are still excessively high in sodium.

One brand that is worth noting is **Healthy Choice**. All of the Healthy Choice meals provide relatively low levels of fat, cholesterol, and sodium. There is an extensive selection, and the products have rated high in consumer taste surveys.

Here is a small sampling of frozen foods that are reasonably low in fat.

ENTREES AND DINNERS

HEALTHY CHOICE

	CALORIES	FAT (g)	CHOLESTEROL (mg)	SODIUM (mg)
Breast of turkey	290	5	45	420
Shrimp marinara	260	1	60	320
Chicken Oriental	230	1	45	460
Sweet-and-sour chicken	280	2	50	260
Pepper fish	300	5	40	370

WEIGHT WATCHERS

Some of Weight Watchers' frozen entrees and dinners are reasonable in fat content, but others are too high. Check the fat grams on the label when choosing from their selection.

	CALORIES	FAT (g)	CHOLESTEROL (mg)	SODIUM (mg)
Low-fat Italian cheese lasagna	290	7	20	510

LEAN CUISINE

These are somewhat high in terms of sodium content.

	CALORIES	FAT (g)	CHOLESTEROL (mg)	SODIUM (mg)
Chicken chow mein	240	5	30	530
Fiesta chicken	240	5	40	560
Chicken tenderloins in herb cream sauce	240	5	20	490
Zucchini lasagna	260	5	20	550

VEGETABLES

BIRDS EYE

Birds Eye offers many frozen vegetables in small boxes or large bags.

	CALORIES	FAT (g)	CHOLESTEROL (mg)	SODIUM (mg)
Broccoli spears	35	0	0	20
Winter squash	45	0	0	0
Cut green beans	25	0	5	5
Green peas	80	0	0	130
Little ears of corn	130	1	0	5
Sweet corn	100	1	5	280

GREEN GIANT

Green Giant also offers many frozen vegetables in small boxes or large bags. To decrease fat intake, buy Green Giant vegetables without added butter sauce.

Two examples of Green Giant vegetables:

	CALORIES	FAT (g)	CHOLESTEROL (mg)	SODIUM (mg)
Cut green beans	25	0	0	0
Harvest fresh sweet peas	50	0	0	135

GREEN GIANT AMERICAN MIXTURES

Green Giant offers several combinations of frozen vegetables.

	CALORIES	FAT (g)	CHOLESTEROL (mg)	SODIUM (mg)
New England–style sweet peas, potatoes, carrots	70	1	0	75

DESSERTS

	CALORIES	FAT (g)	CHOLESTEROL (mg)	SODIUM (mg)
SARA LEE				
Cheesecake (low-fat)	150	2	5	65
Chocolate cake (low-fat)	110	0	0	140
PEPPERIDGE FARM				
Golden pound cake	70	1	0	85

HOW THE OILS AND FATS COMPARE

In general, all added oils and fats should be avoided on the 10% solution. The primary guideline, however, is to limit fat to 10 percent of calories, so it is *possible* to use oil sparingly on the 10% solution as long as you count the fat grams. For example, if using a small amount of oil on your salad is important to you, you could use a teaspoon of olive oil, which adds 4.5 grams of fat. That will be a significant portion of your fat grams, but it is not out of the question (if you eat 2,000 calories per day, 10 percent calories from fat means eating 22 grams of fat per day). Other possible uses of oils include adding small amounts to recipes, such as tomato sauce, or using a very small amount when sautéing.

If you do plan on using oils, then I recommend extra virgin olive oil, which is the oil that is highest in monounsaturated fat, the "less bad" fat. Canola (or rapeseed) oil is also popular because it is very low in saturated fat, although its polyunsaturated fat content is higher than that of olive oil. Also, some of the polyunsaturated fat in canola oil is omega-3 fat, which is another "less bad" fat. Otherwise, I do not recommend any of the other vegetable oils. I also do not recommend any of the meat fats, Crisco, butter, or margarine, all of which are included below for comparison.

The following chart compares these oils and fats in terms of the different types of fat. Eating an excessive level of saturated fat will raise cholesterol levels, which substantially increases the risk of heart disease and other conditions. Consuming polyunsaturated fat is also not healthy and is linked to increased cancer risk and decreased levels of HDL (the good cholesterol). Monounsaturated fat should still be avoided, but it is a "less bad" fat than saturated or polyunsaturated fat.

All amounts below are in teaspoons.

TYPE OF FAT	CALORIES (1 TEASPOON)	TOTAL FAT (G)	SATUR- ATED FAT (G)	POLYUN- SATUR- ATED- FAT (G)	MONOUN- SATUR- ATED- FAT (G)	COMMENT
Olive oil	39.7	4.5	.6	.4	3.5	Highest in monoun-saturated fat
Canola (rapeseed) oil	40	4.5	.3	1.5	2.7	Lowest in saturated fat
Safflower oil	40	4.5	.4	3.4	.8	High in polyun-saturated fat
Corn oil	40	4.5	.6	2.7	1.3	High in polyun-saturated fat
Coconut oil	40	4.5	3.9	.1	.5	Very high in saturated fat
Palm oil	40	4.5	2.2	.4	1.9	High in saturated fat
Peanut oil	39.6	4.5	.8	1.4	2.3	Moderately high in polyunsaturated fat
Sesame oil	40	4.5	.6	1.9	2	Moderately high in polyunsaturated fat
Soybean oil	40	4.5	.7	2.6	1.2	High in polyun-saturated fat
Sunflower oil	40	4.5	.5	3	1.1	High in polyun-saturated fat
Beef tallow, raw	38.7	4.3	2.1	.2	2	High in saturated fat
Chicken fat, raw	38.3	4.2	1.3	.9	2.1	Moderately high in saturated and polyunsaturated fat
Pork fat (lard), raw	38.3	4.3	1.7	.5	2.1	High in saturated fat
Crisco	35.3	4	1	1.2	1.8	Moderately high in saturated and polyunsaturated fat
Butter	36	4.1	2.5	.2	1.4	High in saturated fat
Margarine (stick, corn)	33.3	3.7	.7	1.3	1.7	Moderately high in polyunsaturated fat

RECIPE CONVERSION

Many recipes can be converted to a low-fat equivalent, but use common sense since substituting every ingredient in a recipe may not work well.

Here are some suggested substitutions.

INSTEAD OF	USE
Ricotta cheese	Skim milk (or 1%) ricotta cheese
Oil for sauté	Non-stick pan with low-sodium soy sauce, lemon juice, defatted chicken or fish stock, wine, vegetable stock
Whole-milk products	Non-fat and 1 percent fat milk products, such as skim milk (for a thicker milk product, use evaporated non-fat milk or non-fat milk with additional non-fat milk powder dissolved in it)
1 medium whole egg	2 egg whites or 1/4 cup no-cholesterol, non-fat egg substitute
1 cup sour cream	1 cup skim-milk yogurt 1 cup light or non-fat sour cream
Nuts	Water chestnuts Roasted chestnuts
Ground beef	Ground chicken (without added salt) Ground turkey (without added salt) Ground round or flank steak
White flour	Whole-grain/whole-wheat flour
Oil for baking	Apple sauce Crushed pineapple Mashed banana

INSTEAD OF	USE
Whole-milk cheeses	Low-fat cheeses Hoop cheese Fromage blanc Low-fat soy cheeses
1 cup high-fat yogurt	1 cup skim-milk yogurt
Fruit canned in syrup	Water-packed canned fruit
Fish canned in oil	Water-packed canned fish
Ice cream	Sorbet Non-fat or low-fat frozen yogurt Non-fat frozen desserts
Mayonnaise	Non-fat mayonnaise Non-fat yogurt with mustard or vinegar
Salad dressing with oil	Oil-free salad dressing
Salad dressing with cream or cheese	Yogurt-and-lemon dressing Low-fat salad dressing
Frozen or breaded fish	Fish broiled, baked, poached, steamed
High-fat sauce or gravy	Vinegar marinade Herb/lemon marinade

Butter or cream-based
  vegetable sauces
	Pureed vegetables
	Sauces made with skim milk or
	  low-fat or non-fat sour cream,
	  cottage cheese, or yogurt

Salt	Herbs, spices
Sugar and other sweeteners	Concentrated fruit juice

Butter in pastry recipes	Apple sauce, crushed pineapple,
	  mashed banana, or other fruit to
	  provide moisture and flavor

Note: To thicken sauces, you can use non-fat milk powder, pureed cooked potatoes, pureed cooked vegetables, pureed cooked rice, pureed cooked kasha, and cornstarch.

The following are some samples of full recipe conversion.

■

TRADITIONAL LASAGNA (HIGH-FAT VERSION)
Serves 8

1 medium onion, chopped

4 tablespoons olive oil or salad oil

1½ pounds lean ground beef

1 clove garlic, minced or mashed

16 ounces tomato sauce

1 can (6 ounces) tomato paste

1 cup water

Salt

1 teaspoon oregano

½ teaspoon each pepper and sugar

12 ounces lasagna noodles

1 pound (2 cups) ricotta cheese

½ pound mozzarella cheese, thinly sliced

½ cup grated Parmesan cheese

Optional: 3 medium Italian sausages, spicy

1. In a large frying pan, sauté the onion in oil until soft. Add beef and garlic and cook until the meat is crumbly. Optional: Add sausages to beef, garlic, and onion mixture for flavor.

2. Stir in tomato sauce, tomato paste, and water. Add salt, oregano, pepper, and sugar, stirring until mixed. Cover the pan and simmer for about 1½ hours. Remove sausages, if used.

3. Cook the noodles in boiling salted water as directed on the package. Drain and rinse the noodles. Drain again.

4. Preheat oven to 350°.

5. Arrange ⅓ of the noodles on the bottom of a 9-by-13-inch shallow casserole dish. Spread ⅓ of the tomato sauce over the noodles. Top with ⅓ of the ricotta and mozzarella cheese.

6. Repeat layering two more times. Top with the Parmesan cheese.

7. Bake lasagna for 30 minutes. Remove from oven and cut into rectangles to serve.

Nutritional information per serving:

Calories	681	Cholesterol	126 mg
Fat	33 g	Calories from fat	44%

■

VEGETARIAN LASAGNA (LOW-FAT)
Serves 8

1 medium onion, chopped
(no olive oil)
(no beef)
1 clove garlic, minced
6 ounces fresh mushrooms
16 ounces tomato sauce
1 teaspoon basil
¼ teaspoon oregano
Freshly ground pepper

1½ cups low-fat cottage cheese
(no ricotta cheese)
1 10-ounce package frozen
chopped spinach, defrosted
and drained
1 cup fresh broccoli, pureed
1 8-ounce package lasagna
noodles
6 ounces part-skim mozzarella
cheese, grated

1. Preheat oven to 350°.
2. Using a non-stick skillet, sauté onion, garlic, and mushrooms. Add tomato sauce, basil, oregano, and pepper. Reduce heat.
3. In a bowl, stir cottage cheese, ¾ spinach, and pureed broccoli together.
4. Cook noodles according to directions on package. Do not add salt.
5. Cover bottom of a 13-by-9-inch casserole dish with lasagna noodles. Add ½ of the spinach and broccoli mixtures. Add ⅓ of the tomato sauce and ⅓ of the mozzarella cheese. Repeat layers once.
6. Finish with noodles, the remaining sauce, and the remaining cheese.
7. Cover with aluminum foil. Bake for 35 minutes.

Nutritional information per serving:

Calories	345	Cholesterol	13.8 mg
Fat	5 g	Calories from fat	13%

■

TOMATO SALAD (HIGH-FAT)
Serves 4

5 medium fresh tomatoes, sliced   *3 to 5 tablespoons wine vinegar*
3 medium red onions, sliced thin   *1/4 teaspoon basil leaves, minced*
Salt   *Freshly ground pepper*
1/3 cup olive oil   *1/4 cup parsley, minced*

1. Place sliced tomatoes and red onions in a medium serving bowl.
2. In a small mixing bowl, stir olive oil and pepper together. Pour onto tomatoes and red onions.
3. Sprinkle the tomatoes and red onions with pepper, parsley, and basil. Cover and refrigerate for 2 hours. Serve cold.

Nutritional information per serving:

Calories	206	Cholesterol	0
Fat	18 g	Calories from fat	79%

■

TOMATO SALAD (LOW-FAT)
Serves 4

5 medium fresh tomatoes   *1/4 teaspoon basil leaves, minced*
3 medium red onions   *Freshly ground pepper*
1/4 cup non-fat Italian dressing   *1/4 cup fresh parsley, minced*
Wine vinegar to taste

Follow steps for high-fat Tomato Salad.

Nutritional information per serving:

Calories	46	Cholesterol	0
Fat	0	Calories from fat	0

10% COOKING METHODS MADE SIMPLE

There are many healthy ways to cook food. Several methods are briefly explained below.

1. SAUTÉING

DEFINITION: Cooking or browning food at a high temperature in a small amount of hot liquid in a skillet, continuously stirring food during cooking. Sautéing is similar to stir frying.

Vegetables, fish, meat, and poultry are delicious when sautéed. Ten percent sautéing means replacing butter or oil with:

Defatted chicken or fish stock
Vegetable stock
Wine
Juices from other vegetables, such as finely chopped onions

Do not sauté vegetables in water. Sautéing in water produces tasteless vegetables.

EQUIPMENT FOR SAUTÉING

Teflon skillet or wok: Teflon skillets are useful because you need very little stock to sauté food.

TO SAUTÉ

1. Turn the burner to high.
2. Place a skillet or wok on the burner and add a small amount of the desired liquid.
3. Quickly add food.
4. Stir constantly, keeping heat on high. As the food cooks, you may need to add more liquid.
5. The length of time to sauté the food will depend on the quantity and kind of food cooked. Meats should be browned or golden; vegetables should be tender.

2. STEAMING

DEFINITION: Cooking food in steam given off by boiling water.

Steaming is an excellent way to cook most vegetables (except for large-root vegetables, such as potatoes and yams). Unlike vegetables that have been boiled, steamed vegetables maintain most of their nutritional value.

EQUIPMENT FOR STEAMING

Stainless-steel steamer basket: Different sizes of these inexpensive baskets can be used with different-size pots and are useful for steaming vegetables. However, moisture collects and drips on the metal and may make the food soggy.

Bamboo steamers stacked over a wok: These steamers are handy because several dishes can be steamed over a wok at the same time.

In a pinch: If you have neither bamboo nor stainless steamer baskets, use a metal colander or a wire rack over a pot.

TO STEAM

1. Bring water (no more than an inch) to boil.
2. Lower the heat to simmer.
3. Place steamer basket, colander, or wire rack over, but not touching, water.
4. Add food to the steam basket and cook to desired tenderness. Vegetables will take only a few minutes. Test vegetables to see that they are tender but not limp.
5. Drain food. You can save the water from vegetables, chicken, or fish for stock.

3. GRILLING

DEFINITION: Cooking food over a dry heat source.

Grilling offers a low-fat alternative for cooking poultry, lean meats, and fish that has been marinated. Marinated vegetables may also be grilled.

EQUIPMENT FOR GRILLING

Covered grills: Kettle- or wagon-shaped. These grills are fueled by charcoal, gas, or electricity.

Braisers: Uncovered shallow grills, used for direct-heat grilling only (grilling directly on top of the coals). Note that excessive charcoal-grilling has been linked to stomach cancer.

Hibachis: Portable grills for small servings.

4. MICROWAVE COOKING

MICROWAVE COOKING is moisture producing and needs no added fats to cook foods: Adapt conventional recipes by reducing the cooking time given by one-third to one-quarter. Choose foods that cook well in moist heat: chicken, fish, ground meat, vegetables, sauces, and soups.

1. To help foods cook faster, cover them with dish lids or microwave-safe plastic wrap. If using microwave-safe plastic wrap, allow steam to escape by turning back one corner. (Always leave a gap in a container to allow steam to escape.)
2. Do not use paper plates or towels when cooking food for more than ten minutes.
3. Do not use any dish to microwave food in unless it fits in the microwave!
4. If the microwave doesn't have a turntable to spin food, turn or stir food throughout cooking.

OTHER HEALTHFUL COOKING METHODS

BAKING: Cooking food over a dry heat source, often using a covered container and adding liquid before cooking. Foods to bake: starchy vegetables (potatoes, yams, winter squash), chicken, fish, lean red meat, casseroles.

BROILING: Cooking underneath direct heat (usually in an oven) at high temperatures. Foods to broil: chicken, fish, lean red meat.

POACHING: Cooking by immersing food in simmering liquid. Foods to poach: chicken, fish.

ROASTING: Cooking food with a dry heat source in an uncovered pan. Foods to roast: chicken, lean red meat.

THE 10% PANTRY

The environment that you have the greatest control over is your home. Setting up your pantry to facilitate a low-fat diet is a key step to a successful commitment.

Here are some items that the well-stocked "10% pantry" might include.

DAIRY

1 percent milk	Non-fat or 1 percent	Non-fat yogurt
Dry, non-fat milk powder	cottage cheese	Egg whites
Non-fat or low-fat cheese	Hoop cheese	Egg substitute

BEVERAGES

Seltzer
Mineral water
Fruit juices

Tomato juice
Fruit juice sparklers

1 percent milk
  or skim milk
Herbal teas

GRAINS

Low-fat snacks
Pastas
Vegetables, fruits

Cereals
Breads
Prepared foods (canned and frozen)

HERBS AND SPICES

Basil
Bay leaves
Capers
Chervil
Dill

Fennel
Marjoram
Mint
Mustard
Oregano

Rosemary
Sage
Tarragon
Thyme

CANNED MEAT AND FISH

Unsalted tuna, packed in water
Unsalted salmon, packed in water
Unsalted chicken

CONDIMENTS

Mustard
Vinegar
Salsa
Horseradish
Low-fat salad dressings
Tabasco sauce
Worcestershire sauce

Unsweetened catsup
Non-fat sour cream
Non-fat or 1 percent cottage cheese
Lemon juice
Wine
Sherry

WHERE FAT LURKS

The fat content of food is not always apparent until you acquire some knowledge. One important source of this information is the nutritional breakdown provided on the label of prepared foods. When this is provided, always look at the number of grams of fat. In general, 1 gram of fat per 100 calories represents just slightly less than 10 percent calories from fat. Use appendix 2 of this book, "Nutritional Content of Food," as a further guide. Note that not every food needs to be under 10 percent calories from fat in order for your diet to average 10 percent. Note your overall fat budget. If you eat 2,000 calories per day, then 10 percent calories from fat represents 22 grams of fat.

Following are examples of foods that just don't make it on the 10% solution.

CONDIMENTS

Cocoa butter
Coconut oil
Cream or oil sauces (butter, oils,
   whole-milk solids)
Palm-kernel oil

Palm oil
Peanut oil
Oil-based salad dressings
Vegetable oil
Vegetable shortening

RED MEAT, POULTRY, AND FISH

Bacon
Beef:
   choice grade of chuck rib
   hamburger
   loin, untrimmed
   sirloin
Chicken roasted with skin
Duck, goose
Lamb
Pork:
   ham
   sausage
   spareribs

Processed poultry items
Processed meats
   hot dogs
   bologna
   salami
Roasted turkey, dark meat
Self-basting turkeys
Skin from poultry
Tuna and other fish packed
   in oil

BAKED GOODS

Biscuits
Most cakes (fat is in the cake
   and in the frosting)
Some cereals (check the fat
   grams before you buy cereal)

Most cookies
Croissants
Danish
Doughnuts
Muffins

Pastry
Pie crust
Quiche
Rolls
Scones

DAIRY PRODUCTS

Butter
Cheese: American, blue, Swiss
Cream cheese
Cream soups
Eggs
Egg nog

Ice cream
Margarine
Sour cream
Yogurt (made from whole milk)
Whole milk

SNACKS, APPETIZERS

Crackers
Nuts
Pizza (often made with oily
   tomato sauce and loaded
   with cheese)

Potato chips and other fried
   snack items
Seeds

BEVERAGES

Piña coladas (contains coconut cream)

MISCELLANEOUS

Vegetables prepared in butter or oil
Fried vegetables and other foods
Avocados
Olives
Cream substitutes and non-dairy creamers (some contain coconut
   oil, which is high in saturated fat)
Sour cream substitutes
Whipped toppings (contain coconut or palm-kernel oils)

DINING OUT

TIPS ON DINING OUT

- If possible, call the restaurant ahead of time to find out what's on the menu.
- Ask that food be prepared low-fat.
- Ask if low-fat substitutions may be made for high-fat items.
- For appetizers, choose tomato- or vegetable-based soups. Order salads with low-fat dressing. Order dressing on the side.

■ For an entree, order baked or broiled fish or chicken. Ask to have skin removed from chicken before it is cooked.
■ For a drink, order skim milk, water, fruit juice, or herbal teas.
■ Request that items be prepared without oil, butter, milk, cream, or cheese.
■ Avoid
    Creamy soups
    Fried appetizers
    Butter or margarine on bread or vegetables
    Food cooked "au gratin"
    Anything "Parmesan"
    Anything with cheese, cream, or hollandaise sauce
    Casseroles
    Red meat (except in very small quantities)

Following are a number of suggestions of foods that you can order for each type of restaurant.

1. ITALIAN

■ Vegetable- or tomato-based soup (e.g., minestrone)
■ Salad with balsamic vinegar or lemon juice dressing
■ Seafood and vegetables with fresh tomato sauce
■ Fish or chicken entrees baked, broiled, or poached with wine
■ Vegetarian platters
■ Linguine with white or red clam sauce (but no oil)
■ Pasta with tomato, Marsala, or marinara sauce
■ Pasta primavera with low-fat sauce
■ Italian ice for dessert
■ Low-fat sauce on the side
■ Pizza (no cheese or oil) with tomato sauce and vegetable topping

2. CHINESE

■ Vegetable-based soup:
    Wonton
    Hot-and-sour soup (without egg)
■ Boiled, steamed, or broiled appetizers
■ Boiled, steamed, or broiled entrees, such as chicken with snow peas (ask that no oil be added)
■ Stir-fried vegetables, chicken, fish, or noodle dish (made with a clean wok using soy sauce, chicken broth, or cornstarch)
■ Steamed rice
■ Soft noodles (no fried noodles)

3. JAPANESE

- Sushi
- Sashimi
- Miso soup
- Fish or chicken teriyaki
- Chicken sukiyaki
- Yosenabe (a seafood soup with vegetables and noodles)
- Oshitashi (spinach salad)
- Nabemono
- Yakimono (broiled foods)
- Steamed rice
- Sunomono (marinated fish salad)

4. FRENCH/PROVENÇAL

- Bread (no butter or margarine)
- Vegetable soup with chicken base
- Rice with parsley and herbs
- Roasted new potatoes with herbs
- Broiled, baked, or poached fish or steamed shellfish
- Foods cooked in wine sauces such as Bordelaise
- Provençal items (these are made with tomatoes, garlic, fish, and vegetables; ask the chef to eliminate the oil when cooking these dishes)
- Vegetables with low-fat sauce

5. GREEK

- Tzatziki (yogurt and cucumber appetizer)
- Pita bread
- Greek salad (without feta cheese, anchovies, and olives)
- Plaki (fish with tomatoes, onions, garlic)
- Shish kebob with fish, chicken, or small amount of red meat (no added oil)
- Rice with entree (no butter)
- Vegetarian dolmas or dolmades (grape leaves stuffed with rice and herbs)

6. MEXICAN

- Salsa with vegetables
- Bean salad
- Vegetable salads (without oil)
- Gazpacho

- Tomato-and-onion salad with lemon dressing
- Baked fish
- Steamed corn tortillas or flour tortillas (not fried)
- Steamed tacos or tostadas with vegetable or chicken fillings
- Meatless chili
- Enchiladas stuffed with chicken, crab, or vegetables
- Chicken fajitas (without guacamole; with low-fat sour cream)
- Rice and beans (not refried)
- Seviche

7. INDIAN
- Salad
- Chicken or vegetable curry
- Steamed rice
- Tandoori chicken or fish (cooked with Indian spices and roasted in a clay pot)
- Lentils/dal
- Breads: dried pulkas (unleavened white bread), naan (without butter)

8. MIDDLE EASTERN
- Appetizers: midya dolma (mussels stuffed with rice, pine nuts, and currants)
- Lentil soup
- Tabbouleh (made with a small amount of olive oil)
- Yalanji yaprak (grape leaves with chicken and rice)
- Vegetarian-stuffed grape leaves
- Imam bayildi (baked eggplant stuffed with vegetables)
- Vegetarian or chicken shish kebob
- Couscous or steamed bulgur topped with vegetables or chicken

9. CONTINENTAL
- Fish (swordfish, tuna, scallops, etc.) or chicken broiled, baked, or poached with no oil (wine is a good sauce)
- Baked potato
- Steamed vegetables

FAST-FOOD RESTAURANTS

The typical fast-food restaurant is not the ideal place to follow the 10% solution, but some offered items are better than others. The following items are lower in fat than most, and it would be possible to eat some of these items and still eat no more than 10 percent of your calories from fat (as long as you count your fat grams).

Some of these items are excessively high in sodium, however (particularly those that exceed six hundred mg per serving). These items are listed here as foods that you might eat if necessary, but should be avoided on a regular basis.

	CALORIES	FAT (g)	FAT (%)	CHOLESTEROL (mg)	SODIUM (mg)
ARBY'S®					
Plain potato	240	2	7	0	58
Arby's sauce	30	0	9	0	227
Light roast chicken deluxe*	253	5	17	39	874
Side salad	25	0	0	0	30
Blueberry muffin	200	6	25	22	269
Orange juice	82	0	0	0	2
BASKIN ROBBINS®					
Just Peachy, fat-free frozen dairy dessert	60	1	15	0	45
Just Chocolate, vanilla twist	100	0	0	0	—
Low-fat frozen yogurt	—	—	—	—	—
Non-fat frozen yogurt	—	—	—	—	—
Ice, daiquiri, 1 scoop	140	0	0	0	15
Sherbet, rainbow	160	2	11	6	85
Sorbet, fruit	80	0	0	0	20
Sorbet, red raspberry	140	0	0	0	25
Sugar-free dairy dessert: chunky banana	100	1	9	3	50
BURGER KING®					
B.K. Broiler chicken sandwich*	267	8	27	45	728
Frozen yogurt, vanilla, Breyer's	120	3	23	10	40
Orange juice, 6 oz.	82	0	0	0	2
Salad, chunky chicken salad	142	4	25	49	443
Side salad	25	0	0	0	27
Barbecue sauce	22	—	—	—	47

	CALORIES	FAT (g)	FAT (%)	CHOLESTEROL (mg)	SODIUM (mg)
CARL'S, JR.®					
Baked potato, "lite"	290	1	3	0	60
Charbroiler BBQ chicken sandwich*	310	6	17	30	680
Low-fat milk	138	2	30	12	160
Orange juice, 8 oz.	90	1	10	37	2
Bran muffin	310	7	20	60	370
Blueberry muffin	310	7	20	45	300
Shake, large	459	9	18	19	300
DAIRY QUEEN®					
BBQ beef sandwich*	225	4	16	20	700
Vanilla malt, Mr. Misty	390	7	16	20	95
DUNKIN' DONUTS®					
Bagels	240	1	4	0	450
HARDEE'S®					
Grilled chicken sandwich*	310	9	36	60	890
Side salad	20	0	0	0	15
Yogurt, Nutrasweet	120	0	0	0	75
JACK IN THE BOX®					
Chicken fajita pita*	292	8	25	34	703
Milk shake	330	7	19	25	270
Orange juice, 6 oz.	80	0	0	0	0
KENTUCKY FRIED CHICKEN®					
Baked beans*	133	2	11	1	492
Corn on the cob	176	3	16	0	0
Mashed potatoes and gravy*	71	2	20	0	339
McDONALD'S®					
Apple juice	91	0	0	0	5
Carrot sticks	37	0	0	0	40
Celery sticks	14	0	0	0	100
Cheerios	80	1	11	0	210
English muffin	170	5	26	0	230
Frozen yogurt, cones, vanilla, low-fat	105	1	7	3	80

	CALORIES	FAT (g)	FAT (%)	CHOLESTEROL (mg)	SODIUM (mg)
Frozen yogurt sundae, hot fudge, low-fat	240	3	12	6	170
Grapefruit juice, 6 oz.	80	0	0	0	0
Grilled chicken breast*	252	4	4	50	740
McLean Hamburger (no cheese or mayo)	300	10	30	60	670
Milk shake, chocolate, low-fat	320	2	5	10	240
Milk, 1 percent low-fat	110	2	16	10	130
Muffin, fat-free, apple bran	180	0	0	0	200
Orange drink, 12 fl. oz.	130	0	0	0	10
Orange juice, 6 fl. oz.	80	0	0	0	0
Sorbet ice, orange, cone, 4 oz.	106	0	2	0	25
Salad, chunky chicken	150	4	24	78	230
Wheaties	90	1	10	0	220
TCBY®					
Non-fat frozen yogurt, reg.	267	6	20	20	126
Non-fat frozen yogurt, reg.	226	0	0	0	92
Sugar-free frozen yogurt	164	0	0	0	82
WENDY'S®					

Well-stocked salad bar

*High in sodium

On airplanes: at least twenty-four hours before your departure, order a special meal, either low-fat, low-cholesterol, or vegetarian (no egg, no dairy).

LACTOSE INTOLERANCE AND OTHER FOOD SENSITIVITIES

Do you suffer from excess gas, bloating, stomach cramps, nausea, or other symptoms of gastrointestinal distress (GID)? If so, you may have lactose intolerance. Although not related to the issues raised in this book, lactose intolerance and other food sensitivities are important nutritional issues because of the significant amount of discomfort they cause and the ease of treating these conditions once diagnosed.

At least 25 percent of all American adults are lactose intolerant, but only a small fraction are aware of it. Certain ethnic groups are particularly susceptible. For example, 90 percent of Asians, 70 percent of

North American blacks, 70 percent of Jews, 75 percent of Mexican-Americans, and about 70 percent of Mediterraneans are lactose intolerant. The symptoms can be subtle, although still uncomfortable, and, thus, most instances of lactose intolerance remain undiagnosed.

Lactose intolerance is not an allergy and, consequently, will not respond to allergy medications. Lactose is a simple sugar found in milk and milk products. The body uses a natural enzyme called lactase to digest lactose and to convert it into other simple sugars. Lactose intolerance is caused simply by a lack of lactase. Because the production of lactase normally declines with age, the likelihood of being lactose intolerant increases as one gets older.

The most straightforward way to diagnose lactose intolerance is to stop eating milk and milk products for four to five days. If the symptoms subside, continue to stay away from products containing lactose for another week. If you continue not to have symptoms, then try reintroducing milk products and see if the symptoms return. If so, you are probably lactose intolerant.

Living with lactose intolerance need not be difficult. You can treat milk and other liquid milk products with the lactase enzyme (brand names include Lactaid, Lactogest, and Dairy Ease). For example, using Lactaid drops, you add five drops per quart of dairy product to remove 70 percent of the lactose, ten drops to remove 90 percent, and fifteen drops to remove 99 percent. After adding the lactase drops, gently shake the milk or milk product and wait twenty-four hours for the lactase to convert the lactose. The nutritional qualities of the milk or other dairy products are unaffected, although it may taste slightly sweeter because the lactose is converted into other, more digestible simple sugars. You can also purchase milk that has already been lactose reduced, although lactose-reduced milk is usually only 70 percent reduced in lactose. You can add additional drops of lactase to remove most of the remaining lactose.

You can also take caplets or capsules containing lactase when eating any product containing lactose, to help your system digest the lactose. You take the lactase just before eating the food containing lactose. You have to experiment with the dosage, as different people have different levels of sensitivity.

Yogurt, buttermilk, and other cultured milk products are already very low in lactose because the fermentation process has already predigested most of the lactose. Thus, most lactose intolerant people are able to eat yogurt. Frozen yogurt, however, is usually not made from pure yogurt, but also contains skim or low-fat milk solids.

Although lactose intolerance is the most prevalent food sensitivity, there are many others. Food sensitivities may include reactions to wheat, gluten, onions, garlic, certain spices, nuts, certain fruits, vegetables or grains, beans, eggs, yeast, fructose.... The list is endless. Diagnosing a food sensitivity can be accomplished by removing the food or type of food causing the problem from your diet and then noting that the symptoms have subsided. However, because the number of possible offenders is so large and because many people with food sensitivities will react negatively to more than one category of food, making a successful identification can involve more than a little detective work.

A doctor who is familiar with food sensitivities can assist you in diagnosing this type of problem, but it is important that you choose a physician who is nutritionally oriented. Many cases of food sensitivity are often mislabeled as spastic colon, irritable bowel syndrome, or just a sensitive stomach.

If you have severe or very persistent symptoms, then it is important that you consult your doctor, because you may have an infection, ulcer, tumor, or other serious condition that requires medical attention.

14

■

Quick-and-Lean Cuisine from the Kurzweil Kitchen

The problem with most cookbooks, of course, is that they reflect the high-fat, high-cholesterol, high-sodium, high-sugar, and low-fiber orientation of the Western diet. Japanese cuisine is far superior in terms of fat and cholesterol content, but is very excessive in sodium. There are a number of excellent cookbooks that comply with the guidelines of the 10% solution, some of which I have included here.

Many of the recipes in the books below meet the 10-percent-fat-from-calories guideline. Most are also low-sodium and low-sugar. Most of these books also provide nutritional information, including fat, sodium, cholesterol, and calories. Note that not all of the recipes in these books are sufficiently low in fat, so look at the grams of fat in the nutritional analysis that accompanies many of these recipes.

Barbara Kafka. *Microwave Gourmet Healthstyle Cookbook* (New York: William Morrow and Company, 1989).

Harriet Roth. *Harriet Roth's Cholesterol Control Cookbook* (New York: Penguin Books, 1989).

Harriet Roth. *Deliciously Simple* (New York: Penguin Books, 1986).

Harriet Roth. *Deliciously Low* (New York: Penguin Books, 1983).

Marcia Sabaté Williams. *The No Salt, No Sugar, No Fat, No Apologies Cookbook* (Freedom, CA: The Crossing Press, 1986).

Marcia Sabaté Williams. *More Healthy Cooking with No Apologies* (Freedom, CA: The Crossing Press, 1991).

Rose Dosti and Deborah Kidushim-Allen. *Light Style* (New York: HarperCollins, 1991).

Pritikin Longevity Center Cookbook: Favorite Recipes from our Pritikin Kitchen (Pritikin Systems, 1991). For a copy write to: Pritikin Longevity Center, 1910 Ocean Front Walk, Santa Monica, California 90405.

The problem with many of the recipes in these books, however, is that they (like most recipes) tend to be complicated—lots of ingredients and almost as many preparation steps. If you are like me, you just don't have the time to track down all of the ingredients and spend half the afternoon preparing dinner. The recipes presented here are designed to be quick and easy, just a few ingredients and preparation steps, while also complying with the guidelines for a low-fat, low-cholesterol, high-fiber, low-sodium, and limited-sugar diet. Please keep in mind that the nutritional profiles given assume that you use the "first choice" for any ingredient where alternatives are given.

These recipes are presented in the spirit of showing how it can be done. By trying out these recipes, as well as adapting your own recipes using the guidelines on recipe conversion in chapter 13, "How to Eat Revisited," you will be well on your way toward mastering the art of easy low-fat cuisine.

I would like to express my gratitude to my wife, Sonya, with whom I collaborated on these recipes. These recipes represent our successful experiments. My thanks also to my kids, Ethan and Amy, who had to suffer through the less-successful explorations. All of these recipes have been tested in the Kurzweil Kitchen. Special thanks to Warren Stewart, who enhanced these recipes with his many culinary insights. My thanks also to my assistant, Alison Roberts, who performed an invaluable quality-control and nutritional review of the recipes. *Bon appetit!*

THE 10% BASICS
Pearl Barley
Brown Rice
Bulgur
Cornmeal
Couscous

Hominy Grits
Kasha
Quinoa
Long-Grain Rice
Dried Beans
Millet
Defatted Chicken Stock
Salsa
Tomato Sauce

BREAKFAST
Fat-Free Egg Omelette
Fruit Crepes

SOUPS
Red-Lentil Soup
Barley Soup
Corn Chowder
Potato Cream Soup
Potage de Pomme de Terre

SALADS
Cucumber Salad
Spring Salad
Carrot-Raisin Salad with Dressing

APPETIZERS
Lazy Bean Dip
Bean Dip Mexicano
Mock Peanut Butter

SIDE DISHES
Noodle Pudding
Hummus
Broccoli Piquant

ENTREES
Chicken Supreme Dijon
Chicken in a Pot

Broiled, Marinated Fish
Drunken Scallops
Linguine in Clam Sauce
Vegetarian Lasagna
Chicken and Vegetable Medley
Chicken and Salsa
Pita Pizza

DESSERTS
Whipped Strawberry-Banana Mousse
Frozen Fruit
Carrot Cake
Hot-Fudge Sundae

THE 10% BASICS

Grains are the mainstay of the 10% diet. Following are basic recipes for the common grains. Also included are recipes for salsa, tomato sauce, beans, and defatted chicken stock.

■

PEARL BARLEY
Yield: 3 cups

1 cup barley

1. Bring 3 cups of water to a boil in a medium saucepan.
2. Add barley to boiling water.
3. Cover and simmer for 45 minutes.
4. Drain barley.

Nutritional information for 1 cup, uncooked:

Calories	700	Cholesterol	0
Fat	2 g	Calories from fat	3%

■

BROWN RICE
Yield: 2⅔ cups

1 cup brown rice

1. Bring 3 cups of water to boil in a medium saucepan.
2. Add brown rice to boiling water.
3. Cover and simmer for about 35 minutes.

Nutritional information for 1-cup serving:

Calories	232	Cholesterol	0
Fat	1.2 g	Calories from fat	5%

■

BULGUR
Yield: 2 cups

⅔ cup bulgur

1. Add bulgur to 1½ cups of cold water in a medium saucepan.
2. Bring bulgur and water to boil.
3. Cover and simmer for 12 to 15 minutes.

Nutritional information for 1-cup serving:

Calories	245	Cholesterol	0
Fat	1 g	Calories from fat	4%

■

CORNMEAL
Yield: 3½ cups

1 cup cornmeal

1. In a medium mixing bowl, combine cornmeal and 1 cup cold water.
2. Bring 2¾ cups of water to boil in a medium saucepan.
3. Add cornmeal mixture to boiling water.
4. Cover and simmer for 10 minutes.

Nutritional information for 1-cup serving:

Calories	120	Cholesterol	0
Fat	trace	Calories from fat	0

■

COUSCOUS
Yield: 3 cups

⅔ cup couscous

1. Bring 1 cup of water to a boil.
2. Stir in couscous.
3. Cover; remove from heat. Let stand 5 minutes.

■

HOMINY GRITS (QUICK COOKING)
Yield: 3 cups

¾ cup hominy grits

1. Bring 3 cups of water to a boil.
2. Stir in grits. Cover and simmer for 5 minutes.

Nutritional information for 1-cup serving:

Calories	125	Cholesterol	0
Fat	trace	Calories from fat	0

■

KASHA
Yield: 2 cups

⅔ cup kasha

1. Add kasha to 1½ cups of cold water in a medium saucepan.
2. Bring kasha and water to a boil.
3. Cover and simmer for 10 to 12 minutes.

Nutritional information for ¾-cup serving:

Calories	145	Cholesterol	0
Fat	0	Calories from fat	0

■

QUINOA
Yield: 3 cups

1 cup quinoa
2 cups water, stock, or vegetable juice

1. Rinse quinoa under cold water. Drain.
2. Bring quinoa and 2 cups of water, stock, or vegetable juice to a boil in a medium saucepan.
3. Reduce heat to medium-low. Cover and simmer for 10 to 15 minutes.
4. Drain quinoa.

Nutritional information for ½-cup serving:

Calories	129	Cholesterol	0
Fat	2 g	Calories from fat	14%

■

LONG-GRAIN RICE
Yield: 3 cups

1 cup long-grain rice

1. Bring 2 cups of water to a boil in a medium saucepan.
2. Add rice to boiling water.
3. Cover and simmer for 15 minutes.

Nutritional information for ⅔-cup serving:

Calories	124	Cholesterol	0
Fat	1 g	Calories from fat	7%

■

DRIED BEANS
Yield: 2½ cups

1 cup beans

1. Rinse beans thoroughly in cold water.
2. Soak beans overnight in 3 cups of water.
3. After soaking, simmer beans in a medium saucepan, partially covered, for 2 hours.
4. Drain beans.

Nutritional information for 1-cup serving (great northern beans):

Calories	210	Cholesterol	0
Fat	1 g	Calories from fat	4%

■

MILLET
Yield: 3 cups

¾ cup of millet

1. Bring 2 cups of water to a boil in a medium saucepan.
2. Add millet to boiling water.
3. Cover and simmer for 15 to 20 minutes.
4. Let millet stand covered for 5 minutes.

Nutritional information for 1-ounce serving:

Calories	90	Cholesterol	0
Fat	1 g	Calories from fat	10%

■

DEFATTED CHICKEN STOCK
Yield: 4 quarts

4 pounds chicken bones	*5 quarts water*
2 carrots, peeled	*1 bay leaf*
1 stalk celery	*4 parsley stems*
1 large onion	*Freshly ground pepper*

1. If the chicken bones have not yet been cooked, bake them in a baking pan at 200° for 30 to 40 minutes.
2. In a large stockpot, combine all ingredients and simmer, covered, for 3 hours.
3. Strain broth and discard solids.
4. Cool to room temperature. Cover and refrigerate.
5. Skim fat from surface and discard.

Note: The steps to defat fish and vegetable stock are the same as listed above.

Nutritional information for 1-cup serving:

Calories	24	Cholesterol	0
Fat	0	Calories from fat	0

■

SALSA

Yield: 2 cups

1 cup tomato, finely chopped
 and peeled

½ cup tomato sauce

½-ounce can diced green
 chili peppers, drained

¼ cup sliced green onion

¼ cup chopped green or
 red bell pepper

1 tablespoon parsley

2 tablespoons lemon juice

1 clove garlic, minced

Freshly ground pepper

1. In a medium mixing bowl, combine all ingredients.
2. Place half of the tomato mixture in a blender or food processor. Blend mixture until it is smooth. Stir in remaining tomato mixture.
3. Cover and chill for at least 3 hours before serving.

Nutritional information for 1 tablespoon:

Calories	4	Cholesterol	0
Fat	0	Calories from fat	0

■

TOMATO SAUCE

Yield: 1 quart

1 cup onion, diced

1 cup green pepper, diced

1 cup mushrooms, sliced thin

1 28-ounce can Italian plum
 tomatoes

3 tablespoons no-salt-added
 tomato paste

½ teaspoon ground black pepper

½ teaspoon oregano

½ teaspoon basil

1. Combine all ingredients in a heavy saucepan over medium-high heat.
2. Bring to a boil, reduce heat, and simmer about 20 minutes.

Nutritional information for 1 tablespoon:

Calories   4   Cholesterol   0

Fat   0   Calories from fat   0

BREAKFAST

▪

FAT-FREE EGG OMELETTE

Serves 2

¼ cup skim milk

10 small mushrooms, sliced

1 small onion, diced

1 small potato, baked or microwaved until just tender, then cubed

1 tablespoon fines herbes *(or 1 teaspoon each dried tarragon, parsley, marjoram). If using fresh herbs, mince 1 teaspoon tarragon, ⅛ cup parsley, 1 teaspoon marjoram or thyme.*

8 egg whites
    (or equivalent egg substitute)

Optional: ½ teaspoon turmeric or pinch saffron to color eggs. Soak saffron strands, if not using powdered, in a teaspoon of cold water before adding to eggs. Let color develop.

1. In a medium sauté pan, bring the milk to a boil.

2. Add the mushroom slices and diced onion to the milk. The liquid volume will increase as the mushrooms cook. Reduce the amount of liquid to 3 tablespoons. The mushrooms will have darkened, but not nearly as much as when cooked in butter or fat.

3. On low heat (the heat retained in the pan will probably be enough), toss the cooked, diced potato and the *fines herbes* with the mushrooms. This will absorb the remaining liquid.

4. In a 10-inch skillet, either non-stick or sprayed with Pam, cook the egg whites (perhaps previously colored with turmeric or saffron).

5. Cook at a high temperature and coat the bottom of the pan with the eggs to make a flat disk.

6. Arrange the vegetables in the middle of the disk and fold the two side flaps over. Serve immediately.

Note: Mushrooms prepared in this manner, without the potato, are also excellent pureed. This *duxelles blanc* is fine with eggs and chicken and as a general-purpose thickener.

Nutritional information per serving:

Calories	147	Cholesterol	1 mg
Fat	0.8 g	Calories from fat	5%

■

FRUIT CREPES
Serves 6*

1 cup all-purpose flour (or ½ cup all-purpose flour and ½ cup whole-wheat flour)

2 cups skim milk

2 egg whites

1½ cups fresh fruit, sliced (suggestions: blueberries, strawberries, bananas, kiwis) or 4 liquid ounces fruit preserves without sugar

6 ounces plain, non-fat yogurt

1. In a blender, mix the flour, milk, and egg whites. Let stand for 1 hour in the refrigerator. It will have the consistency of cream.
2. For each pancake, spray an 8-inch non-stick skillet with Pam and brown on both sides over medium-high heat. The crepes will be very delicate and cook quickly, about ½ minute per side.
3. Stack the crepes (with layers of wax paper in between, if possible), and keep them warm under a towel.
4. Fill each crepe with fruit, or if using preserves, spread the preserves thinly over the whole crepe.
5. Roll the crepe and top with a dollop of yogurt.

*One serving = 2 crepes.

Note: Fruit may be flavored and macerated with a tablespoon of kirsch. Alternately, the fruit may be given a more exotic flavor with 1 teaspoon of chat masala, a spice mixture available at Indian grocers. One-half teaspoon of vanilla extract gives the yogurt a pleasant flavor.

Nutritional information per serving:

Calories	141	Cholesterol	2 mg
Fat	1 g	Calories from fat	7%

SOUPS

■

RED-LENTIL SOUP
Serves 4

Spices: 1 teaspoon cumin,
2 teaspoons ground coriander,
1 teaspoon turmeric,
1 teaspoon freshly grated ginger,
and 2 garlic cloves

1 medium onion, diced

1 cup red lentils, cleaned of chaff,
washed, and drained

1 large boiling potato, diced

1 large carrot, sliced

4 cups water

½ cup chard or spinach, chopped

½ teaspoon sea salt

1. In a medium-size Dutch oven or a stock pot with a tight-fitting lid (non-stick or sprayed with Pam), roast spices over medium heat until aromatic (about 4 minutes).
2. Add onion and sauté until tender.
3. Add the lentils, potato, carrot, and water.
4. Bring to a boil and reduce the heat.
5. Simmer for 30 minutes.
6. Add the greens and cook for an additional 5 minutes. Season to taste with the sea salt.

Note: Parsnips may be used if preferred to potatoes, but potatoes are in keeping with the Indian spicing. The roasting of the spices approximates the Indian technique of frying spices before adding liquid to release the aroma and oils.

Nutritional information per serving:

Calories	144	Cholesterol	0
Fat	0.8 g	Calories from fat	5%

■

BARLEY SOUP
Serves 6

8½ cups broth (thoroughly defatted chicken stock or low-sodium vegetable)

¼ cup pearl barley

2 potatoes, diced

1 cup carrots, sliced

½ cup celery, chopped

¼ cup onions, chopped

Low-sodium soy sauce to taste (approximately 1 teaspoon)

½ cup lima beans (fresh or already reconstituted dried)

1 cup frozen peas (or fresh if in season and tender)

½ cup fresh parsley, chopped

Optional: 1 tablespoon minced fresh dill; ¼ pound lean chicken white meat, microwaved or baked, and cubed

1. In a large Dutch oven or suitable stock pot, bring the broth to a boil.
2. Add the barley, lower the heat, and simmer for 40 minutes.
3. Add the potatoes and simmer for 20 minutes more or until the barley is tender.
4. Add the remaining ingredients, including optional ingredients, except the peas and the parsley. Cover and cook until the vegetables are tender.
5. Add the peas and cook for one minute longer.
6. Remove from the heat and add the parsley.

Note: An alternative, which gives the soup a darker color and a heartier texture, is to substitute lentils for the lima beans. Add them with the barley.

Nutritional information per serving:

Calories	164	Cholesterol	12 mg
Fat	0.9 g	Calories from fat	5%

■

CORN CHOWDER
Serves 2

1 garlic clove

1 small onion or 4 scallions, coarsely chopped

16 ounces canned corn

⅓ cup skim milk

⅓ cup non-fat dry-milk powder

Optional: Sea salt to taste

1. Blend the ingredients in a food processor, the garlic and onion first, then the corn with its liquid, and then the skim and powdered milk.
2. If using scallions, do not blend them. Instead, add them coarsely chopped.
3. Heat in a medium saucepan and serve. Optionally, season to taste with sea salt.

Note: For a fresher taste, use one pound of frozen corn with one cup of water or, if in season, fresh corn kernels cut off the cob. Try reserving a portion of either the fresh or frozen corn—do not puree this portion—and add the kernels whole after blending other ingredients and before heating for a chunky texture. Sea salt may be added to taste.

Nutritional information per serving:

Calories	178	Cholesterol	5 mg
Fat	0.5 g	Calories from fat	2%

■

POTATO CREAM SOUP
Serves 4

2 large potatoes, baked
1½ cups non-fat milk
2 tablespoons non-fat dry-milk
   powder
1½ to 2 teaspoons low-sodium
   soy sauce

Garlic and onion powder to taste
   (or, better yet, use freshly
   chopped onion and garlic)
Black pepper to taste

1. Blend all the ingredients in a food processor and warm in a medium-size saucepan. Season to taste with black pepper.

Variation: Reduce skim milk to ½ cup, soy sauce to 1 tablespoon, and garlic to 1 teaspoon to make flavorful whipped potatoes.

Nutritional information per serving:

Calories	86	Cholesterol	2 mg
Fat	0.3 g	Calories from fat	3%

■

POTAGE DE POMME DE TERRE
Serves 4

2 cups leeks or onions, thinly sliced
3 tablespoons fines herbes *(or
   1 teaspoon tarragon,
   1 teaspoon thyme, 1 tablespoon
   parsley, 1 teaspoon marjoram,
   1 teaspoon rosemary)*

6 cups water or thoroughly
   defatted chicken stock
4 potatoes, cubed

1. In a medium Dutch oven or suitable stock pot, non-stick or sprayed with Pam, sauté the leeks or onions over medium heat until translucent.
2. Add the *fines herbes* and cook a moment longer.

3. Pour the liquid (water or defatted chicken stock) over the onions and herbs and add the potatoes. Raise the heat and bring to a boil.

4. Cook for 1 hour or until the vegetables are tender.

5. Mash the vegetables with a potato masher or puree in a blender or food processor. (If you use a food processor, you will have to work in batches.) Serve.

Note: This base is remarkably versatile. Though appealing as is, you may add a puree of practically any green (suggestions: spinach, watercress, rabe, sorrel) at the end of cooking, and, *voilà*! Another soup! Adding pureed mushrooms is also delicious. The addition of powdered non-fat milk creates a mock creamed version of whatever is selected as a flavoring.

Nutritional information per serving:

Calories	98	Cholesterol	0
Fat	1 g	Calories from fat	9%

SALADS

■

CUCUMBER SALAD
Serves 4

2 medium-size cucumbers	1/4 teaspoon sugar
1/2 teaspoon salt	1 tablespoon fresh dill, finely
1/3 cup plain, non-fat yogurt	chopped (or dill powder)
2 tablespoons lemon juice	Optional: Paprika

1. Peel and slice the cucumbers in half lengthwise. Scoop out the seeds in the center.

2. Cut the cucumbers crosswise into paper-thin slices and spread in one layer in a shallow dish. Sprinkle with salt and set aside at room temperature for 20 minutes.

3. In a small serving bowl, stir the yogurt, lemon juice, and sugar together until well combined.

4. One handful at a time, squeeze the cucumber slices gently to remove excess liquid and pat dry with paper towels.

5. Drop the slices into the yogurt mixture to coat evenly with the sauce.

6. Cover with aluminum foil or plastic wrap and refrigerate for 2 hours.

7. Sprinkle with dill and paprika (optional) before serving.

Nutritional information per serving:

Calories	23	Cholesterol	0
Fat	0.1 g	Calories from fat	5%

■

SPRING SALAD
Serves 6

2 medium-size cucumbers, peeled and cut into ½-inch cubes (to make about 2 cups)

2 medium-size firm, ripe tomatoes cut into ½-inch cubes (to make about 2 cups)

4 scallions, including 1 inch of green stems, sliced crosswise (to make about ¼ cup)

6 radishes, sliced crosswise (to make about ¾ cup)

12 ounces 1 percent fat cottage cheese

12 ounces plain, non-fat yogurt

¼ teaspoon salt

Freshly ground black pepper

1. In a large mixing bowl, combine all the ingredients.

2. Toss together and divide into 6 portions.

Note: Individual portions fit nicely on a cupped leaf of iceberg lettuce or other suitable green.

Nutritional information per serving:

Calories	96	Cholesterol	4 mg
Fat	1.1 g	Calories from fat	11%

▪

CARROT-RAISIN SALAD WITH DRESSING
Serves 4

4 large carrots, grated
2 stalks celery, chopped
½ cup red cabbage, shredded

¼ cup minced parsley
¼ cup scallions, minced
⅓ cup raisins

1. Mix all ingredients together.

Carrot Salad Dressing
Serves 4

2 teaspoons blackstrap molasses
    (if not available, maple syrup)
1 tablespoon lemon juice

2 tablespoons water
½ teaspoon mustard

1. Toss salad ingredients with combined dressing ingredients.

Nutritional information per serving:

Calories	108	Cholesterol	0
Fat	0.4 g	Calories from fat	3%

APPETIZERS

■

LAZY BEAN DIP
Serves 16

2 cups pinto beans, cooked

¾ cup salsa—mild!

1 cup 1 percent fat cottage cheese or
  fromage blanc (a non-fat cheese)

1 cup plain, non-fat yogurt

2 tomatoes, chopped

Mini rice cakes

1. Drain liquid off the beans. Place the beans and 1/4 cup salsa in a blender or food processor and puree.
2. Spread the beans on a large serving platter.
3. Cream cottage cheese in a food processor. Add the yogurt and mix together, making a sour cream–like mixture. Alternatively, use the fromage blanc in place of this mixture.
4. Spread this mixture over pureed beans layer to about 1/2 inch from the edge of the platter so the bean layer can be seen.
5. Add a layer of tomatoes and spoon remaining salsa on top. Refrigerate until ready to serve.
6. Serve with mini rice cakes.

Nutritional information per serving:

Calories   88

Fat   0.4 g

Cholesterol   1 mg

Calories from fat   4%

■

BEAN DIP MEXICANO
Serves 16

Salsa Cruda (Raw Sauce)

1 large tomato, chopped
  (saving juice)

1 small onion, chopped

3 very mild chilies, perhaps
  serrano, but not bell pepper

8 sprigs fresh coriander, chopped

¼ cup cold water (or tomato
  juice)

Frijoles Refritos (Refried Beans)

1 small onion, chopped

1 garlic clove, crushed

2 cups reconstituted dry pinto beans plus remaining liquid. If remaining liquid is less than 1 cup, after soaking, add water to make 1 cup.

1 cup 1 percent fat cottage cheese or fromage blanc (a non-fat cheese)

1 cup plain, non-fat yogurt

1 package raw corn tortillas

1. Mix the ingredients for the Salsa Cruda. (If the chilies are too hot, remove the seeds and filament.)
2. In a large skillet, non-stick or sprayed with Pam, sauté the onion and garlic over medium heat until slightly golden. Add the beans and continue cooking
3. As the beans dry out, add some of their liquid, until all the liquid is absorbed. The beans should be a thick paste.
4. Continue cooking, folding the beans over themselves, until they pull away from the skillet and leave a slightly crusty residue.
5. Puree the cottage cheese in a food processor, being careful to process only to the point of puree, not to whip and lighten.
6. Add the yogurt and mix together, making a sour cream–like mixture. Alternatively, use the fromage blanc in place of this mixture.
7. Spread the refried beans over a large serving platter.
8. Cover with cheese-yogurt mixture or fromage blanc, spreading it to ½ inch of the edge of the beans.
9. Add a layer of Salsa Cruda.
10. Toast the tortillas under broiler or in a toaster oven. They will brown and crispen very quickly. Brown only one side or they will become too fragile.
11. Break the tortillas into large triangles and serve while still warm with the dip.

Note: You may alternatively use ¾ cup of commercially prepared mild salsa mixed with 8 sprigs of chopped, fresh coriander.

Nutritional information per serving:
Calories   108   Cholesterol   1 mg
Fat   1.5 g   Calories from fat   13%

■

MOCK PEANUT BUTTER
Serves 8

½ pound roasted chestnuts   *Optional: Peanut extract*
4 ounces apple juice concentrate

1. Mash the roasted chestnuts in a food processor. Add the apple juice concentrate until you achieve the consistency of peanut butter. Blend.
2. Optionally, add the peanut extract to flavor, although the chestnut puree is delicious without the peanut flavor.

Nutritional information per serving:
Calories   82   Cholesterol   0
Fat   0.5 g   Calories from fat   5%

SIDE DISHES

■

NOODLE PUDDING
Serves 8

16 ounces eggless noodles, cooked   *2 peeled apples, chopped*
8 egg whites (or low-fat, no-   *½ cup raisins*
cholesterol egg substitute   *½ cup pineapple, crushed*
to equal 4 eggs)   *½ cup Grape Nuts cereal*
½ cup apple juice concentrate   *1 teaspoon cinnamon*

1. Preheat the oven to 350°.
2. Boil the noodles until firm.

3. Spray a baking dish or a lasagna pan with Pam, or use a non-stick dish.
4. Blend the other ingredients except the Grape Nuts cereal and cinnamon.
5. Alternate layers of cooked noodles and blended ingredients in the dish.
6. Top with the Grape Nuts cereal and cinnamon.
7. Bake for 1 hour (until brown) at 350°.

Nutritional information per serving:

Calories	322	Cholesterol	0
Fat	1.2 g	Calories from fat	3%

▪

HUMMUS
Serves 6

12 ounces canned garbanzo
  beans/chick-peas

¼ cup lemon juice

2 garlic cloves, peeled

½ teaspoon Tabasco sauce

⅓ cup parsley, chopped

Mini rice cakes or toasted
  pita bread

1. Combine all the ingredients except the parsley in the food processor.
2. Stir in the chopped parsley.
3. Serve with mini rice cakes or toasted pita bread.

Nutritional information per serving:

Calories	146	Cholesterol	0
Fat	1.4 g	Calories from fat	9%

■

BROCCOLI PIQUANT
Serves 6

1 large bunch of broccoli

1 teaspoon fresh garlic, chopped

1/3 cup 1 percent fat cottage
    cheese

1 cup salsa—mild! (Alternatively,
    make a fresh salsa; see Bean
    Dip Mexicano, pages 232–234)

1 tablespoon lemon juice

1. Steam the broccoli for about 5 minutes.
2. Rinse in cold water.
3. Chop the broccoli in a food processor, then puree.
4. Blend in all other ingredients.

Nutritional information per serving:

Calories	47	Cholesterol	0
Fat	0.3 g	Calories from fat	6%

ENTREES

■

CHICKEN SUPREME DIJON
Serves 4

2 cups cooked long-grain rice

2 skinless, boned chicken breasts
    or 1 pound chicken cutlets

1 garlic clove, finely minced or
    crushed

1 medium onion, sliced into wedges
    and separated from root end

1/4 pound mushrooms, sliced

1/2 cup defatted chicken stock
    or white wine

2 tablespoons Dijon mustard

1/2 cup skim milk

1 teaspoon dried tarragon or
    1 tablespoon fresh
    tarragon, minced

Freshly ground pepper to taste

1. Cook rice according to package directions and set aside, keeping warm.

2. In a large non-stick skillet, brown the chicken breasts or cutlets at medium-high heat, until golden.

3. Add the garlic and onion and cook until the onion is slightly colored.

4. Add the mushrooms, chicken stock or white wine, mustard, and milk. The liquid should boil promptly.

5. Stir, scraping loose any browned bits that have stuck to the pan, and mix into the liquid (this is called "deglazing.") The mushrooms will liberate additional liquid, but keep boiling until the total liquid is about ⅛ cup.

6. Add the tarragon and pepper and stir, simmering until the sauce is thick.

7. Serve with cooked rice.

Nutritional information per serving:

Calories	320	Cholesterol	92 mg
Fat	4.3 g	Calories from fat	12%

▪

CHICKEN IN A POT
Serves 6

1 pint Brussels sprouts

3 pounds white-meat chicken (without skin)

16 baby carrots or 4 large carrots, sliced

1 cup turnips, cubed, or rutabaga, cubed

1 cup parsnips (¼-inch chunks)

1 cup leeks, white only, thoroughly cleaned and cut

12 small white onions, peeled

½ teaspoon dried thyme or 2 sprigs thyme

1 bay leaf

1 tablespoon grated ginger

1 teaspoon turmeric

2 whole cloves

2 cups defatted chicken stock or water

½ cup white wine

2 tablespoons Worcestershire sauce

1. Cover and simmer all of the above ingredients except the Worcestershire sauce in a large pot for 30 minutes.
2. Add the Worcestershire sauce. *Voilà!*

Note: You can also experiment with different assortments of vegetables.

Nutritional information per serving:

Calories	488	Cholesterol	175 mg
Fat	9.8 g	Calories from fat	18%

■

BROILED, MARINATED FISH
Serves 4

Marinade

½ cup low-sodium soy sauce
2 garlic cloves, chopped
2 tablespoons lemon juice
¼ cup parsley, chopped

1 teaspoon oregano
½ cup orange juice
Freshly ground pepper
Freshly grated ginger root

1 pound swordfish (or tuna),
divided into four pieces

1. In a shallow baking dish, combine all of the marinade ingredients.
2. Add the fish to the marinade and refrigerate for 6 to 8 hours.
3. When ready to cook, broil in the oven for 7 to 8 minutes on each side.

Nutritional information per serving:

Calories	195	Cholesterol	0
Fat	5 g	Calories from fat	23%

▪

DRUNKEN SCALLOPS

Serves 6

Marinade

1 tablespoon whiskey

1/4 teaspoon pepper

2 scallions, chopped (or
*   2 tablespoons onion, chopped)*

1 garlic clove, finely minced

1 slice ginger, finely minced

1 pound scallops

1 cup frozen peas

1 red pepper, sliced

1 tablespoon cornstarch

Water

1. Combine all of the marinade ingredients in a medium bowl.
2. Add the scallops to the marinade, mix well, and refrigerate for 30 minutes to 1 hour.
3. Steam the scallops, peas, and pepper in the marinade for 12 to 15 minutes, add water as needed. Water should not touch bottom of basket.
4. Mix in the cornstarch at the end.

Nutritional information per serving:

Calories	101	
Fat	1.8 g	

Cholesterol   0

Calories from fat   16%

▪

LINGUINE IN CLAM SAUCE

Serves 4

1 pound linguine
*   (cooked and set aside)*

1 medium onion, chopped

3 garlic cloves

Clam juice (you can use the clam
*   juice packed with the clams,*
*   if available) or white wine*

1 can minced clams or whole
*   baby clams (try to obtain a*
*   brand that is not excessively*
*   salty)*

1 zucchini, sliced

1 pepper, sliced

1/8 cup fresh parsley, chopped

1. Cook the linguine according to package instructions and set aside, keeping it warm.
2. In a large skillet, stir-fry the onions and garlic in the clam juice or white wine.
3. Add the clams with some of their liquid.
4. Add the zucchini and pepper and stir-fry with the above ingredients.
5. Add the parsley and cook briefly.
6. Toss with the cooked linguine and serve.

Nutritional information per serving:

Calories	492	Cholesterol	40 mg
Fat	3.6 g	Calories from fat	6%

■

VEGETARIAN LASAGNA
Serves 8

½ package (½ pound) cooked
  lasagna

2 cups 100 percent skim ricotta cheese

3 tablespoons fresh parsley,
  chopped

½ cup fresh spinach, chopped

2 garlic cloves, chopped
  (or, if not available,
  1½ teaspoons garlic powder)

Pepper to taste

2½ cups low-sodium tomato
  sauce (chunky-style
  preferred)

1 teaspoon dried oregano

6 tablespoons fresh basil,
  minced (if available)

Optional: 1 large eggplant
  sliced

1. Preheat the oven to 350°.
2. Cook the lasagna according to the package instructions and set aside.
3. Combine the cheese, parsley, spinach, 1/3 of the garlic, and pepper.
4. Spice the tomato sauce with oregano, basil, and the rest of the garlic.

5. Spread a thin layer of tomato sauce in the bottom of an 8-by-11-inch baking pan.

6. Arrange alternate layers of lasagna, cheese, tomato sauce (and, optionally, the eggplant), ending with a layer of tomato sauce.

7. Bake at 350° for 40 minutes.

Nutritional information per serving:

Calories	250	Cholesterol	0
Fat	1.3 g	Calories from fat	5%

▪

CHICKEN AND VEGETABLE MEDLEY
Serves 6

2 cups water

1 cup uncooked medium-grain rice

2 chicken breasts (without skin), cubed

¼ cup white wine or sherry

½ teaspoon five-spice powder (available at Asian markets and in some supermarkets in the international-food aisle)

1 garlic clove, sliced into tiny slivers

1 teaspoon grated ginger

1 medium onion, cut in wedges and separated from root end

1 stalk broccoli, florets removed and stalk sliced thin

5 large mushrooms, sliced

1 large red pepper, cut in 1-inch squares

Low-sodium soy sauce to taste

1. Bring the water to a boil in a medium-size saucepan, and add the rice to the water.

2. Boil for 5 minutes. Cover and let stand for 15 minutes.

3. In a wok, sauté the chicken in the wine or sherry. When the chicken is nearly done, add the spice powder, garlic, and grated ginger. Toss vigorously.

4. Add the vegetables and cook, stirring for about 5 minutes until the vegetables are bright in color—tender, but still crispy. Season to taste with the soy sauce. Add water if the mixture becomes too dry.

5. Toss with the rice, or serve over rice, if preferred.

Nutritional information per serving:

Calories	203	Cholesterol	49 mg
Fat	2.3 g	Calories from fat	10%

■

CHICKEN AND SALSA

Serves 4

2 boneless chicken breasts (without skin)

Salsa—mild! (Alternatively, make a fresh salsa; see Bean Dip Mexicano, pages 232–234)

Optional: 8 sprigs cilantro, chopped

1. Put the chicken breasts in a broiling pan that has been sprayed with Pam or the equivalent.

2. Spoon on the mild salsa generously (approximately 10 tablespoons per breast).

3. Broil at 450° or medium-high for 15 to 20 minutes on a side, or until done.

4. Optionally, add the cilantro at the end.

Nutritional information per serving:

Calories	169	Cholesterol	98 mg
Fat	3.3 g	Calories from fat	18%

▪

PITA PIZZA
Serves 2

½ cup low-sodium tomato sauce (or mild salsa)

4 mini pita breads

Oregano or mixed Italian herbs to taste

Garlic powder to taste

4 thin slices low-fat mozzarella cheese*

Optional: ¼ cup chopped onions and and/or ¼ cup red or green peppers

1. Preheat oven.
2. Spoon the tomato sauce on each round pita bread and sprinkle with the seasonings.
3. Add one slice of cheese and ¼ of the onions and peppers (optional) to each piece of bread. You may also use salsa instead of the tomato sauce (then you do not need additional onions or peppers).
3. Cook in a conventional oven or microwave until the cheese melts—about 10 to 15 minutes at 450° in an oven, 1 minute on high in a microwave.

*Available in some health-food stores; 2 grams of fat per ounce.

Nutritional information per serving:

Calories	246	Cholesterol	7 mg
Fat	4 g	Calories from fat	15%

DESSERTS

▪

WHIPPED STRAWBERRY-BANANA MOUSSE
Serves 4

1 banana

4 ice cubes, crushed

4 tablespoons non-fat milk powder

8 ounces fresh strawberries

Optional: 2 teaspoons cocoa

1. Peel and slice the banana.
2. If you have a cheese-grater disk (or a small shredder disk) for your food processor, run the ice through the disk to fully pulverize it. If not, just crushing the ice is adequate.
3. Place all of the ingredients, including optional ingredient, in a food processor (using the normal steel blade) and blend for a couple of minutes until smooth.
4. This mousse is intended to be eaten right after blending; it will fall and lose its consistency if you wait.

Note: You can also experiment with other fruits. If you do not use a high-water-content fruit (such as strawberries), then you will need to add some liquid (such as water, fruit juice, or skim milk).

The dessert is based on the discovery that skim milk whips! This is interesting because regular milk (even low-fat milk) does not whip. Instead of the non-fat milk powder, you can also use ordinary skim milk. Because of the additional liquid, the dessert will then come out more like a milk shake than a pudding.

Nutritional information per serving:

Calories	45	Cholesterol	0
Fat	0.3 g	Calories from fat	6%

■

FROZEN FRUIT
Serves 6

1 large banana, peeled and sliced   *1 cup pineapple, sliced*
¾ cup raspberries

1. Put the banana pieces and raspberries in the freezer for at least 6 hours.
2. Blend the frozen banana pieces, frozen raspberries, and cold (but not frozen) pineapple pieces in a food processor until smooth. This makes a creamy, but fat-free, soft dessert.

Variations: Try ½ cup fruit juice (such as apple juice) instead of the pineapple pieces. Or try ½ cup of skim milk.

Nutritional information per serving:

Calories 38 Cholesterol 0
Fat 0.3 g Calories from fat 6%

▪

CARROT CAKE
Serves 8

*1 cup all-purpose flour (or ½
cup all-purpose flour and
½ cup whole-wheat flour)*

1 teaspoon baking powder

1 teaspoon baking soda

1 teaspoon cinnamon

½ teaspoon nutmeg

1 teaspoon ground cloves

6 egg whites, beaten

½ cup apple juice concentrate

1 teaspoon vanilla extract

*4 large carrots, grated
(to make about 2½ cups)*

*2 teaspoons freshly grated orange
zest (the colored part of the
rind, not the pith, or white part
of the rind)*

*1 large orange, peeled and cut into
small pieces (with no seeds)*

*Apricot preserves (or other
fruit preserves)*

Optional: 3 tablespoons raisins

1. Preheat the oven to 350°.
2. In one bowl, combine flour, baking powder, baking soda, cinnamon, nutmeg, and ground cloves.
3. In another bowl, combine egg whites, apple juice concentrate, and vanilla. Mix.
4. Combine the contents of the two bowls together and mix well.
5. Add the carrots, orange zest, chopped oranges, and raisins (optional), and mix well.
6. Pour the batter into a cake pan that has been sprayed with Pam or the equivalent.
7. Bake for 40 to 45 minutes at 350°.
8. Cool for 10 to 15 minutes and remove from pan.
9. Warm the fruit preserves in a small saucepan.

10. Glaze the cake with the preserves. Optionally, a middle layer of preserves can be spread as well.

Nutritional information per serving:

Calories	159	Cholesterol	0
Fat	0.6 g	Calories from fat	3%

■

HOT-FUDGE SUNDAE

Serves 6

Hot-Fudge Sauce

1 cup apple juice concentrate
   (alternatively, try peach and/or
   pear juice concentrate)
1 cup cocoa powder
   (or carob powder)

2 teaspoons vanilla
2 teaspoons chocolate extract
Your favorite non-fat frozen
   yogurt

1. Mix the apple juice concentrate and the cocoa or carob powder.
2. In a saucepan, bring mixture to a boil and simmer for 4 to 6 minutes.
3. Add the vanilla and chocolate extract and stir.
4. Serve over your favorite non-fat frozen yogurt.

Variation: Start with a peeled banana for a banana split. (Now who says you can't splurge on the 10% solution?!)

Nutritional information per serving:

Calories	193	Cholesterol	0
Fat	2.4 g	Calories from fat	11%

15

■

Ranking the Killers: How to Save a Million American Lives a Year

From the evidence summarized here, there is every reason to conclude, based on all seven criteria set forth, that the epidemiologic associations among dietary lipid (cholesterol and saturated fat), serum cholesterol, and CHD [coronary heart disease] incidence represent etiologically significant relationships. In the multifactorial causation of this disease, at least four major factors are operative—diet high in cholesterol and saturated fat, hypercholesterolemia, hypertension, and cigarette smoking. However, since the data from both animal and human studies indicate that high blood pressure and cigarette smoking are minimally significant in the absence of the nutritional-metabolic prerequisites for atherogenesis, it is further reasonable and sound to designate rich diet as a *primary, essential, necessary cause* of the current epidemic of premature atherosclerotic disease raging in the Western industrialized countries. Cigarette smoking and hypertension are then secondary or complementary causes. (This designation, of both practical and theoretical importance, in no way detracts from their relevance in terms of medical care and public-health approaches to the prevention and control of the epidemic.)

—Jeremiah Stamler,
"Population Studies," in
*Nutrition, Lipids and
Coronary Heart Disease*,
ed. R. Levy, et al.

1. Overview

In reviewing the eating and dying patterns of different societies, we find two basic patterns. The poor nations of the world cannot afford the high-fat, "refined" foods characteristic of the wealthier nations and, thus, eat a diet that tends to be high in starch (complex carbohydrates) and fiber and low in fat and cholesterol. Heart disease, diabetes, and various forms of cancer (colon-rectal, breast, ovarian, and others) are very rare in these societies. Individuals in such societies also cannot afford medical care and proper food storage. The primary causes of death are, therefore, infectious diseases. If salt and pickling are commonly used to preserve foods, then stomach cancer may also be high. These are the diseases of poverty.

In contrast, the wealthier nations typically eat diets that are high in fat and cholesterol and low in fiber. In these societies, most of the deaths are caused by heart disease, thrombotic and embolic stroke (stroke caused by atherosclerosis), and cancers of the colon, breast, lung, and reproductive organs. These are the diseases of affluence.

Several questions come to mind. First, might the low rates of heart disease, colon cancer, breast cancer, and the other degenerative diseases in the undeveloped nations be due to the fact that these people succumb at an earlier age to infectious diseases and, thus, do not live long enough to get the degenerative diseases, which tend to develop in middle age and beyond? The answer is that death from infectious diseases occurs at different ages. Those who do survive into old age still have extremely low rates of heart disease and the other diseases typical of advanced societies. Furthermore, the elderly in these societies lead more productive lives. For example, in the regions of Japan that consume a traditional diet there is a significantly higher percentage of people over 70 who lead active, productive lives, when

THE LINK OF DIET TO DOLLARS

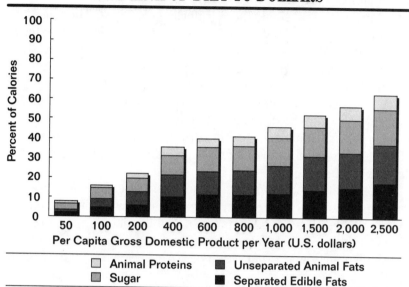

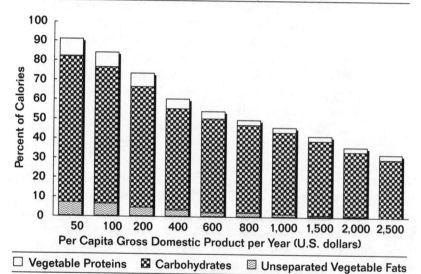

Percent of calories derived from various food categories according to the income of the countries. Data is based on eighty-four countries. Note that as income rises, consumption of meat and fat go up and consumption of carbohydrates and vegetables goes down.

Data from: J. Stamler, "Population Studies," in <u>Nutrition, Lipids, and Coronary Heart Disease</u>, ed. R. Levy et al. (New York: Raven Press, 1979).

compared with regions of Japan, such as Tokyo, where people now eat a diet higher in fat.[1]

Second, can we attribute these patterns to genetics? There are two responses here. It would be quite a coincidence, given the consistency of this pattern across the world. Furthermore, extensive studies of population migration show that people who move from one society to another adopt the disease patterns of the society they move to. The crucial and dominant role of nutrition as a primary causative factor in the development of heart disease, stroke, and the most prevalent forms of cancer is also supported by a vast literature of both animal and human studies, including recent human intervention studies.

Among the low-fat societies, we see two basic patterns. Japan is typical of the first pattern, a society that eats relatively little fat but an extremely high level of sodium (salt). The people have, as a result, very low rates of heart disease and breast and colon cancer, but the high level of salt causes a very high rate of hypertension. In the United States and other high-fat societies, hypertension is a risk factor for heart disease. But hypertension is a secondary, not a primary, factor. A high-fat, high-cholesterol diet is the primary factor and, thus, heart disease remains low in Japan despite the high level of hypertension (as well as the high rate of smoking). Still, the hypertension does cause a high level of intracerebral hemorrhage, a form of stroke caused by excessive pressure on the cerebral arteries. The other primary forms of stroke, thrombotic and embolic strokes, which are caused by atherosclerosis, remain at a low level in Japan, but are the primary forms of stroke in the United States. The extensive use of salt as a preservative and an affinity for blackened, charbroiled food also causes a high rate of stomach cancer. With the increasing affluence and resulting Westernization of Japan, the eating patterns and resulting disease patterns are moving gradually (although slowly) toward American and European patterns. Beef has become a symbol of luxury in Japan, and the consumption of meat and other fatty foods has been rising along with the rate of heart disease since World War II. The percentage of calories from fat, as well as the rates of heart disease and other "affluent" diseases, still remain, however, far below Western levels. There has also been a trend toward healthier methods of food preservation, and the rate of stomach cancer has also been falling. One interesting finding from studying Japanese patterns is the very low rate of lung cancer despite the very high rate of smoking. Smoking causes initiation of the cancer, but the growth phase of the cancer requires a diet high in fat.

Some parts of China are similar to Japan in having a low-fat but high-sodium diet, and the disease patterns are similar to Japan. Other parts of China are typical of the second pattern of diet in low-fat societies, where people eat a low-fat and low-sodium diet. Here we see very low rates of heart disease and other degenerative diseases as well as low lifetime blood pressure and very low rates of all forms of stroke. We do see high rates of infectious diseases in many of these societies due to the absence of medical care and the high level of pathogens in the food supply. There are also sections of China that eat a relatively high-fat diet (for China), and here we see higher rates of heart disease and other diseases typical of Western countries. China is, therefore, an ideal laboratory for assessing the impact of nutrition on disease because of its homogeneous genetic composition and diverse nutritional patterns. The massive study conducted at Cornell University discussed earlier has shown clearly the dramatic link of nutrition to disease.

Among Western societies, we also see two basic patterns. The worst pattern is that found in the United States and the northern European countries. High levels of saturated and polyunsaturated fats and cholesterol cause very high rates of heart disease, colon, breast, ovarian, and lung cancer, along with high rates of obesity and type II diabetes. In southern European countries, we see some amelioration of this pattern. Here, the primary form of oil is virgin (first-pressed) olive oil, which is low in both saturated and polyunsaturated fat. The fat is primarily monounsaturated. This has led many people to comment that the monounsaturated fat in olive oil is "good" for you and lowers blood cholesterol levels. Actually, it is simply "less bad," and death rates from heart disease, while substantially lower than American and northern European levels, are still much higher here than in the Asian nations that eat very low levels of all forms of fat. France, despite its reputation for rich cream sauces and desserts, actually eats a day-to-day diet not too dissimilar in many regards to the southern Europeans' and its disease patterns are also similar.

The link of prosperity to high-fat diets and in turn to atherosclerotic diseases goes back to antiquity. Egyptian mummies of the nobility and priesthood contain bits of arteries with gross atherosclerosis. There are also many reports of angina pain and sudden death among the Roman aristocracy.[2]

In summary, we have the opportunity for the best of all worlds. We can enjoy a diverse and appealing diet that avoids both the diseases of affluence and the diseases of poverty.

2. A Comment on the Title to Part One

With regard to the reference to the "civilized" diet, it is certainly not my intention to imply that Asian diets are in some way "uncivilized." Clearly, it is the Western "civilized" diets that are the most objectionable. However, we do find a very strong worldwide link between the industrialization that is associated with civilization and the adoption of an unhealthy diet. As Japan has grown in wealth since World War II, its fat consumption has grown from around 10 percent to more than 20 percent, and heart disease rates have correspondingly increased. In China, we find the wealthier counties eating substantially higher levels of fat and cholesterol (as compared to the less-wealthy counties) and, not surprisingly, experiencing much higher rates of heart disease, cancer, and other diseases of affluence.

3. The United States

Of all countries, the United States has close to the worst profile in terms of eating patterns and the resulting degenerative diseases of affluence. Percentage of calories from fat is still around 37 percent, down somewhat from the mid-40s about ten years ago. Since the 1960s, there has been about a 40 percent reduction in saturated fat consumption, which has resulted in about a 35 percent reduction in heart disease. Along with the decrease in saturated fat, there has been, up until recently, a corresponding increase in other types of fat, notably polyunsaturated fat, which has caused an increase in cancer rates.

The change in Native Americans' health represents a good example of the impact of a Western diet on an indigenous population. Prior to the twentieth century, the diet of American Indians was high in grains, corn, and other high-fiber foods. Obesity and diabetes were unknown, and rates of coronary heart disease were extremely low. In those U.S. tribes that are still relatively isolated from the rest of American society, such as the Alaskan Athapaskans, the people's situation remains the same in terms of diet and patterns of disease. Prior to 1940, tribes in Oklahoma continued to eat a low-fat, high-fiber diet and had very low rates of heart disease, diabetes, and gallbladder disease. Since 1940, the diet and disease patterns for most tribes of American Indians have changed dramatically to those of the rest of American society. With the

UNITED STATES

HOW TO SAVE 1,138,200 AMERICAN LIVES A YEAR

CAUSE OF DEATH[1]	NUMBER PER YEAR[2]	HOW TO AVOID	NUMBER THAT COULD BE SAVED BY ADOPTING THE 10% SOLUTION[3,4]
Heart disease[5]	765,100	The 10% solution	**654,200**
Cancer	469,400	The 10% solution	**363,300**
Lung	125,500	The 10% solution, particularly no smoking and very low fat	115,900
Colon	47,900	The 10% solution	45,500
Breast	40,500	The 10% solution	35,700
Prostate	27,300	The 10% solution	24,900
Stroke	149,600	The 10% solution, including low sodium	**120,700**
Pulmonary diseases[6]	101,100		
Accidents	95,300		
Pneumonia and influenza	69,200		
Diabetes mellitus	37,200		
Suicide	30,900		
Liver disease and cirrhosis	26,200	Moderate alcohol	
TOTAL:	**1,985,200**		**1,138,200**

[1]Data from WHO, 1988.
[2]All numbers rounded to the nearest hundred.
[3]Data based on Korea, Guatemala, Thailand, and the Philippines. WHO, 1982, 1987, 1989.
[4]If everyone followed the recommendations of the 10% solution, people who otherwise would have died of degenerative diseases would grow older and subsequently succumb to other causes, thus eventually increasing the figures for these other diseases. The charts in this section do not reflect this effect, but rather demonstrate the impact of life-style on current patterns of disease.
[5]Including atherosclerosis.
[6]Including bronchitis, asthma, emphysema.

increased level of fat and decreased fiber, the rates of obesity, diabetes, heart disease, and the other characteristic conditions associated with a "civilized" diet have become very high. Liver cancer is also very high, due to high rates of alcoholism.[3]

The table above represents the leading causes of death in the United States and what can be done to avoid these diseases. The 10%

solution represents all of the dietary and life-style recommendations detailed in chapter 12, "The Ten-Minute Guide to the 10% Solution," and discussed extensively throughout this book. The number of deaths that can be avoided through adoption of the 10% solution has been calculated based on corresponding rates of these diseases in the countries that follow these guidelines. Obviously, if everyone followed the recommendations of the 10% solution, people who otherwise would have died of degenerative diseases would grow older and subsequently succumb to other causes, thus eventually increasing the figures for these other diseases. The charts in this section do not reflect this effect, but rather demonstrate the impact of life-style on current patterns of disease.

4. Europe

As noted, the northern European countries have eating and disease patterns similar to those of the United States. With the campaign in the United States to cut down on saturated fat to some extent, rates of heart disease in some northern and eastern European countries (such as Finland, Poland, Hungary, Ireland, and the United Kingdom) are even higher than in the United States. Cancer rates are also very high.

In southern European countries, such as Italy and Greece, the extensive use of olive oil, with its high monounsaturated fat content as a primary oil for cooking and salad dressing, has resulted in a rate of death from coronary heart disease in between that of the low-fat Asian countries and the high–saturated-fat northern European countries and the United States. Consumption of fruits and vegetables and low-fat breads are also high in these southern European countries. On the other hand, rates of cancer of the breast, colon, and lung remain relatively high in these countries due to the high overall level of fat in the diet.

France is interesting in that it fits into the southern European model despite its reputation for cream sauces and rich desserts. Actually, the rich French cuisine is not typical of everyday eating and is reserved for special occasions. The French eat a lot of low-fat French bread and are avid consumers of fresh fruits and vegetables. The French typically do not overeat and obesity is rare. Also, much of the fat in their diet is in the form of cheese. While cheese is high in saturated fat, it is also high in calcium. Studies have shown that the high calcium content of cheese may provide some protection from its fat content. Apparently, the calcium may limit the absorption of the fat and cause a substantial fraction of it to be excreted. Other dairy products that are lower in calcium do not have this protective effect. Also, the consumption of wine may have a protective effect on heart disease (but not cancer).[4]

SEVERAL NORTHERN EUROPEAN COUNTRIES (FINLAND, GERMANY, IRELAND, AND THE U.K.)

HOW TO SAVE 216,200 LIVES A YEAR IN FINLAND, GERMANY, IRELAND, AND THE UNITED KINGDOM

CAUSE OF DEATH[1]	NUMBER PER YEAR[2]	HOW TO AVOID	NUMBER THAT COULD BE SAVED BY ADOPTING THE 10% SOLUTION[3,4]
Heart disease[5]	118,700	The 10% solution	**104,400**
Cancer	85,400	The 10% solution	**71,500**
Lung	17,800	The 10% solution, particularly no smoking and very low fat	16,500
Breast	7,800	The 10% solution	7,200
Colon	7,700	The 10% solution	7,400
Prostate	4,400	The 10% solution	4,100
Stroke	44,100	The 10% solution, including low sodium	**40,300**
Pulmonary diseases[6]	13,000		
Pneumonia and influenza	11,800		
Accidents	9,300		
Diabetes mellitus	5,100		
Suicide	4,500		
Liver disease and cirrhosis	4,400	Moderate alcohol	
TOTAL:	**334,000**		**216,200**

[1]Data from WHO, 1988, 1989.
[2]All numbers rounded to nearest hundred.
[3]Data based on Korea, Guatemala, Thailand, and the Philippines. WHO, 1982, 1987, 1989.
[4]If everyone followed the recommendations of the 10% solution, people who otherwise would have died of degenerative diseases would grow older and subsequently succumb to other causes, thus eventually increasing the figures for these other diseases. The charts in this section do not reflect this effect, but rather demonstrate the impact of life-style on current patterns of disease.
[5]Including atherosclerosis.
[6]Including bronchitis, asthma, emphysema.

SEVERAL SOUTHERN EUROPEAN COUNTRIES (GREECE, ITALY, PORTUGAL, AND SPAIN)

HOW TO SAVE 138,700 LIVES A YEAR IN GREECE, ITALY, PORTUGAL, AND SPAIN

CAUSE OF DEATH[1]	NUMBER PER YEAR[2]	HOW TO AVOID	NUMBER THAT COULD BE SAVED BY ADOPTING THE 10% SOLUTION[3,4]
Heart disease[5]	69,900	The 10% solution	**56,300**
Cancer	57,900	The 10% solution	**44,900**
Lung	10,800	The 10% solution, particularly no smoking and very low fat	9,600
Breast	4,100	The 10% solution	3,500
Colon	3,300	The 10% solution	3,000
Prostate	2,600	The 10% solution	2,300
Stroke	41,100	The 10% solution, including low sodium	**37,500**
Accidents	10,700		
Liver disease and cirrhosis	7,700	Moderate alcohol	
Diabetes mellitus	7,600		
Pulmonary diseases[6]	6,200		
Pneumonia and influenza	5,300		
Suicide	2,100		
TOTAL:	**228,400**		**138,700**

[1]Data from WHO, 1988.
[2]All numbers rounded to nearest hundred.
[3]Data based on Korea, Guatemala, Thailand, and the Philippines. WHO, 1982, 1987, 1989.
[4]If everyone followed the recommendations of the 10% solution, people who otherwise would have died of degenerative diseases would grow older and subsequently succumb to other causes, thus eventually increasing the figures for these other diseases. The charts in this section do not reflect this effect, but rather demonstrate the impact of life-style on current patterns of disease.
[5]Including atherosclerosis.
[6]Including bronchitis, asthma, emphysema.

5. Japan

In comparison to other highly industrialized countries, Japan offers a sharp contrast in its low rates of heart disease. The traditional Japanese diet is very low in fat and cholesterol, and correspondingly in areas that eat the traditional diet, there are extremely low rates of atherosclerosis and the diseases produced by atherosclerosis, including coronary heart disease, thrombotic and embolic stroke, claudication, and others. The Japanese diet is also extremely high in sodium, which causes a high rate of hypertension. As a result, the form of stroke caused by a burst blood vessel (intracerebral hemorrhage) is one of the leading causes of death in Japan. There is also a high rate of stomach cancer, which has been linked to the high intake of salted, smoked, and pickled foods, particularly salted, dried fish, as well as the extensive use of charbroiling and blackening in food preparation, which produces a potent carcinogen.

The Japanese diet has been changing gradually since World War II with the influence of Western society. There has been a 650 percent increase in the consumption of meat, poultry, and eggs, a 1,400 percent increase in the consumption of milk, a 97 percent decrease in the consumption of barley, a 50 percent decrease in the consumption of potatoes, and a 30 percent decrease in the consumption of rice. Fat levels are still substantially lower than in the United States and Europe, although they have doubled since 1950. This trend toward a Western-style diet is mostly restricted to the wealthy non-farmers and urban dwellers. Farmers, rural dwellers, and other less-wealthy people have largely retained the traditional diet. Also, older Japanese people tend to eat a more traditional diet. Along with the gradual change in diet has been a corresponding increase in heart disease, although still running at only 30 percent of American levels. Rates of diabetes have also increased. For example, the mortality rate from type II diabetes increased by 133 percent from 1950 to 1984. With a decrease in salt consumption, pickling as a food-preservation method, and charbroiling, there has been a gradual decrease in intracerebral hemorrhage and stomach cancer. Along with the change in disease patterns, the change in diet has caused the Japanese to become taller and heavier, as well as caused the onset of menstruation in Japanese girls to start earlier by three to six years. With the earlier sexual development of Japanese girls has been a parallel increase in the mortality rates of the cancers of the reproductive organs and breast, which were traditionally uncommon among the Japanese. However, Japanese rates of these diseases are still substantially lower than the rates in other industrialized nations.[5]

JAPAN

HOW TO SAVE 344,800 JAPANESE LIVES A YEAR

CAUSE OF DEATH[1]	NUMBER PER YEAR[2]	HOW TO AVOID	NUMBER THAT COULD BE SAVED BY ADOPTING THE 10% SOLUTION[3,4]
Cancer	199,600		**146,100**
Stomach	48,300	Less pickling, charbroiling, salt	43,400
Lung	31,700	The 10% solution, particularly no smoking and very low fat	26,800
Liver	15,500	Avoid alcohol, pesticides, and other chemicals	14,500
Colon	12,700	The 10% solution	11,500
Heart disease[5]	146,600	The 10% solution	**90,700**
Stroke	123,600	The 10% solution, including low sodium	**109,000**
Pneumonia and influenza	49,000		
Accidents	28,300		
Pulmonary diseases[6]	26,800		
Senility	25,300		
Suicide	23,800		
Liver disease and cirrhosis	16,700	Moderate alcohol	
TOTAL:	**747,900**		**344,800**

[1]Data from WHO, 1988.
[2]All numbers rounded to nearest hundred.
[3]Data based on Korea, Guatemala, Thailand, the Philippines, and Honduras. WHO, 1982, 1986, 1987, 1989.
[4]If everyone followed the recommendations of the 10% solution, people who otherwise would have died of degenerative diseases would grow older and subsequently succumb to other causes, thus eventually increasing the figures for these other diseases. The charts in this section do not reflect this effect, but rather demonstrate the impact of life-style on current patterns of disease.
[5]Including atherosclerosis.
[6]Including bronchitis, asthma, emphysema.

6. China

As detailed earlier (see chapter 1), a massive study conducted at Cornell University tracking 6,500 Chinese, comprising 100 people from each of China's 65 counties, has confirmed the link of total fat and saturated fat in the diet to the incidence of heart disease and cancers of the colon, breast, prostate, and ovaries. One important aspect of the Cornell Study is that the subjects vary in their diet, but are relatively homogeneous genetically. We also find all three primary dietary patterns: high-fat, high-salt; low-fat, high-salt; and low-fat, low-salt.

In general, the Chinese eat a very low fat diet, consuming about one-third of the fat that Americans consume. Only 7 percent of the protein in the average Chinese diet comes from animal products, compared to 70 percent in the average American diet. In those regions that eat very low fat diets (which account for most of the population), heart disease, diabetes, and the above forms of cancer are very rare. In rural counties with very low fat consumption, rates of heart disease are 155 times lower than in the United States. In those regions that have more fat in the diet, mostly in the form of meat and oils, these diseases are correspondingly higher.

As in Japan, there is a link between certain methods of food preservation, most notably salt, fermentation, and pickling, and rates of stomach cancer. There is also a link between the ingestion of moldy food and rates of both stomach and esophageal cancer. A study in Shandong, China (in the eastern part of the country), found that risks of stomach cancer were increased by 50 percent by heavy (one or more packs a day) cigarette smoking in men, by 40 percent among those who ate large amounts of salt, and by 50 percent among families with moldy grain supplies. Conversely, decreased risk was associated with the consumption of fresh fruits and vegetables.[6]

There are regions of China that have high rates of liver cancer, which have been linked to high rates of hepatitis B infection and high levels of aflatoxins (a potent carcinogen excreted by the fungus *Aspergillus flavus*, which often grows on potatoes, corn, and peanuts) in the food supply, although some recent studies have not found the link to aflatoxins.[7]

As in Japan, there is a strong link between salt intake and blood pressure. Studies have shown a significant intrapopulation correlation between systolic blood pressure and salt intake. In those regions where salt intake is high, usually because of its use as a food preservative, hypertension and intracerebral hemorrhage are very common. In those regions where salt is not added to the food, people have lifelong low blood pressure. No exceptions to this generalization appear to have been traced anywhere in the world.

7. East Africa

Historically, east African communities have relied on grains, vegetables, and fruits. For example, the Kikuyu diet in Kenya in 1930 was typical of that eaten by other east African agricultural peasants and consisted primarily of maize, millet, sweet potatoes, beans, and plantains, with very small amounts of meat on occasion and almost no milk. Calories derived from fat were under 10 percent. These communities had lifelong low blood pressure and no or very low incidence of coronary heart disease, cerebrovascular disease (stroke), obesity, and diabetes.

Beginning in the 1940s, Kenya, Uganda, and other east African communities underwent rapid Westernization, particularly in the urban regions. And beginning in the 1940s, the above-mentioned diseases began to show a large and progressive increase in east Africa. Today, obesity, diabetes, and heart disease are common in the urban areas where the Westernization has been most pronounced.[8]

Appendixes

∎

APPENDIX 1

Reference Notes

INTRODUCTION

1. W. B. Kannel, W. P. Castelli, and T. Gordon, "Cholesterol in the Prediction of Atherosclerotic Disease. New Perspectives Based on the Framingham Study," *Annals of Internal Medicine* 90 (Jan. 1979): 85–91.

    T. Gordon et al., "Diabetes, Blood Lipids, and the Role of Obesity in Coronary Heart Disease Risk for Women: The Framingham Study," *Annals of Internal Medicine* 87 (Oct. 1977): 393–97. One of the first conclusions of the Framingham Study is that the risk of coronary heart disease is "strikingly related to the serum total cholesterol level. Within so-called normal limits, risk has been found to mount over a fivefold range."

    Subsequent analysis of the Framingham data revealed that an even more reliable estimate of coronary risk could be obtained by considering the ratio of the total serum cholesterol to the HDL cholesterol.

$$\text{Let } X = \text{total cholesterol / HDL cholesterol}$$

Risk for men $= 1.357 \ln X - 1.1875$
(note Ln is natural logarithm, i.e., logarithm base e)
$= 3.125 \log X - 1.1875$
(note Log is logarithm base 10)

Risk for women $= 2.069 \ln X - 2.042$
$= 4.766 \log X - 2.042$

Note that the two formulas for men give the same answer, as do the two formulas for women.

    The risk derived from the above formula is expressed as a multiple of "average" risk.

    For example, if a male has a total cholesterol of 180 and an HDL of 60, then X (the cholesterol-to-HDL ratio) = 3. The risk = .30, which means this person has 30 percent of the average risk for coronary heart disease. This figure may then be subsequently adjusted for other risk factors, such as obesity, type II diabetes, hypertension, cigarette smoking, etc.

    The graph on the following page shows the risk (Y) (expressed as a multiple of average American risk) as a function of the total cholesterol-to-HDL ratio for both men and women.

2. World Health Organization, *Statistics Annual*, 1988.

    Approximately 40 percent of all Americans die from heart disease. Of those who die from other causes (such as cancer), more than half have had a previous heart attack. Interestingly, not all of these heart attacks are diagnosed. Autopsies often reveal evidence of ischemic damage (damage to the heart muscle resulting from deficiency of blood due to diminished arterial flow) caused by a previously undiagnosed heart attack in patients who succumb to other diseases.

CONVERSION OF RISK FACTOR TO RISK

$$\text{Risk Factor} = \frac{\text{Total Cholesterol}}{\text{HDL Cholesterol}}$$

Female: $Y = 2.069\ln X - 2.042$ Male: $Y = 1.357\ln X - 1.1875$
        $Y = 4.766\log X - 2.042$ $Y = 3.125\log X - 1.1875$

Where   X = Risk Factor
        Y = Risk

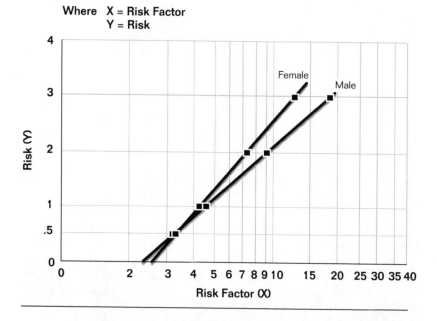

3.   For a detailed account of Nathan Pritikin's life and pioneering research in nutrition see the biography coauthored by his wife: T. Monte with I. Pritikin, *Pritikin: The Man Who Healed America's Heart* (Emmaus, PA: Rodale Press, 1988).

4.   J. D. Hubbard, S. Inkeles, and R. J. Barnard, "Nathan Pritikin's Heart," *New England Journal of Medicine* 313 (July 1985): 52.

CHAPTER 1: ASIDE FROM THAT, MRS. LINCOLN, HOW DID YOU ENJOY THE PLAY?

1.   National Research Council, *Diet and Health: Implications for Reducing Chronic Disease Risk* (Washington, D.C.: National Academy Press, 1989), 140. A veritable encyclopedia of nutrition and disease, this comprehensive volume is an informative

and scholarly guide for the researcher and layperson alike. In addition to the plethora of material contained in the text, an exhaustive array of research is cited.

2.   I. Romieu et al., "Energy Intake and Other Determinants of Relative Weight," *American Journal of Clinical Nutrition* 47 (1988): 406–12. The results of this study suggest that weight gain is not dependent on calorie intake alone. Fat calories are more fattening than other calories because the body is able to store the fat calories more efficiently, leaving more calories to be stored in the body's tissues to contribute to weight gain.

Another study with similar findings and some interesting discussion on the subject is D. M. Dreon et al., "Dietary Fat: Carbohydrate Ratio and Obesity in Middle-Aged Men," *American Journal of Clinical Nutrition* 47 (1988): 995–1000. Background support for these findings can be found in L. Lissner et al., "Dietary Fat and the Regulation of Energy Intake in Human Subjects," *American Journal of Clinical Nutrition* 46 (1987): 886–92. The Lissner study suggests that reducing calorie intake may not be the best approach to weight loss because of calorie deficits. Rather, decreasing the amount of fat in the diet allows individuals to eat more, induces spontaneous weight loss, and may be more readily incorporated into an individual's life-style.

The following study also supports efforts to alter food selection rather than limiting food intake in weight loss by comparing the effects of high- and low-fat diets, caloric intake, and eating time among obese and nonobese individuals: K. H. Duncan, J. A. Bacon, and R. L. Weinsler, "The Effects of High- and Low-Energy Density Diets on Satiety, Energy Intake, and Eating Time of Obese and Nonobese Subjects," *American Journal of Clinical Nutrition* 37 (May 1983): 763–67. Among the findings was that subjects on the low-fat diets were able to reach their satiety point by consuming only about one-half the calories of those on the high-fat diets.

3.   V. W. Brown, "Changing the Diet to Reduce Plasma Cholesterol Levels," *Cholesterol and Coronary Disease … Reducing the Risk* 1 (Apr. 1987): 1.

W. E. Connor and S. L. Connor, "The Key Role of Nutritional Factors in the Prevention of Coronary Heart Disease," *Preventive Medicine* 1 (1972): 49–83. Beginning with a thorough and informative discussion on the epidemiological link between diet and coronary heart disease, the critical role of diet in the development of heart disease is emphasized. A dietary prescription for the prevention of coronary heart disease is provided—complete with dietary recommendations and several low-fat recipes.

S. Inkeles and D. Eisenberg, "Hyperlipidemia and Coronary Atherosclerosis: A Review," *Medicine* 60 (1981): 110–23. This is an excellent overview of the pathogenesis of atherosclerosis and coronary heart disease and its various modes of treatment. In conclusion, the authors discuss the limitations of conventional medical treatment and recommend treating coronary heart disease patients with low-fat diets aimed at lowering cholesterol to threshold levels (where heart disease is virtually unheard of).

A. Keys, *Seven Countries: A Multivariate Analysis of Death and Coronary Heart Disease* (Cambridge, MA: Harvard University Press, 1980). This is Ancel Keys's opus, the culmination of a ten-year study as well as a long professional career dating back to the late 1940s. Keys, a pioneer in the field, masterminded the renowned Seven Countries Study, which was unprecedented in its scope. Involving seven countries (comprising of sixteen cohorts) over the span of ten years, it was the first study to compare the epidemiology of heart disease in different countries. The outcome of the Seven

Countries Study provided a foundation for many contemporary studies—it is rare to find a study on the epidemiology of heart disease that does not cite Keys's classic work. The 1990 study in China (see n. 23, below) is perhaps the only study since Seven Countries to offer such rich evidence on the patterns of disease and diet.

National Cholesterol Education Program, *Report of the Expert Panel on Detection, Evaluation, and Treatment of High Blood Cholesterol in Adults* (U. S. Department of Health and Human Services, 1988).

S. Renaud and M. de Lorgeril,"Dietary Lipids and Their Relation to Ischaemic Heart Disease: From Epidemiology to Prevention," *Journal of Internal Medicine* 225, suppl. 1 (1989). A particularly interesting finding of this study is that cheese, unlike other dairy products, is not closely related to the mortality rate of ischemic heart disease—perhaps because cheese contains a high level of calcium, which inhibits the absorption of saturated fatty acids.

4. A. M. Gotto and E. H. Wittels, "Diet, Serum Cholesterol, Lipoproteins, and Coronary Heart Disease," in *Prevention of Coronary Heart Disease: Practical Management of the Risk Factors*, ed. N. M. Kaplan and J. Stamler (Philadelphia: W. B. Saunders Company, 1983), 37.

5. Gotto and Wittels, 34 (see n. 4, above).

6. K. Byrne, *Understanding and Managing Cholesterol: A Guide for Wellness Professionals* (Illinois: Human Kinetics Books, 1991), 17.

7. Brown, 1 (see n. 3, above).

M. C. Lueg and R. H. Anding, "Hypercholesterolemia: New Values, New Strategies," *Hospital Practice* (Jan. 30, 1986): 112.

National Research Council, 168 (see n. 1, above).

D. Steinberg and J. L. Witzum, "Lipoproteins and Atherogenesis," *Journal of the American Medical Association* 264 (Dec. 1990): 3047–52.

D. Steinberg et al., "Beyond Cholesterol: Modifications of Low-Density Lipoprotein That Increase Its Atherogenicity," *New England Journal of Medicine* 320 (Apr. 6, 1989): 915–24.

8. W. F. Enos, J. C. Beyer, and R. H. Holmes, "Pathogenesis of Coronary Disease in American Soldiers Killed in Korea," *Journal of the American Medical Association* 158 (July 1955): 912–14. This autopsy study provides clear evidence that the significant majority (77 percent) of young (22-year-old) American males autopsied had significant atherosclerosis. Atherosclerosis is a progressive condition, and the percentage of Americans with it (on the order of 77 percent of American males by age 22) will significantly increase with age.

Another indication of the prevalence of atherosclerosis is the incidence of heart disease among all Americans (male and female), the vast majority of which is linked to atherosclerosis. Half of all Americans die from heart disease and related complications.

The average American has a 75 percent chance of having a heart attack during his or her lifetime (see introduction, n. 2, above), indicating an advanced stage of atherosclerosis at the time of such event. A significant fraction of the 25 percent of Americans who will not have experienced a heart attack at the time of their death nonetheless have some level of atherosclerosis; they will have died from other causes (such as cancer) prior to having their atherosclerosis advance sufficiently to cause an acute atherosclerosis-triggered event. On the basis of these observations, an estimate that 90 percent of Americans have at least some level of atherosclerosis appears reasonable.

9. R. Virag, P. Bouilly, and D. Frydman, "Is Impotence an Arterial Disorder?" *Lancet* 1 (Jan. 26, 1985): 181.

10. J. A. Hall et al., "Effects of Diet and Exercise on Peripheral Vascular Disease," *Physician and Sportsmedicine* 10 (May 1982): 91–92.

11. H. E. Aldridge and A. S. Trimble, "Progression of Proximal Coronary Artery Lesions to Total Occlusion after Aorta-Coronary Saphenous Vein Bypass Grafting," *Journal of Thoracic and Cardiovascular Surgery* 62 (July 1971): 7–11.

W. L. Cashin et al., "Accelerated Progression of Atherosclerosis in Coronary Vessels with Minimal Lesions That Are Bypassed," *New England Journal of Medicine* 311 (Sept. 1984): 824–28.

12. E. L. Alderman et al., "Ten-Year Follow-up of Survival and Myocardial Infarction in the Randomized Coronary Artery Surgery Study," *Circulation* 82 (Nov. 1990): 1629–46.

13. W. A. Check, "Ventricular Arrhythmias May Not Be Primary Cause of Sudden Death," *Journal of the American Medical Association* 246 (Aug. 1981): 581–89.

14. V. Manninen et al., "Joint Effects of Serum Triglyceride and LDL Cholesterol and HDL Cholesterol Concentrations on Coronary Heart Disease Risk in the Helsinki Heart Study," *Circulation* 85 (Jan. 1992): 37–45.

15. D. J. Gordon and B. M. Rifkind, "High-Density Lipoprotein: The Clinical Implications of Recent Studies," *New England Journal of Medicine* 321 (Nov. 1989): 1311–12.
Lueg and Anding, 112–13 (see n. 7, above).
W. B. Kannel, W. P. Castelli, and T. Gordon, "Cholesterol in the Prediction of Atherosclerotic Disease," *Annals of Internal Medicine* 90 (1979): 85–91, 88–89.
Gotto and Wittels, 37–42 (see n. 4, above).

16. T. Gordon et al., "High-Density Lipoprotein as a Protective Factor against Coronary Heart Disease: The Framingham Study," *American Journal of Medicine* 62 (1977): 707–14.
W. P. Castelli et al., "Incidence of Coronary Heart Disease and Lipoprotein Cholesterol Levels: The Framingham Study," *Journal of the American Medical Association* 256 (1986): 2835–38.
D. H. Blankenhorn et. al., "Beneficial Effects of Combined Colestipol-Niacin Therapy on Coronary Atherosclerosis and Coronary Venous Bypass Grafts," *Journal of the American Medical Association* 257 (1987): 3233–40.

17. See introduction, n. 2, above.

18. W. B. Kannel and D. J. Lerner, "Present Status of Risk Factors for Atherosclerosis," *Medical Times* 112 (Sept. 1984): 33–45.

19. W. E. Connor et al., "The Plasma Lipids, Lipoproteins, and Diet of the Tarahumara Indians of Mexico," *American Journal of Clinical Nutrition* 31 (July 1978):

1131–42. Coauthored by William Connor, a physician, researcher, and nutritionist at the Oregon Health Sciences University, this study offers a classic example of an unacculturated society with very low levels of blood cholesterol, a very low fat diet, intense physical activity, and nonexistent heart disease and hypertension throughout life.

20. Gordon and Rifkind, 1313 (see n. 15, above).

21. M. L. Armstrong, E. D. Warner and W. E. Connor, "Regression of Coronary Atheromatosis in Rhesus Monkeys," *Circulation Research* 27 (July 1970): 59–67.
    A. S. Daoud et al., "Regression of Advanced Atherosclerosis in Swine," *Archives of Pathological and Laboratory Medicine* 100 (July 1976): 372–79.
    R. G. de Palma et al., "Regression of Atherosclerotic Plaques in Rhesus Monkeys," *Archives of Surgery* 115 (Nov. 1980): 1268–78.

22. Enos, Beyer, and Holmes (see n. 8, above). This is an important autopsy study offering clear-cut evidence that atherosclerosis starts at an early age in the vast majority of American males. Autopsy findings from Japanese males of comparable age are cited for comparison since they reveal little or no evidence of coronary occlusion. The authors conclude that diet, as it affects the cholesterol levels in the blood, is an important factor in the development of coronary disease in young males.

23. J. Chen et al., *Diet, Life-style, and Mortality in China: A Study of the Characteristics of Sixty-Five Chinese Counties* (Oxford: Oxford University Press, 1990). The most extensive study on the relationship of diet and disease to be done to date, this 920-page publication documents the initial findings of the study conducted in China. The study offers an impressive and diverse array of information that gives evidence to the importance of a low-fat diet in maintaining health.

24. J. B. Hannah, "Civilization, Race, and Coronary Atheroma with Particular Reference to Its Incidence and Severity in Copperbelt Africans," *Central African Journal of Medicine* 4 (Jan. 1958): 1–5.
    D. Pazzanese et al., "Serum-Lipid Levels in a Brazilian Indian Population," *Lancet* (Sept. 1964): 615–17.

25. M. S. de Wolfe and H. M. Whyte, "Serum Cholesterol and Lipoproteins in Natives of New Guinea and Australians," *Australasian Annals of Medicine* 7 (1958): 51.

26. H. M. Whyte, "Body Fat and Blood Pressure of Natives in New Guinea: Reflections on Essential Hypertension," *Australasian Annals of Medicine* 7 (1958): 41–42.

27. A. Keys et al., "Lessons from Serum Cholesterol Studies in Japan, Hawaii, and Los Angeles," *Annals of Internal Medicine* 48 (Jan. 1958): 83–94.

28. A. Leaf, "Management of Hypercholesterolemia: Are Preventive Interventions Advisable?" *New England Journal of Medicine* 321 (Sept. 1989): 681.

29. N. D. Barnard, *The Power of Your Plate* (Summertown, TN: Book Publishing Company, 1990), 16. This publication includes interview material with several medical experts, including William Castelli, M.D., Denis Burkitt, M.D., and William Connor, M.D.

30. T. R. Dawber, *The Framingham Study: The Epidemiology of Atherosclerotic Disease* (Cambridge, MA: Harvard University Press, 1980), 133. Thomas R. Dawber of Boston

University Medical School and leader of the renowned Framingham Study summarizes this extensive research project, which has spawned innumerable journal articles over the years. The Framingham Study has yielded landmark evidence in establishing the link between dietary-fat consumption, serum cholesterol levels, high blood pressure, smoking, obesity, and diabetes and coronary heart disease. Interestingly, the results of the Framingham Study confirm the inadequacy of the recommendation of cutting back to only 30 percent calories from fat.

31. H. C. McGill, Jr., ed., *The Geographic Pathology of Atherosclerosis* (Baltimore: Williams and Wilkins Company, 1968).

32. National Research Council, 102 (see n. 1, above). For further details on the impact of cardiovascular health in Japanese migrating to Hawaii and California, see M. G. Marmot et al., "Epidemiologic Studies of Coronary Heart Disease and Stroke in Japanese Men Living in Japan, Hawaii, and California: Prevalence of Coronary and Hypertensive Heart Disease and Associated Risk Factors," *American Journal of Epidemiology* 102 (1975): 514–25, and T. L. Robertson et al., "Epidemiologic Studies of Coronary Heart Disease and Stroke in Japanese Men Living in Japan, Hawaii, and California: Incidence of Myocardial Infarction and Death from Coronary Heart Disease," *American Journal of Cardiology* 39 (1977): 239–43.

33. A. Kagan et al., "Epidemiologic Studies of Coronary Heart Disease and Stroke in Japanese Men Living in Japan, Hawaii, and California: Demographic, Physical, Dietary, and Biochemical Characteristics," *Journal of Chronic Diseases* 27 (Sept. 1974): 346.

34. Y. Kagawa, "Impact of Westernization on the Nutrition of Japanese: Changes in Physique, Cancer, Longevity, and Centenarians," *Preventive Medicine* 7 (1978): 205–7. This is a thought-provoking article on the effect of the Western diet on the health of the Japanese.

35. H. Malmros, "The Relation of Nutrition to Health: A Statistical Study of the Effect of the War-Time on Arteriosclerosis, Cardiosclerosis, Tuberculosis, and Diabetes," *Acta Medica Scandinavia* 246, suppl. (1950): 141–49. Despite its title, this article is surprisingly nontechnical. The dramatic effect of food rationing on heart disease in several European countries during World War II is presented in standard prose and charts.

A. Keys, "Coronary Heart Disease: The Global Picture," *Atherosclerosis* 22 (1975): 153–54. A comprehensive overview on coronary heart disease by the author of the eminent Seven Countries Study, this article cites extensive evidence from around the world covering a broad range of topics related to the disease, including studies of global peoples; the effects of wartime; social class and occupation; the impact of exercise, stress, and personality type; the role of risk factors, dietary factors, and genetics; and a discussion on the prevention of coronary heart disease. The varied selection of reference notes makes this an excellent resource for the professional, student, and interested reader.

36. J. Stamler, "Population Studies," in *Nutrition, Lipids, and Coronary Heart Disease*; ed. R. Levy et al. (New York: Raven Press, 1979), 52. A leading figure in cardiovascular research, Jeremiah Stamler, offers a comprehensive overview of research on the

relationship of diet to coronary heart disease in varied populations. Providing extensive information that is accessible to the general reader, this article reviews a rich body of evidence on the impact of diet on heart disease. Although most of the article focuses on international epidemiological studies, economic and political issues and their effects on diet and disease are also discussed.

37. American Heart Association, "Dietary Guidelines for Healthy American Adults," *Circulation* 77 (March 1988): 721A.

38. D. Ornish et al., "Can Life-style Changes Reverse Coronary Heart Disease? *Lancet* 336 (July 1990): 129–33. This is Dean Ornish's highly publicized study on the regression of heart disease without drugs or surgery. The dramatic results of this study led Ornish to develop his Opening-Your-Heart Program, featured in his book *Dr. Dean Ornish's Program for Reversing Heart Disease* (New York: Random House, 1990). In his book, Ornish presents his research on the regression of heart disease through life-style factors, stressing inner peace, happiness, and other spiritual factors as much as he does a low-fat vegetarian diet. In addition, Ornish outlines his Opening-Your-Heart program, which consists of stress management and smoking cessation techniques, advice on how to exercise, and his reversal and prevention diets, including an extensive section of recipes.

39. Chen et al. (see n. 23, above).

40. J. E. Brody, "Huge Study of Diet Indicts Fat and Meat," *New York Times,* 8 May 1990, sec. C.

41. Brody (see n. 40, above).
     Chen et al. (see n. 23, above).

42. U.S. Department of Commerce, *Statistical Abstract of the United States,* 109th ed., 1989, 119.

43. See introduction for discussion on the derivation of this statistic.

44. T. J. Moore, "The Cholesterol Myth," *The Atlantic* (Sept. 1989): 37–70.

45. Multiple Risk Factor Intervention Trial Research Group, "Risk Factor Changes and Mortality Results," *Journal of the American Medical Association* 248 (Sept. 1982): 1465–77.

46. American Heart Association Special Report, "Recommendations for Treatment of Hyperlipidemia in Adults," *Circulation* 69 (May 1984): 1067A–90A.

47. K. A. Matthews et al., "Menopause and Risk Factors for Coronary Heart Disease," *New England Journal of Medicine* 321 (Sept. 1989): 641–46.

CHAPTER 2: WHAT DOES THIS MEAN?

1.   J. W. Anderson, "Fiber and Health: An Overview," *The American Journal of Gastroenterology* 81 (1986): 892–97. Anderson is best known for his work with high-carbohydrate, high-fiber diets in treating diabetics. In this article he gives a brief

summary of the benefits of fiber in reducing the risk of various degenerative diseases.

M. L. Slattery et al., "Diet and Colon Cancer: Assessment of Risk by Fiber Type and Food Source," *Journal of the National Cancer Institute* 80 (Nov. 1988): 1474–80.

2.   The evidence on lifelong low blood pressure in acculturated societies is abundant. For specific examples see W. J. Oliver, E. L. Cohen, and J. V. Neel, "Blood Pressure, Sodium Intake, and Sodium Related Hormones in the Yanomamo Indians, a 'No-Salt' Culture," *Circulation* 52 (July 1975): 146–51, and Whyte (see chap. 1, n. 26, above). For a general discussion see L. B. Page, "Hypertension and Atherosclerosis in Primitive and Acculturating Societies," in *Hypertension Update: Mechanisms, Epidemiology, Evaluation, Management*, Proceedings of Hypertension Update Symposium, ed. J. C. Hunt et al. (Washington, D.C.: Health Learning Systems, 1979), 1–12, and H. C. Trowell, "Hypertension, Obesity, Diabetes Mellitus, and Coronary Heart Disease," in *Western Diseases: Their Emergence and Prevention*, ed. H. C. Trowell and D. P. Burkitt (Cambridge: Harvard University Press, 1981): 3–4, 12–13. Also see S. B. Eaton, M. Shostak, and M. Konner, *The Paleolithic Prescription: A Program of Diet and Exercise and a Design for Living* (New York: Harper and Row, 1988): 45, 49–50, for a brief discussion of hypertension within a broader overview on nutrition and health.

3.   S. Addanki, "Roles of Nutrition, Obesity, and Estrogens in Diabetes Mellitus: Human Leads to an Experimental Approach to Prevention," *Preventive Medicine* 10 (1981): 577–89.

J. W. Anderson, "Effect of High-Glucose and High-Sucrose Diets on Glucose Tolerance of Normal Men," *American Journal of Clinical Nutrition* 26 (June 1973): 600–7.

4.   R. Tannahill, *Food in History* (New York: Stein and Day, 1973): 320–72.

5.   National Research Council, 42 (see chap. 1, n. 1, above). In fact, an estimated 60 percent of food available in supermarkets in 1960 came into existence during the 15 years after the end of World War II. Innovations such as sugared breakfast cereals and many snack items were unheard of before World War II.

6.   S. B. Eaton and M. Konner, "Paleolithic Nutrition: A Consideration of Its Nature and Current Implications," *New England Journal of Medicine* 313 (Jan. 1985): 283–89. Eaton and Konner give an anthropological perspective on the evolution of the human diet. For those interested in further reading and a more clinical approach see M. A. Crawford, "Fatty-Acid Ratios in Free-Living and Domestic Animals," *Lancet* (June 1968): 1329–33.

7.   T. B. Clarkson et al., "Psychosocial Influences on the Pathogenesis of Atherosclerosis among Nonhuman Primates, *Circulation* 76, suppl. One (July 1987): I29–40, I30. This is a methodical review of a series of studies designed to investigate the effects of high- and low-fat diets and psychosocial stress on the development of coronary heart disease in monkeys. The monkeys in the high-fat group were fed a diet designed to approximate both the type and level of fat typical in the Western diet, and consequently they developed atherosclerosis.

R. W. Wissler et al., "Atherogenesis in the Cebus Monkey," *Archives of Pathology* 74 (1962): 312–22.

8.   P. D. Wood and W. L. Haskell, "The Effect of Exercise on Plasma High Density Lipoproteins," *Lipids* 14 (1979): 417–27.

9.   W. Speiser et al, "Increased Blood Fibrinolytic Activity after Physical Exercise: Comparative Study in Individuals with Different Sporting Activities and in Patients after Myocardial Infarction Taking Part in a Rehabilitation Sports Program," *Thrombosis Research* 51 (Sept. 1988): 543–55.
     S. Williams et al., "Physical Conditioning Augments the Fibrinolytic Response to Venous Occlusion in Healthy Adults," *New England Journal of Medicine* 302 (May 1980): 987–91.

10.   L. H. Calabrese, "Exercise, Immunity, Cancer, and Infection," in *Exercise, Fitness, and Health: A Consensus of Current Knowledge,* ed. C. Bouchard et al. (Champaign, IL: Human Kinetics Books, 1990), 569–71.
     M. Gerhardsson de Verdier et al., "Physical Activity and Colon Cancer: A Case-Referent Study in Stockholm," *International Journal of Cancer* 46 (Dec. 1990): 985–89.

11.   J. F. Aloia et al., "Prevention of Involutional Bone Loss by Exercise," *Annals of Internal Medicine* 89 (1978): 356–58.
     E. L. Smith, Jr., W. Reddan, and P. E. Smith, "Physical Activity and Calcium Modalities for Bone Mineral Increase in Aged Women," *Medicine and Science in Sports and Exercise* 13 (1981): 60–64.
     M. K. White et al., "The Effects of Exercise on the Bones of Postmenopausal Women," *International Orthopaedics* 7 (1984): 209–14. The results of this study found that aerobic dancing had a significant positive effect on both bone width and mineral content (important factors in osteoporosis), while walking improved only bone width and sedentary subjects continued to worsen.

12.   V. F. Froelicher, "Exercise, Fitness, and Coronary Heart Disease," in Bouchard, ed., 430 (see n. 10, above).

13.   P. O. Astrand and K. Rodahl, *Textbook of Work Physiology: Physiological Bases of Exercise*, 3d. ed. (New York: McGraw-Hill, 1986), 140–41.
     Bouchard, 19 "The Consensus Statement" (see n. 10, above).

14.   R. E. Dustman et al., "Aerobic Exercise Training and Improved Neuropsychological Function of Older Individuals," *Neurobiology of Aging* 5 (1984): 35–42. Studies have shown that intellect, memory, and perception decline with age. This decrease in our ability to think as we age is a result of a lack of oxygen to the brain caused by atherosclerosis and a sedentary life-style. The results of this study indicate that aerobic exercise can decrease this "natural" deterioration of mental functioning by increasing oxygen to the brain.
     R. E. Dustman et al., "Age and Fitness Effects on EEG, ERPs, Visual Sensitivity, and Cognition," *Neurobiology of Aging* 11 (1990): 193–200. A follow-up to the above study, this article studies aerobic exercise and cognition in more detail. Among the results: The effects of aerobic exercise improved central nervous system functioning, leading to significant improvement in cognitive ability (memory, perception) and visual sensitivity. Another important finding was that mental decrements occurred at a relatively early age, 50–62 years, in subjects who had been screened for good health.

M. Elsayed, A. H. Ismail, and R. J. Young, "Intellectual Differences of Adult Men Related to Age and Physical Fitness before and after an Exercise Program," *Journal of Gerontology* 35 (1980): 383–87. Studying the benefits of exercise on mental functioning in both the young as well as the older population, these researchers found that regardless of age, physically fit individuals had a significantly higher total fluid intelligence score than low-fit individuals.

C. F. Merzbacher, "A Diet and Exercise Regimen: Its Effect upon Mental Acuity and Personality, A Pilot Study," *Perceptual and Motor Skills* 48 (1979): 367–71.

15. M. N. Janal et al., "Pain Sensitivity, Mood, and Plasma Endocrine Levels in Man Following Long-Distance Running: Effects of Naloxone," *Pain* 19 (1984): 13–25.

W. D. McArdle, F. I. Katch, and V. L. Katch, *Exercise Physiology: Energy, Nutrition, and Human Performance*, 2d ed. (Philadelphia: Lea and Febiger, 1986), 338–39.

CHAPTER 3: THE BENEFITS

1. H. C. Pitot, "Chemicals and Cancer: Initiation and Promotion," *Hospital Practice* (July 1983): 101–13.

B. S. Reddy et. al., "Nutrition and Its Relationship to Cancer," *Advances in Cancer Research* 32 (1980): 237–345. Over one hundred pages in length (facilitated by a detailed table of contents), this article is a rich resource for those interested in the role of dietary factors in the development of cancer. Six different forms of cancer are covered with respect to epidemiology, etiology, and experimental studies. After considering a wealth of international information, the authors conclude that none of the risk factors for cancer is more significant than diet and nutrition.

For a less clinical approach to diet and cancer see the interview with Leonard A. Cohen, a leading researcher on nutrition and breast cancer and a coauthor in the Reddy study (above): "Reducing the Risk of Breast Cancer," *Nutrition Action Healthletter* (March 1988): 4–6. Although the topic of the interview is breast cancer, Cohen outlines the relationship of dietary fat to the process of carcinogenesis in general.

K. K. Carroll, "Role of Lipids in Tumorigenesis," *Journal of the American Oil Chemists' Society* 61 (Dec. 1984): 1888–91.

2. J. W. Berg, "Can Nutrition Explain the Pattern of International Epidemiology of Hormone-Dependent Cancers?" *Cancer Research* 35 (Nov. 1975): 3345–50.

K. K. Carroll, "Experimental Evidence of Dietary Factors and Hormone-Dependent Cancers," *Cancer Research* 35 (Nov. 1975): 3374–83.

Reddy, 237–345 (see n. 1, above).

3. D. P. Burkitt, "Epidemiology of Cancer of the Colon and Rectum," *Cancer* 28 (July 1971): 3–13.

S. L. Gorbach, "Estrogens, Breast Cancer, and Intestinal Flora," *Reviews of Infectious Diseases* 6, suppl. 1 (Mar.–Apr. 1984): S85–90.

M. J. Hill, "Bile Acids and Human Colorectal Cancer," in *Dietary Fiber in Health and Disease*, ed. G. V. Vahouny and D. Kritchevsky, (New York: Plenum Press, 1982), 299–312.

M. J. Hill, "Gut Bacteria and Aetiology of Cancer of the Breast," *Lancet* 2 (Aug. 1971): 472–73.

D. Kritchevsky, "Diet, Nutrition, and Cancer," *Cancer* 58, suppl. (Oct. 1986): 1830–36.

Reddy, 241–71 (see n. 1, above).

4.   A. S. Whittemore et al., "Diet, Physical Activity, and Colorectal Cancer among Chinese in North America and China," *Journal of the National Cancer Institute* 82 (June 1990): 915–26.

For further reading on the relationship of colon cancer to diet in Chinese and Chinese Americans, see K. S. Yeung et al., "Comparisons of Diet and Biochemical Characteristics of Stool and Urine between Chinese Populations with Low and High Colorectal Cancer Rates," *Journal of the National Cancer Institute* 83 (Jan. 1991): 46–50. The findings of this study indicate that colorectal cancer risk is increased by the consumption of high-fat, high-protein, and low-carbohydrate diets.

5.   J. J. DeCosse, H. H. Miller, and M. L. Lesser, "Effect of Wheat Fiber and Vitamins C and E on Rectal Polyps in Patients with Familial Adenomatous Polyposis," *Journal of the National Cancer Institute* 81 (Sept. 1989): 1290–97. The results of this study found that subjects consuming a high-fiber diet had significant decreases in rectal polyps (precursors of colon cancer) in comparison to subjects consuming a low-fiber diet. Furthermore, the greater the subject's fat intake, the greater the number of polyps (in both groups), suggesting that a high-fiber, low-fat diet is the most beneficial in preventing colon cancer. Although all the subjects in this study had a genetic susceptibility to developing colon cancer, Dr. Jerome DeCosse in an interview with the *New York Times* (J. E. Brody, "Stronger Data Show Fiber Reduces Colon Cancer," 6 Sept. 1989) stated that the findings should apply to all Americans at risk of developing colon-rectal cancer since there is no difference in the type of polyps that form in people with a genetic susceptibility.

6.   B. S. Reddy et al., "Metabolic Epidemiology of Large Bowel Cancer: Fecal Bulk and Constituents of High-Risk North American and Low-Risk Finnish Population," *Cancer* 42 (1978): 2832–38.

S. Tornberg et al., "Risks of the Colon and Rectum in Relation to Serum Cholesterol and Beta-Lipoprotein," *New England Journal of Medicine* 315 (Dec. 1986): 1629–33. The results of this study found that men with high cholesterol levels (above 250 mg/dl) were approximately 60 percent more likely than those with normal cholesterol levels to get rectal and colon cancer.

7.   P. Toniolo et al., "Calorie-Providing Nutrients and Risk of Breast Cancer," *Journal of the National Cancer Institute* 81 (Feb. 1989): 278–86. The findings of this study indicate that a high-fat diet places women at a significantly increased risk of breast cancer. In addition, a high consumption of dairy products (butter, whole milk, cheese), especially high-fat cheeses, is particularly associated with increased risk.

8.   E. L. Wynder et al., "Comparative Epidemiology of Cancer Between the United States and Japan: A Second Look," *Cancer* 67 (Feb. 1991): 746–63.

World Health Organization, *World Health Statistics Annual*, 1987, 1988.

9.   G. E. Fraser, W. L. Beeson, and R. L. Phillips, "Diet and Lung Cancer in California Seventh-Day Adventists," *American Journal of Epidemiology* 133 (Apr. 1991): 683–93.

10. E. Giovannucci et al., "Relationship of Diet to Risk of Colorectal Adenoma in Men," *Journal of the National Cancer Institute* 84 (Jan. 1992): 91–98.

11. International Collaborative Group, "Circulating Cholesterol Level and Risk of Death from Cancer in Men Aged 40 to 69 Years," *Journal of the American Medical Association* 248 (Dec. 1982): 2853–59.
    A. J. McMichael et al., "Dietary and Endogenous Cholesterol and Human Cancer," *Epidemiologic Reviews* 6 (1984): 192–216.
    R. W. Sherwin et al., "Serum Cholesterol Levels and Cancer Mortality in 361,662 Men Screened for the Multiple Risk Factor Intervention Trial," *Journal of the American Medical Association* 257 (Feb. 1987): 943–48. During a seven-year follow-up of men screened for the Multiple Risk Factor Intervention Trial, mortality analysis revealed that there was a significant correlation between cancer and low levels of cholesterol in subjects who died in the early years of the study. However, those subjects who died of cancer in later years of the study did not have significantly lower cholesterol levels at the beginning of the study.
    The authors of this study conclude that the subjects with low cholesterol at the beginning of the study actually had preclinical cancer since they developed cancer within a few years of the low cholesterol reading. Thus, it was not the low cholesterol levels that caused cancer, but it was the cancer that caused the low cholesterol levels. These findings are supported by other research that indicates a two- to five-year period of significance between cancer and low cholesterol readings. After six years from cholesterol measurement, the significant relationship between cancer and low cholesterol disappears.

12. Prevention Magazine, *The Complete Book of Cancer Prevention: Foods, Life-styles and Medical Care to Keep You Healthy* (Emmaus, PA: Rodale Press, 1988), 138.

13. R. P. Mensink and M. B. Katan, "Effect of Dietary Trans–Fatty-Acids on High-Density and Low-Density Lipoprotein Cholesterol Levels in Healthy Subjects," *New England Journal of Medicine* 323 (Aug. 1990): 3439–45.

14. D. H. Blankenhorn et. al., "The Influence of Diet on the Appearance of New Lesions in Human Coronary Arteries," *Journal of the American Medical Association* 263 (Mar. 1990): 1646–52.

15. Carroll (see n. 1, above).
    K. L. Erikson and N. E. Hubbard, "Dietary Fat and Tumor Metastasis," *Nutrition Reviews* 48 (Jan. 1990): 6–14.
    National Research Council, 213–14 (see chap. 1, n. 1, above).

16. R. K. Chandra, "Effects of Overnutrition on Immune Responses and Risk of Disease," *Nutrition and Immunology* (New York: Alan R. Liss, 1988), 315–28.

17. Inkeles and Eisenberg, 113–14 (see chap. 1, n. 3, above).
    M. Friedman, S. O. Byers, and R. H. Rosenman, "Effect of Unsaturated Fats Upon Lipemia and Conjuctival Circulation," *Journal of the American Medical Association* 193 (Sept. 1965): 110–14.
    A. V. Williams, A. C. Higginbotham, and M. H. Knisely, "Increased Blood Cell Agglutination Following Ingestion of Fat: A Factor Contributing to Cardiac Ischemia, Coronary Insufficiency, and Anginal Pain," *Angiology* 8 (1957): 29–39.

18. J. L. Swank and H. Nakamura, "Oxygen Availability in Brain Tissues after Lipid Meals," *American Journal of Physiology* 198 (1960): 217–20.

19. Friedman (see n. 17, above).

20. Reddy, 306 (see n. 1, above).

21. S. M. Grundy et al., "Basis for Dietary Treatment," *Circulation* 80 (Sept. 1989): 729–34, esp. 730.
     R. A. L. Sturdevant et al., "Increased Prevalence of Cholelithiasis in Men Ingesting a Serum Cholesterol Lowering Diet," *New England Journal of Medicine* 288 (Jan. 1973): 24–27.

22. Mensink and Katan, 3439 (see n. 13, above).

23. S. M. Grundy et al., "Comparison of Monounsaturated Fatty Acids and Carbohydrates for Reducing Raised Levels of Plasma Cholesterol in Man," *American Journal of Clinical Nutrition* 47 (1988): 965–69.

24. National Research Council, 594 (see chap. 1, n. 1, above).
     Reddy, 275–77 (see n. 1, above).

25. T. Pollare, H. Lithell, and C. Berne, "A Comparison of the Effects of Hydrochlorothiazide and Captopril on Glucose and Lipid Metabolism in Patients with Hypertension," *New England Journal of Medicine* 321 (Sept. 1989): 868–73.

26. Multiple Risk Factor Intervention Trial, "Risk Factor Changes and Mortality Results," *Journal of the American Medical Association* 248 (Sept. 1982): 1465–77.

27. G. R. Boss and J. E. Seegmiller, "Hyperuricemia and Gout: Classification, Complications, and Management," *New England Journal of Medicine* 300 (June 1979): 1459–68, esp. 1463.
     V. J. Dzau, "Treatment Strategies: An Evaluation of Antihypertensive Therapy," *American Journal of Medicine* 86, suppl. 1B (Jan. 1989): 113–15.

28. S. H. Croog et al., "The Effects of Antihypertensive Therapy on the Quality of Life," *New England Journal of Medicine* 314 (June 1986): 1657–64.
     M. H. Weinberger, "Antihypertensive Therapy and Lipids: Paradoxical Influences on Cardiovascular Disease Risk," *American Journal of Medicine* 80, suppl. 2A (Feb. 1986): 64–70.

29. Oliver, Cohen, and Neel (see chap. 2, n. 2, above).
     A. S. Truswell et al., "Blood Pressures of !Kung Bushmen in Northern Botswana," *American Heart Journal* 84 (July 1972): 5–12.
     Whyte (see chap. 1, n. 26, above).

30. H. Blackburn and R. Prineas, "Diet and Hypertension: Anthropology, Epidemiology, and Public-Health Implications," *Progress in Biochemical Pharmacology* 19 (1983): 31–79.

31. Kunio Owada et al., "Epidemiology of Cerebrovascular Disease in Japan," *Osaka City Medical Journal* 19 (1973): 37–49.

H. Tanaka et al., "Risk Factors for Cerebral Hemorrhage and Cerebral Infarction in a Japanese Rural Community," *Stroke* 13 (1982): 62–73.

National Research Council, 103, 195 (see chap. 1, n. 1, above).

H. Ueshima, "Multivariate Analysis of Risk Factors for Stroke: Eight-Year Follow-Up Study of Farming Villages in Akita, Japan," *Preventive Medicine* 9 (1980): 722–40.

32. O. G. Kolterman, "Etiology and Pathogenesis of Diabetes Mellitus," in *Clinical Guide to Diabetes Mellitus,* ed. K. E. Sussman, B. Draznin, and W. E. James, (New York: Alan R. Liss, 1987), 5–8.

33. Kolterman, 8–12 (see n. 32, above).

34. D. M. Kipnis, "Insulin Secretion in Normal and Diabetic Individuals," in *Advances in Internal Medicine* 16, ed. G. H. Stollerman (Year Book Medical Publishers, 1970), 112–13

35. Dawber, 190–201 (see chap. 1, n. 30, above).

N. B. Ruderman and C. Haudenschild, "Diabetes as an Atherogenic Factor," *Progress in Cardiovascular Diseases* 26 (Mar./Apr. 1984): 373–412. Rudderman and Haudenschild present a scholarly analysis of the various mechanisms that accelerate atherosclerosis in diabetics.

L. P. Krall, ed., *Joslin Diabetes Manual,* 11th ed. (Philadelphia: Lea and Febiger, 1978), 23, 163–87.

36. R. J. Barnard et al., "Response of Non-Insulin-Dependent Diabetic Patients to an Intensive Program of Diet and Exercise," *Diabetes Care* 5 (July/Aug. 1982): 370–74.

R. J. Barnard et al., "Long-Term Use of a High-Complex-Carbohydrate, High-Fiber, Low-Fat Diet, and Exercise in the Treatment of NIDDM Patients," *Diabetes Care* 6 (May/June 1983): 268–73.

37. P. Ducimetiere et al., "Relationship of Plasma Insulin Levels to the Incidence of Myocardial Infarction and Coronary Heart Disease Mortality in a Middle-Aged Population," *Diabetologia* 19 (1980): 205–10.

G. L. King et al., "Receptors and Growth-Promoting Effects of Insulin and Insulin-like Growth Factors on Cells from Bovine Retinal Capillaries and Aorta," *Journal of Clinical Investigation* 75 (Mar. 1985): 1028–36.

Ruderman and Haudenschild (see n. 35, above).

R. W. Stout, "Overview of the Association between Insulin and Atherosclerosis, *Metabolism* 34, suppl. 1 (Dec. 1985): 7–12.

I. Zavaroni et al., "Risk Factor for Coronary Artery Disease in Healthy Persons with Hyperinsulinemia and Normal Glucose Tolerance," *New England Journal of Medicine* 320 (Mar. 1989): 702–6.

38. C. Gopalan et al., "Effect of Calorie Supplementation on Growth of Undernourished Children," *American Journal of Clinical Nutrition* 26 (May 1973): 563–66.

M. H. N. Golden, "Protein Deficiency, Energy Deficiency, and the Oedema of Malnutrition," *Lancet* 1 (June 1982): 1261–65.

39. National Research Council, 15, 62–63 (see chap. 1, n. 1, above).

40. Barnard, 129 (see chap. 1, n. 29, above).

41. A. B. Gutman and T. F. Yü, "Prevention and Treatment of Chronic Gouty Arthritis," *Journal of the American Medical Association* 157 (Mar. 1955): 1096–1102.

C. P. Lucas and L. Power, "Dietary Fat Aggravates Active Rheumatoid Arthritis," *Clinical Research* 29 (1981): 754A.

J. Mayer, "Nutrition and Gout," *Postgraduate Medicine* 45 (May 1969): 277–78.

M. A. Ogryzlo, "Hyperuricemia Induced by High-Fat Diets and Starvation," *Arthritis and Rheumatism* 8 (Oct. 1965): 799–817.

A. L. Parke and G. R. V. Hughes, "Rheumatoid Arthritis and Food: A Case Study," *British Medical Journal* 282 (June 1981): 2027–29.

42. Dustman et al. (see chap. 2, n. 14, above). High-fat diets lead to elevated lipid levels, which results in lack of oxygen (hypoxia) in muscle tissues, most notably the brain (see n. 18, above). As noted previously, the Dustman study found that by increasing oxygen availability through exercise, not only did subjects show improved cognitive ability, but their visual sensitivity (visual threshold and field) was also increased. Thus, the degenerative effects of hypoxia, including a reduced visual field, may be avoided by adhering to a low-fat diet and by exercising.

R. Gray, "Disappearing Gallstones: Report of Two Cases," *British Journal of Surgery* 61 (1974), 101–3.

A. H. Ismail and H. Tolson, "Deafness Linked to Heart Attacks, Strokes," *Science News* 94 (Dec. 1968): 641.

S. L. Malhotra, "Epidemiological Study of Cholelithiasis among Railroad Workers in India with Special Reference to Causation," *Gut* 9 (1968): 290.

T. Matushiro et al., "Effects of Glucaric Acid Concentration in Bile and the Formation of Calcium Bilirubinate Gallstones," *Gastroenterology* 72 (1977): 630–33.

S. Rosen and P. Olin, "Hearing Loss and Coronary Heart Disease," *Archives of Otolaryngology* 82 (Sept. 1965): 236–43.

E. Wolf and A. S. Nadroski, "Extent of the Visual Field: Changes with Age and Oxygen Tension," *Archives of Ophthalmology* 86 (Dec. 1971): 637–642. The Dustman study (cited above) found that increased oxygen availability improved visual sensitivity in older subjects, 50 to 62 years of age. The Wolf and Nadroski study came to the same conclusion by showing that decreased oxygen availability in younger subjects resulted in reduced visual sensitivity. Subjects in their mid-teens to mid-twenties inhaled air with reduced oxygen, which had the effect of lowering their visual sensitivity to the same level measured in individuals 30 to 50 years older.

43. Matthews et al. (see chap. 1, n. 47, above).

B. W. Walsh et al., "Effects of Postmenopausal Estrogen Replacement on the Concentrations and Metabolism of Plasma Lipoproteins," *New England Journal of Medicine* 325 (Oct. 1991): 1196–1204.

44. G. A. Colditz et al., "Prospective Study of Estrogen Replacement Therapy and Risk of Breast Cancer in Postmenopausal Women," *Journal of the American Medical Association* 264 (Nov. 1990): 2648–53. Current users of estrogen replacement therapy were found to be at increased risk of breast cancer. A stronger relationship was observed with increasing age but not with increasing duration of use.

S. M. Wolfe, "New Evidence that Menopausal Estrogens Cause Breast Cancer; Further Doubts About Prevention of Heart Disease," *The Public Citizen Health Research Group Health Letter* 7 (June 1991): 4–6.

H. Jick et al., "Replacement Estrogens and Endometrial Cancer," *New England Journal of Medicine* 300 (Feb. 1979): 218–22.

M. I. Whitehead, "Controversies Concerning the Safety of Estrogen Replacement Therapy," *American Journal of Obstetrics and Gynecology* 156 (May 1987): 1313–21.

45. Clarkson et al. (see chap. 2, n. 7, above). In studying the effects of diet and stress on the development of coronary heart disease in monkeys, Clarkson et al. found that monkeys fed a high-fat diet and exposed to a high-stress environment were more than thirty times as likely to develop advanced atherosclerosis as high-stress monkeys consuming a low-fat diet. Findings also revealed that stress influenced the development of minimal atherosclerosis in monkeys on the low-fat diet, but these cases of disease were much less advanced, indicating that stress can be harmful independent of dietary factors but not nearly as harmful as stress combined with a high-fat diet. Other studies have also indicated that stress in combination with an atherogenic diet can accelerate atherosclerosis: C. M. Land, "Effects of Psychic Stress on Atherosclerosis in the Squirrel Monkey (*Saimiri sciureus*)," *Proceedings of the Society of Experimental and Biological Medicine* 126 (1967): 30–34, and H. N. Uhley and M. Friedman, "Blood Lipids, Clotting, and Coronary Atherosclerosis in Rats Exposed to a Particular Form of Stress," *American Journal of Physiology* 197 (1959): 396–98.

H. Benson with M. Z. Klipper, *The Relaxation Response* (New York: William Morrow, 1975), 23–25, 68–74.

R. M. Sapolsky, "Stress in the Wild," *Scientific American* (Jan. 1990): 116–24.

N. Schneiderman, "Behavior, Autonomic Function, and Animal Models of Cardiovascular Pathology," in *Biobehavioral Bases of Coronary Heart Disease,* ed. T. M. Dembroski, T. H. Schmidt, and G. Blümchen (Basel Switzerland: Karger, 1983), 304–64, 317–22.

46. R. S. Eliot and J. C. Buell, "Role of the Central Nervous System in Sudden Cardiac Death," in Dembroski, ed. (see n. 45, above), 262.

J. I. Haft and Y. S. Arkel, "Effect of Emotional Stress on Platelet Aggregation in Humans," *Chest* 70 (Oct. 1976): 501–5.

47. V. Riley, "Psychoneuroendocrine Influences on Immunocompetence and Neoplasia," *Science* 292 (June 1981): 1100–9.

48. D. Remington, G. Fisher, and E. Parent, *How to Lower Your Fat Thermostat: The No-Diet Reprogramming Plan for Lifelong Weight Control* (Provo, UT: Vitality House International, 1983), 68.

49. See chap. 1, n. 2, above.

50. R. E. Keesey, "A Set-Point Theory of Obesity," in *Handbook of Eating Disorders,* ed. K. D. Brownell and J. P. Foreyt (New York: Basic Books, 1986), 63–87.

Remington, 4 (see n. 48, above).

CHAPTER 4: A PARABLE

1. For further information on Nathan Pritikin's work please refer to any of the several books he authored during his nutrition career.

N. Pritikin with J. N. Leonard and J. L. Hofer, *Live Longer Now* (New York: Grosset and Dunlap, 1974). This best-selling book is Nathan Pritikin's first and most comprehensive book on the relationship between diet and disease in the modern world. The wealth of information contained in *Live Longer Now* was the foundation for Pritikin's lectures at the Pritikin Longevity Centers in addition to the many lectures and speeches he presented over the years to lay and professional audiences around the country.

N. Pritikin with Patrick M. McGrady, Jr., *The Pritikin Program for Diet and Exercise* (New York: Grosset and Dunlap, 1979).

N. Pritikin, *The Pritikin Permanent Weight-Loss Manual* (New York: Grosset and Dunlap, 1981).

N. Pritikin, *The Pritikin Promise: Twenty-eight Days to a Longer and Healthier Life* (New York: Simon and Schuster, 1983).

N. Pritikin with Ilene Pritikin, *The Official Pritikin Guide to Dining Out* (Indianapolis, N.Y.: Bobbs-Merrill Co., 1984).

N. Pritikin, *Diet for Runners* (New York: Simon and Schuster, 1985).

2.   Wolf and Nadroski (see chap. 3, n. 42, above).
Ismail and Tolson (see chap. 3, n. 42, above).
Rosen and Olin (see chap. 3, n. 42, above).

3.   See chap. 3, n. 41, above.

4.   D. S. Freedman et al., "Atherosclerosis in Early Life: The Bogalusa Heart Study," *Cardiology Board Review* 3 (Aug. 1986): 26–40.

5.   According to J. A. T. Pennington, *Food Values of Portions Commonly Used,* 15th ed. (New York: Harper and Row, 1989), one twelve-fluid ounce can of Coca-Cola has 46 mg of caffeine, and 1 cup of coffee prepared from one rounded teaspoon of instant coffee has 57 mg of caffeine. Thus a 50-pound child consuming 3 cans of Coca-Cola and a 150-pound adult consuming 7.3 cups of coffee are both ingesting 2.76 mg of caffeine per pound of body weight.

6.   T. O. Scholl et al., "Maternal Weight Gain, Diet, and Infant Birth Weight: Correlations during Adolescent Pregnancy," *Journal of Clinical Epidemiology* 44 (1991): 423–28.

7.   J. Robbins, *Diet for a New America* (Walpole, NH: Stillpoint Publishing, 1987), 351.

CHAPTER 5: YOUR WEIGHT

1.   A. Miller et al., "Diets Incorporated," *Newsweek* (11 Sept. 1989), 56–60.
2.   G. K. Goodrick and J. P. Foreyt, "Why Treatments for Obesity Don't Last," *Journal of the American Dietetic Association* 91 (Oct. 1991): 1243–47.

F. M. Kramer et al., "Long-term Follow-up of Behavioral Treatment for Obesity: Patterns of Weight Regain among Men and Women," *International Journal of Obesity* 13 (1989): 123–36.

Miller (see n. 1, above).

3. K. D. Brownell, "Weight Cycling," *American Journal of Clinical Nutrition* 49 (1989): 937.
G. L. Blackburn et al., "Weight Cycling: the Experience of Human Dieters," *American Journal of Clinical Nutrition* 49 (1989): 1105–9.

4. Remington, 53 (see chap. 3, n. 48, above).

5. F. W. Ashley, Jr., and W. B. Kannel, "Relation of Weight Change to Changes in Atherogenic Traits," *Journal of Chronic Diseases* 27 (Mar. 1974): 103–14.
National Center for Health Statistics, 1981.

6. D. V. Schapira et al., "Upper-Body Fat Distribution and Endometrial Cancer Risk," *Journal of the American Medical Association* 266 (Oct. 1991): 1808–11.

7. Romieu (see chap. 1, n. 2, above).
Dreon et al. (see chap. 1, n. 2, above).

8. Keesey (see chap. 3, n. 50, above).

9. A. W. Williams-Larson, "Urinary Calculi Associated with Purine Metabolism: Uric Acid Nephrolithiasis," *Endocrinology and Metabolism in Clinics of North America* 19 (1990): 821–38.

CHAPTER 7: HOW TO EXERCISE

1. Wood and Haskell (see chap. 2, n. 8, above).

2. N.A., *The Fit Body: Building Endurance* (Alexandria, VA: Time-Life Books, 1987), 24.

3. American College of Sports Medicine, *Guidelines for Exercise Testing and Prescription*, 3d ed. (Philadelphia: Lea and Febiger, 1986), 1–3.

4. S. N. Blair et al., "Physical Fitness and All-Cause Mortality," *Journal of the American Medical Association* 262 (Nov. 1989): 2395–401.

5. Pritikin, *Diet for Runners,* 78–79 (see chap. 4, n. 1, above).

CHAPTER 8: THE MIND-BODY CONNECTION

1. J. A. Herd, "Physiological Basis for Behavioral Influences in Arteriosclerosis," in Dembroski (see chap. 3, n. 45, above).
Sapolsky (see chap. 3, n. 45, above).
R. Williams, *The Trusting Heart* (New York: Times Books, 1989), 75–82.

2. R. B. Williams, Jr., "Psychological Factors in Coronary Artery Disease: Epidemiologic Evidence," *Circulation* 76, suppl. I (July 1987): I117–23.

3. J. C. Barefoot et al., "The Cook-Medley Hostility Scale: Item Content and Ability to Predict Survival," *Psychosomatic Medicine* 51 (1989): 46–57.

4.   J. C. Barefoot, G. Dahlstrom, and R. B. Williams, "Hostility, CHD Incidence, and Total Mortality: A Twenty-Five-Year Follow-up Study of 255 Physicians," *Psychosomatic Medicine* 45 (Mar. 1983): 59–63.

5.   J. C. Barefoot et al., "Suspiciousness, Health and Mortality: A Follow-up Study of Five Hundred Older Adults," *Psychosomatic Medicine* 49 (1987): 450–57.

6.   M. Friedman and D. Ulmer, *Treating Type A Behavior and Your Heart* (New York: Alfred A. Knopf, 1984), 175–237.

7.   U. S. Department of Health and Human Services, *The United States Surgeon General's Report on Smoking*, 1989.

8.   U.S. Department of Health and Human Services, Centers for Disease Control, "Alcohol-Related Mortality and Years of Potential Life Lost: United States, 1987," *Morbidity and Mortality Weekly Report* 39 (Mar. 1990): 173–77.

     U. S. Department of Health and Human Services, *Seventh Special Report to the U. S. Congress on Alcohol and Health from the Secretary of Health and Human Services*, Jan. 1990.

9.   R. D. Moore and T. A. Pearson, "Moderate Alcohol Consumption and Coronary Artery Disease: A Review," *Medicine* 65 (1986): 242–67.

10. A. G. Shaper, G. Wannamethee, and M. Walker, "Alcohol and Mortality in British Men: Explaining the U-Shaped Curve," *Lancet* (Dec. 1988): 1267–73.

11. E. B. Rimm et al., "Prospective Study of Alcohol Consumption and Risk of Coronary Heart Disease in Men," *Lancet* 338 (Aug. 1991): 464–68.

12. W. C. Willett et al., "Moderate Alcohol Consumption and the Risk of Breast Cancer," *New England Journal of Medicine* 316 (May 1987): 1174–80.

     For a general analysis of case-control studies on alcohol and breast cancer which supports the findings of the article above see S. Graham, "Alcohol and Breast Cancer," which appears in the same issue of *NEJM*: 1211–12.

13. J. P. Boulenger et al., "Increased Sensitivity to Caffeine in Patients with Panic Disorders," *Archives of General Psychiatry* 41 (Nov. 1984): 1067–71.

14. S. M. Wolfe et al., *Worst Pills Best Pills* (Washington, D.C.: Public Citizen Health Research Group, 1988), 145.

15. University of California, *Berkeley Wellness Letter* 5.7 (Apr. 1989): 5.

16. *The Public Citizen Health Research Group Health Letter* 6.1 (Jan. 1990): 1.

17. E. V. Nunes and J. S. Rosecan, "Human Neurobiology of Cocaine," in *Cocaine Abuse: New Directions in Treatment and Research,* ed. H. I Spitz and J. S. Rosecan (New York: Brunner/Mazel Publishers, 1987), 48–97.

     S. Shiffman and T. A. Wills, eds., *Coping and Substance Use* (San Diego: Academic Press, 1985), 41–42.

18. H. Benson, J. F. Beary, and M. P. Carol, "The Relaxation Response," *Psychiatry* 37 (Feb. 1974): 37–46.

H. Benson, M. M. Greenwood, and H. Klemchuk, "The Relaxation Response: Psychophysiologic Aspects and Clinical Applications," *International Journal of Psychiatry in Medicine* 6 (1975): 87–98.

19. H. Benson et al., "Decreased Blood Pressure in Borderline Hypertensive Subjects Who Practiced Meditation," *Journal of Chronic Diseases* 27 (1974): 163–69.

20. C. N. Alexander et al., "Transcendental Meditation, Mindfulness, and Longevity: An Experimental Study with the Elderly," *Journal of Personality and Social Psychology* 57 (Dec. 1989): 950–64.

21. Benson with Klipper (see chap. 3, n. 45, above).

22. D. Shapiro and R. S. Surwit, "Biofeedback," in *Behavioral Medicine: Theory and Practice,* ed. O. F. Pomerleau and J. P. Brady (Baltimore: Wilkins and Williams, 1979).

23.   Although Benson derived his technique largely from transcendental meditation (TM), proponents of TM point out that Benson's technique is not the same as TM and differs from it in subtle, but important, ways. There has been extensive research reported on the health benefits of TM, which includes papers in over one hundred refereed journals. A summary of this research and a complete listing of references is contained in D. Orme-Johnson and C. N. Alexander, "Summary of Research on the Transcendental Meditation and TM-Sidhi Program," available from TM centers.
       For information on centers that teach transcendental meditation in your area, contact: Maharishi National Council of the Age of Enlightenment, 2021 North Main St., Fairfield, IA 52556-2062; (515) 472-0108.

24. Benson with Klipper, 158–66 (see chap. 3, n. 45, above).

CHAPTER 10: THE SECOND FOUNTAIN

1.   R. L. Walford, S. B. Harris, and R. Weindruch, "Dietary Restriction and Aging: Historical Phases, Mechanisms, and Current Directions," *Journal of Nutrition* 117 (1987): 1650–54.

2.   B. P. Yu et al., "Life Span Study of SPF Fischer 344 Male Rats Fed *Ad Libitum* or Restricted Diets: Longevity, Growth, Lean Body Mass, and Disease," *Journal of Gerontology* 37 (1982): 130–41.

3.   N. Angier, "Diet Offers Tantalizing Clues to a Long Life," *New York Times*, 17 April 1990, sec. C.

4.   D. Kritchevsky, "Influence of Caloric Restriction and Exercise on Tumorigenesis in Rats," *Proceedings of the Society for Experimental Biology and Medicine* 193 (1990): 35–38. Caloric restriction has been shown to inhibit the growth of spontaneous, transplanted, or chemically induced tumors in rats and mice. At 40 percent caloric restriction, growth of chemically induced breast and colon tumors was significantly inhibited. Exercise has also been shown to inhibit tumor growth. Sedentary rats who were

allowed to eat freely had 108 percent higher incidence of induced colon tumors than free-eating rats subjected to vigorous treadmill exercise.

Walford, Harris, and Weindruch (see n. 1, above).

5.   Angier (see n. 3, above).

6.   A. Cerami, "Hypothesis: Glucose as a Mediator of Aging," *Journal of the American Geriatric Society* 33 (1985): 626–34.

E. J. Masoro, M. S. Katz, and C. A. McMahan, "Evidence for the Glycation Hypothesis of Aging from the Food-Restricted Rodent Model," *Journal of Gerontology: Biological Sciences* 41 (1989): B20–22.

7. D. Harman, "Free Radical Theory of Aging: Role of Free Radicals in the Origination and Evolution of Life, Aging, and Disease Processes," in *Free Radicals, Aging, and Degenerative Diseases*, ed. J. E. Johnson et al. (New York: Alan R. Liss, 1986), 3–50.

8.   A. Koizumi, R. Weindruch, and R. L. Walford, "Influences of Dietary Restriction and Age on Liver Enzyme Activities and Lipid Peroxidation in Mice," *Journal of Nutrition* 117 (Feb. 1987): 361–67.

9.   R. Licastro, R. Weindruch, and R. L. Walford, "Dietary Restriction Retards the Age-Related Decline of DNA Repair Capacity in Mouse Splenocytes," in *Topics in Aging Research in Europe* 9, ed. A. Facchini, J. J. Haaijman, and G. Labo (Rijswijk: EURAGE, 1986), 53–61.

R. J. Tice and R. B. Setlow, "DNA Repair and Replication in Aging Organisms and Cells," in *Handbook of the Biology of Aging,* ed. C. E. Finch and E. L. Schneider (New York: Van Nostrand Reinhold, 1985), 173–224.

10.   R. K. Liu and R. L. Walford, "'The Effect of Lowered Body Temperature on Lifespan and Immune and Non-Immune Processes," *Gerontologia* 18 (1972): 363–88.

11.   Kagawa (see chap. 1, n. 34, above).

C. Kahn, "His Theory Is Simple: Eat Less, Live Longer. A Lot Longer," *Longevity* (Oct. 1990): 61–66, esp. 64.

12.   Angier (see n. 3, above).

CHAPTER 15: RANKING THE KILLERS

1.   Kagawa (see chap. 1, n. 34, above).

2.   Stamler, 26 (see chap. 1, n. 36, above).

3.   K. W. West, "North American Indians," in Trowell and Burkitt, eds., 129–37 (see chap. 2, n. 2, above).

4.   E. Dolnick, "Le Paradoxe Français," *In Health* (May/June) 1990): 41–47.

5.   Kagawa (see chap. 1, n. 34, above).

6.   W. C. You et al., "Diet and High Risk of Stomach Cancer in Shandong, China," *Cancer Research* 48 (June 1988): 3518–23.

7.   Chen et al. (see chap. 1, n. 23, above). The results of this study, the most extensive to date that addresses the subject of liver cancer in the Chinese, did not find a correlation between liver cancer and aflatoxins. According to the findings of Chen et al., high rates of liver cancer in China are primarily linked to chronic rates of hepatitis B infection and high serum cholesterol levels.

National Research Council, 596–97 (see chap. 1, n. 1, above).

Earlier research on liver cancer and aflatoxins does suggest a link, although the hepatitis B virus has similar world distribution as aflatoxins, indicating that earlier studies may not have controlled independent influence of these two factors.

8.   Trowell, in Trowell and Burkitt, eds., 3–32. (see chap. 2, n. 2, above).

APPENDIX 2

Nutritional Content of Food

(Tables adapted from *Food Values of Portions Commonly Used,* 15th edition by Jean A. T. Pennington and Helen Nichols Church. Copyright © 1989 by Jean A. T. Pennington. Copyright © 1980, 1985 by Helen Nichols Church and Jean A. T. Pennington. Reprinted by permission of HarperCollins Publishers, Inc.)

Please note that blank spaces in the following nutritional guide denote lack of information. Do not assume that missing values are zero.

	CALORIES	FAT (g)	CHOLESTEROL (mg)	SODIUM (mg)
BEVERAGES				
COFFEE, TEA, CEREAL GRAIN BEVERAGES				
Coffee				
Brewed	4	0	0	4
6 fl. oz.				
From instant	4	0	0	6
1 rounded tsp. powder in 6 fl. oz. water				
Decaffeinated, from instant	4	0	0	0
1.8 g powder in 6 fl. oz. water				
Tea				
Brewed, 3 min.	2	0	0	5
6 fl. oz.				
From instant	2	0	0	8
1 tsp. powder in 8 fl. oz. water				
Herb, brewed	1	0	0	2
6 fl. oz.				
Tea, iced				
Lemon-flavored, from instant	4	0	0	14
1 rounded tsp. powder in 8 fl. oz. water				

	CALORIES	FAT (g)	CHOLESTEROL (mg)	SODIUM (mg)
Cereal grain beverage, Postum	11	0	0	3
1 tsp. in 6 fl. oz. water				

CARBONATED, WITH SUGAR

	CALORIES	FAT (g)	CHOLESTEROL (mg)	SODIUM (mg)
Coca-Cola	155	0		6
12 fl. oz.				
Ginger ale	124	0	0	25
12 fl. oz.				
Sprite	142	0		46
12 fl. oz.				
Tonic water	125	0	0	15
12 fl. oz.				

CARBONATED, LOW-CALORIE

	CALORIES	FAT (g)	CHOLESTEROL (mg)	SODIUM (mg)
Club soda	0	0		75
12 fl. oz.				
Seltzer	0	0		0
12 fl. oz.				
Sparkling Water	0	0		0
12 fl. oz.				
Diet Coke	1	0		8
12 fl. oz.				
Diet Sprite	4	0		0
12 fl. oz.				
Tab	1	0		8
12 fl. oz.				

NONCARBONATED (PUNCHES, JUICE DRINKS, FRUIT ADES)

	CALORIES	FAT (g)	CHOLESTEROL (mg)	SODIUM (mg)
Apple juice drink, Campbell's	97	0.1		30
6 fl. oz.				

	CALORIES	FAT (g)	CHOLESTEROL (mg)	SODIUM (mg)
Grape drink, canned	84	0	0	12
6 fl. oz.				
Lemonade, from frozen concentrate	100	0.1	0	8
6 fl. oz.				
Orange drink, canned	94	0	0	31
6 fl. oz.				

CANDY AND CANDY BARS[1]

CANDY

Fudge, chocolate	113	3.5		54
1 oz.				
Hard candy	109	0.3		9
1 oz.				
Lifesavers	9.1	0		1
1 piece				
Chocolate chips, Bakers	196	8.8	0	26
1/4 cup				

CANDY BARS

Almond Joy, Peter Paul	136	2.3	1	58
1 oz.				
Chocolate almond, Cadbury	153	8.9	6	41
1 oz.				
Chew, chocolate, strawberry, vanilla, Charleston	240	6		80
2 oz.				
Milk chocolate, Hershey	254	14.5		35
1.65 oz.				

[1]Not recommended. Information included for comparison.

	CALORIES	FAT (g)	CHOLESTEROL (mg)	SODIUM (mg)
CEREALS				
COOKED CEREALS				
Bulgur wheat, canned	227	0.9		809
1 cup				
Cream of Wheat, quick, cooked	96	0.4		104[2]
3/4 cup				
Oatmeal, regular or quick, cooked	108	1.8	0	1[3]
3/4 cup[4]				
READY-TO-EAT CEREALS				
All-Bran	71	0.5		320
1/3 cup (1 oz.)				
Cheerios	111	1.8		290
1 1/4 cups (1 oz.)				
Cornflakes, Kellogg's	110	0.1		351
1 1/4 cup (1 oz.)				
Granola, Nature Valley	126	4.9		58
1/3 cup (1 oz.)				
Grape-Nuts, Post	104	0.1	0	188
1/4 cup (1 oz.)				
Life, Quaker	111	1.8		150
2/3 cup (1 oz.)				
Nutri-Grain, corn, Kellogg's	108	0.7		187
2/3 cup (1 oz.)				
Nutri-Grain, wheat, Kellogg's	102	0.3		193
3/4 cup (1 oz.)				
Puffed rice	57	0.1		0
1 cup (1/2 oz.)				

[2]Sodium is 347 mg if salt is added according to label directions.
[3]Sodium is 280 mg if salt is added according to label directions.
[4]1/3 cup (1 oz.) dry.

	CALORIES	FAT (g)	CHOLESTEROL (mg)	SODIUM (mg)
Puffed wheat	52	0.2		1
1 cup (½ oz.)				
Raisin Bran, Post	86	0.4	0	178
½ cup (1 oz.)				
Rice Krispies	112	0.2		340
1 cup (1 oz.)				
Shredded wheat	83	0.3		0
1 biscuit				
Special K, Kellogg's	111	0.1		265
1⅓ cups (1 oz.)				
Total, General Mills	100	0.6		280
1 cup (1 oz.)				
Wheat Chex	100	0.7		200
⅔ cup (1 oz.)				

CHEESE[5]

	CALORIES	FAT (g)	CHOLESTEROL (mg)	SODIUM (mg)
Blue	100	8.2	21	396
1 oz.				
Brie	95	7.9	28	178
1 oz.				
Cheddar	114	9.4	30	176
1 oz.				
Cottage cheese, creamed	217	9.5	31	850
1 cup, not packed				
Cottage cheese, dry curd[6]	123	0.6	10	19
1 cup, not packed				
Cottage cheese, 1 percent fat[7]	164	2.3	10	918
1 cup				

[5]Not recommended (except for very low fat varieties). Information included for comparison.
[6]Within the low-fat guidelines of the 10% solution.
[7]Within the low-fat guidelines of the 10% solution.

	CALORIES	FAT (g)	CHOLESTEROL (mg)	SODIUM (mg)
Cream cheese	99	9.9	31	84
2 tbsp. (1 oz.)				
Feta	75	6	25	316
1 oz.				
Mozzarella	80	6.1	22	106
1 oz.				
Mozzarella, part skim	72	4.5	16	132
1 oz.				
Parmesan, grated	23	1.5	4	93
1 tbsp.				
Ricotta, part skim	171	9.8	38	155
½ cup				
Ricotta, whole milk	216	16.1	63	104
½ cup				
Swiss	107	7.8	26	74
1 oz.				

CHIPS AND PROCESSED SNACKS[8]

	CALORIES	FAT (g)	CHOLESTEROL (mg)	SODIUM (mg)
Cheese straws	272	17.9		433
10 pieces				
Corn chips	153	8.8		218
1 oz.				
Party mix, Chex	130	4.7		3
⅔ cup (1 oz.)				
Popcorn[9]	23	0.3		0
1 cup				
Potato chips	148	10.1	0	133
1 oz.				

[8]Not recommended. Information included for comparison.
[9]Popcorn is within the low-fat guidelines of the 10% solution if it is air-popped and eaten without butter.

	CALORIES	FAT (g)	CHOLESTEROL (mg)	SODIUM (mg)
Pretzels	111	1		451
1 oz.				
Tortilla chips, Planters	150	8.0	0	155
1 oz.				

CREAMS, CREAM SUBSTITUTES[10]

Half-and-half	20	1.7	6	6
1 tbsp.				
Light (coffee/table)	29	2.9	10	6
1 tbsp.				
Sour, cultured	26	2.5	5	6
1 tbsp.				
Whipped, pressurized	8	0.7	2	4
1 tbsp.				
Whipping, heavy, fluid	52	5.6	21	6
1 tbsp.				

DESSERTS[11]

CAKE

Angel-food, homemade	161	0.1		161
1 piece				
Brownies, chocolate, from mix, Duncan Hines	120	2.8	0	98
1 brownie				
Carrot cake, from mix, Duncan Hines	187	4	0	253
¹/₁₂ cake				

[10]Not recommended. Information included for comparison.
[11]Not recommended (unless low-fat). Information included for comparison.

	CALORIES	FAT (g)	CHOLESTEROL (mg)	SODIUM (mg)
Cheesecake	257	16.3		189
1 piece				
Chocolate chip, from mix, Duncan Hines Deluxe	189	4.4	0	249
$1/_{12}$ cake				
Coffee cake, from mix	232	6.9		310
$1/_6$ cake				
Gingerbread, homemade	267	12.9		99
1 piece				
Lemon, from mix, Pillsbury	220	9		260
$1/_{12}$ cake				
Pound, old-fashioned, homemade	142	8.9		33
1 piece				
Yellow, homemade	283	12.4		329
1 piece				

CAKE ICING

	CALORIES	FAT (g)	CHOLESTEROL (mg)	SODIUM (mg)
Chocolate fudge, Pillsbury	150	6.5		82
For $1/_{12}$ cake				
Vanilla, Pillsbury	160	6.1		74
For $1/_{12}$ cake				

COOKIES

	CALORIES	FAT (g)	CHOLESTEROL (mg)	SODIUM (mg)
Animal crackers	112	2.4		79
10 cookies				
Chocolate chip, Chips Ahoy	130	6		110
2 cookies				
Chocolate chip, homemade	46	2.7		21
1 cookie				
Fig bars	53	1		45
1 bar				

	CALORIES	FAT (g)	CHOLESTEROL (mg)	SODIUM (mg)
Gingersnaps	59	1.2		80
2 cookies				
Oatmeal, homemade	62	2.6		45
1 cookie				
Peanut butter, Almost Home	140	7		95
2 cookies				

MISCELLANEOUS

	CALORIES	FAT (g)	CHOLESTEROL (mg)	SODIUM (mg)
Apple brown betty, homemade	325	7.5		329
1 cup				
Danish pastry	161	8.8		161
1 piece				
Doughnut, old-fashioned, Hostess	180	10	9	220
1 doughnut				
Doughnut, powdered-sugar, Hostess	110	5	6	140
1 doughnut				
Popsicle	65	0		
1 bar				
Turnover, apple, Pillsbury	170	7.8		320
1 turnover				

ICE CREAM, SHERBET, FROZEN YOGURT

	CALORIES	FAT (g)	CHOLESTEROL (mg)	SODIUM (mg)
Chocolate, Häagen-Dazs	280	17		120
½ cup				
Strawberry, Häagen-Dazs	270	16		80
½ cup				
Vanilla, Häagen-Dazs (10 percent fat)	269	14.3	59	116
1 cup				

	CALORIES	FAT (g)	CHOLESTEROL (mg)	SODIUM (mg)
Sherbet, fruit flavors, Land o' Lakes	127	1.7	4	24
¼ cup				
Yogurt, frozen, Honey Hill Farms	118	3.5		
4.5 fl. oz.				

PIE

Apple, homemade	282	11.9		181
⅛ pie				
Blueberry, homemade	286	12.7		316
⅛ pie				
Chocolate cream, homemade	301	17.3		311
⅛ pie				
Pecan, homemade	431	23.6		228
⅛ pie				

EGGS AND EGG SUBSTITUTES

CHICKEN EGGS[12]

Boiled, hard or soft	79	5.6	274	69
1 large				
Fried	83	6.4	246	144
1 large				
Omelette	95	7.1	248	155
With 1 large egg				
White, fresh or frozen	16	0	0	50
White of 1 large egg				
Yolk, fresh or frozen	63	5.6	272	8
Yolk of 1 large egg				

[12]Not recommended. Information included for comparison.

	CALORIES	FAT (g)	CHOLESTEROL (mg)	SODIUM (mg)
EGG SUBSTITUTES				
Frozen[13]	96	6.7	1	120
¹⁄₄ cup				
Liquid[14]	40	1.6	0	33
1¹⁄₂ fl. oz.				
Egg Beaters, Fleischmann's	25	0	0	80
¹⁄₄ cup				

FAST FOODS[15]

	CALORIES	FAT (g)	CHOLESTEROL (mg)	SODIUM (mg)
BURGER KING ®				
Cheeseburger, double, with bacon	510	31	104	728
Hamburger, Whopper	640	41	94	842
Hamburger, Whopper, double beef	950	60		
with cheese				
Shake, chocolate	320	12		202
1 medium				

	CALORIES	FAT (g)	CHOLESTEROL (mg)	SODIUM (mg)
KENTUCKY FRIED CHICKEN ®				
Chicken, fried				
1 piece				
Breast, extra crispy	354	23.7	66	797
Drumstick, extra crispy	173	10.9	65	346
Thigh, extra crispy	371	26.3	121	766
Wing, extra crispy	218	15.6	63	437

[13]Contains egg white, corn oil, and non-fat dry-milk solids. Not recommended. Information included for comparison.
[14]Contains egg white, hydrogenated soybean oil, and soy protein.
[15]Not recommended. Information included for comparison.

	CALORIES	FAT (g)	CHOLESTEROL (mg)	SODIUM (mg)
McDONALD'S ®				
Big Mac	570	35	83	979
Chicken McNuggets	323	21.3	73	512
1 serving				
Egg McMuffin	340	15.8	259	885
Filet-o-fish	435	25.7	45	799
Quarter Pounder, with cheese	525	31.6	107	1,220
Shake, chocolate	383	9	30	300
PIZZA				
Cheese	290	8.6	56	698
1 piece				

FISH, SHELLFISH, AND CRUSTACEA

	CALORIES	FAT (g)	CHOLESTEROL (mg)	SODIUM (mg)
Bass, striped, raw	82	2	68	59
3 oz.				
Bluefish, raw	105	3.6	50	51
3 oz.				
Clams, raw	63	.8	29	47
3 oz.				
Cod, broiled	89	0.7	47	66
3 oz.				
Crab, steamed	87	1.5		237
3 oz.				
Flounder, sole, baked	202	8.2		237
3 1/2 oz.				
Haddock, broiled	95	0.8	63	74
3 oz.				
Halibut, broiled	119	2.5	35	59
3 oz.				

	CALORIES	FAT (g)	CHOLESTEROL (mg)	SODIUM (mg)
Herring, Atlantic, broiled *3 oz.*	172	9.9	65	98
Lobster, northern, raw *3 oz.*	77	0.8	81	
Mackerel, Atlantic, broiled fillet *3 oz.*	223	15.1	64	71
Mussels, blue, raw *3 oz.*	73	1.9	24	243
Ocean perch, Atlantic, raw *3 oz.*	80	1.4	36	64
Oysters, eastern, raw *6 medium*	58	2.1	46	94
Perch, raw *3 oz.*	77	0.8	76	52
Roe, mixed species, raw *1 oz.*	39	1.8	105	
Salmon, pink, raw *3 oz.*	99	2.9	44	57
Sardines, Pacific, canned in tomato sauce *1 sardine*	68	4.6	23	157
Scallops, raw *3 oz. (6 large or 14 small)*	75	0.6	28	137
Shrimp, raw *3 oz. (12 large)*	90	1.5	130	126
Sole, fillet *1 serving*	80	0.8		162
Swordfish, raw *3 oz.*	103	3.4	33	76
Trout, rainbow, raw *3 oz.*	100	2.9	48	23

	CALORIES	FAT (g)	CHOLESTEROL (mg)	SODIUM (mg)
Tuna albacore, raw, Starkist	100	5	20	310
2 oz.				
Tuna, yellowfin, raw	92	0.8	38	31
3 oz.				

FLOUR

	CALORIES	FAT (g)	CHOLESTEROL (mg)	SODIUM (mg)
Barley flour, pearled light	698	2		6
1 cup				
Bisquick, mix, General Mills	240	8		700
½ cup (2 oz.)				
Corn meal, white or yellow, enriched, dry, Quaker/Aunt Jemima	102	0.5		1
3 tbsp. (1 oz.)				
Rye flour, medium, Pillsbury's Best	400	2.2		5
1 cup				
Wheat flour, all-purpose, enriched	499	1.4		3
1 cup				
Whole-wheat flour	400	2.4		4
1 cup				

FRUITS

	CALORIES	FAT (g)	CHOLESTEROL (mg)	SODIUM (mg)
Apple, raw, with skin	81	0.5	0	1
1 medium				
Applesauce, canned, unsweetened	53	0.1		2
½ cup				
Apricots, raw	51	0.4	0	1
3 medium				

	CALORIES	FAT (g)	CHOLESTEROL (mg)	SODIUM (mg)
Banana, raw	105	0.6	0	1
1 medium				
Blueberries, raw	82	0.6	0	9
1 cup				
Canteloupe, raw	57	0.4	0	14
1 cup pieces				
Cherries, sweet, raw	49	0.7	0	0
10 cherries				
Cranberries, raw	46	0.2	0	1
1 cup whole				
Figs, dried	477	2.2	0	20
10 figs				
Grapefruit, pink and red	37	0.1	0	0
½ medium				
Grapes, American (slip-skin), raw	58	0.3	0	2
1 cup				
Honeydew melon, raw	33	0.3		12
¼ cup				
Kiwifruit, raw	46	0.3		4
1 medium				
Lemon, raw	17	0.2	0	1
1 medium				
Lime, raw	20	0.1	0	1
1 medium				
Mango, raw	135	0.6	0	4
1 medium				
Nectarine, raw	67	0.6	0	0
1 medium				
Orange, navel, raw	65	0.1	0	1
1 medium				

	CALORIES	FAT (g)	CHOLESTEROL (mg)	SODIUM (mg)
Peach, raw	37	0.1	0	0
1 medium				
Pear, raw	98	0.7	0	1
1 medium				
Pineapple, raw	77	0.7	0	1
1 cup pieces				
Plum, raw	36	0.4	0	0
1 medium				
Prunes	201	0.4	0	3
10 prunes				
Raisins, seedless	300	0.5	0	12
⅔ cup				
Raspberries, raw	61	0.7	0	0
1 cup				
Strawberries, raw	45	0.6	0	2
1 cup				
Tangerine, raw	37	0.2	0	1
1 medium				
Watermelon, raw	50	0.7	0	3
1 cup				

GRAIN PRODUCTS (BREAD, CRACKERS, PASTAS, ETC.)

BREAD

Bagel	163	1.4		198
1 bagel				
Biscuits, from mix	93	3.3		262
1 biscuit				
French or Vienna	70	1	0	138
1 slice				
Mixed grain	64	0.9		103
1 slice				

	CALORIES	FAT (g)	CHOLESTEROL (mg)	SODIUM (mg)
Raisin	70	1		94
1 slice				
Rye, American	66	0.9		174
1 slice				
Rye, pumpernickel	82	0.8		173
1 slice				
Sourdough, DiCarlo	70	1	0	140
1 slice				
Wheat[16]	61	1	0	129
1 slice				
White	64	0.9		123
1 slice				
Whole-wheat	61	1.1		159
1 slice				

CRACKERS

	CALORIES	FAT (g)	CHOLESTEROL (mg)	SODIUM (mg)
Cheese	81	4.9		180
5 pieces				
Graham	60	1.5		66
2 squares				
Oyster	33	1		83
10 crackers				
Ritz	70	4		120[17]
4 crackers				
Rye-Krisp, sesame	60	1.4		148
2 triple crackers				
Saltines	26	0.6		80
2 crackers				

[16]Made with white enriched flour and colored brown; not the same as whole-wheat bread.
[17]Low-sodium Ritz crackers contain 60 mg sodium.

	CALORIES	FAT (g)	CHOLESTEROL (mg)	SODIUM (mg)
Triscuits	60	2		90[18]
3 crackers				
Wheat Thins, Nabisco	70	3		120[19]
8 crackers				
MUFFINS				
Blueberry, from mix	126	4.3		200
1 muffin				
Bran, homemade	112	5.1		168
1 muffin				
Corn, with enriched cornmeal, homemade	126	4		192
1 muffin				
PASTAS				
Macaroni, enriched, cooked	159	0.7	0	1
1 cup				
Noodles, enriched, cooked	200	2.4	50	3
1 cup				
Spaghetti, enriched, cooked	159	0.7	0	1
1 cup				
MISCELLANEOUS GRAIN PRODUCTS				
Bread crumbs, dry, grated, enriched	392	4.6		736
1 cup				
Croutons	60	3		155
½ oz.				
English muffin	135	1.1	0	364
1 muffin				
French toast, homemade	153	6.7		257
1 slice				

[18]Low-salt Triscuits contain 35 mg sodium.
[19]Low-salt Wheat Thins contain 35 mg sodium.

	CALORIES	FAT (g)	CHOLESTEROL (mg)	SODIUM (mg)
Pancakes, plain, homemade	62	1.9		115

1 4-inch pancake

JUICES, FRUIT AND VEGETABLE

	CALORIES	FAT (g)	CHOLESTEROL (mg)	SODIUM (mg)
Apple juice, from frozen concentrate	111	0.3	0	17

8 fl. oz.

Cranberry juice cocktail, bottled	147	0.1	0	10

8 fl. oz.

Grape juice, canned or bottled	155	0.2	0	7

8 fl. oz.

Grapefruit juice, canned	93	0.2	0	3

8 fl. oz.

Orange juice, from frozen concentrate	112	0.1	0	2

8 fl. oz.

Pineapple juice, canned	139	0.2	0	2

8 fl. oz.

Tomato juice cocktail, canned	51	0.2		486

8 fl. oz.

Vegetable juice cocktail, canned, V-8, Campbell's	37	0.1		593

6 fl. oz.

MEATS[20]

BEEF

	CALORIES	FAT (g)	CHOLESTEROL (mg)	SODIUM (mg)
Brisket, separable lean and fat, braised	391	32.4	93	61

3.5 oz.

[20]Most meats are too high in fat and cholesterol.

	CALORIES	FAT (g)	CHOLESTEROL (mg)	SODIUM (mg)
Corned beef, cured brisket, cooked	251	19	98	1,134
3.5 oz.				
Flank steak, lean only, broiled	243	15	70	83
3.5 oz.				
Frankfurter, beef	180	16.3	35	585
1 frank (8 per 1-pound package)				
Ground, extra-lean, broiled	256	16.3	84	70
3.5 oz.				
Ground, lean, broiled	272	18.5	87	77
3.5 oz.				
Ground, regular, broiled	289	20.7	90	83
3.5 oz.				
Rib eye, separable lean, broiled	225	11.6	80	69
3.5 oz.				
Short loin porterhouse steak, separable lean, broiled	218	10.8	80	66
3.5 oz.				
Short loin tenderloin, separable lean, broiled	204	9.3	84	63
3.5 oz.				
Short loin wedge-bone sirloin, separable lean, broiled	208	8.7	89	66
3.5 oz.				

LAMB

	CALORIES	FAT (g)	CHOLESTEROL (mg)	SODIUM (mg)
Leg, separable lean, roasted	158	6		60
3 oz.				
Loin chop, separable lean, broiled	92	3.7	39	34
1 chop				

	CALORIES	FAT (g)	CHOLESTEROL (mg)	SODIUM (mg)
PORK				
Bacon, cured, broiled or fried	109	9.4	16	303
3 medium pieces				
Ham, cured, lean, canned	120	4.6	38	1,255
3.5 oz.				
Sausage, fresh, cooked	48	4.1	11	168
1 link				
Sirloin, separable lean, roasted	236	13.2	90	62
3.5 oz.				
Spareribs, separable lean and fat, braised	397	30.3	121	93
3.5 oz.				
Tenderloin, separable lean, roasted	166	4.8	93	67
3.5 oz.				
VEAL				
Loin, braised or broiled	199	11.4		55
3 oz.				
Round with rump, braised or broiled	184	9.4		56
3 oz.				
ORGAN MEATS				
Brains, beef, pan-fried	196	15.8	1995	158
3.5 oz.				
Kidneys, beef, simmered	144	3.4	387	134
3.5 oz.				
Liver, beef, braised	161	4.9	389	70
3.5 oz.				

	CALORIES	FAT (g)	CHOLESTEROL (mg)	SODIUM (mg)

MILK AND YOGURT[21]

COW MILK

	CALORIES	FAT (g)	CHOLESTEROL (mg)	SODIUM (mg)
Buttermilk, cultured	99	2.2	9	257
1 cup				
Low-fat, 1 percent fat	102	2.6	10	123
1 cup				
Low-fat, 2 percent fat	121	4.7	18	122
1 cup				
Skim	86	0.4	4	126
1 cup				
Whole, 3.7 percent fat	157	8.9	35	119
1 cup				

OTHER

Goat milk	168	10.1	28	122
1 cup				
Soy milk	79	4.6	0	30
1 cup				

YOGURT (FROM COW MILK)

Plain

Low-fat with nfdm[22]	144	3.5	14	159
1 cup				
Skim with nfdm[23]	127	0.4	4	174
1 cup				
Whole milk	139	7.4	29	105
1 cup				

[21]Only non-fat and 1 percent fat dairy products are recommended.

[22] Non-fat dry-milk solids.

[23] Non-fat dry-milk solids.

	CALORIES	FAT (g)	CHOLESTEROL (mg)	SODIUM (mg)
Flavored				
Fruit-flavored, low-fat with nfdm[24]	225	2.6	10	121
1 cup				
Fruit-flavored, whole milk, Yoplait[25]	190	4		105
6 fl. oz.				

NUTS[26]

	CALORIES	FAT (g)	CHOLESTEROL (mg)	SODIUM (mg)
Almonds, dry-roasted, unsalted	167	14.7	0	3[27]
1 oz.				
Brazil nuts	186	18.8	0	0
1 oz. (8 medium)				
Cashews, dry-roasted, unsalted	163	13.2	0	4[28]
1 oz.				
Chestnuts, Chinese, raw	64	0.3	0	1
1 oz.				
Chestnuts, European	60	0.6	0	1
1 oz. (2½ nuts)				
Coconut, raw	159	15.1	0	9
1 piece (2 × 2 × ½ inches)				
Mixed, dry-roasted, unsalted	169	14.6	0	3[29]
1 oz.				
Peanut butter, creamy	95	8.2	0	3[30]
1 tbsp.				

[24] Non-fat dry-milk solids.
[25] Values are averages for nine flavors.
[26] Not recommended (except for chestnuts). Information included for comparison.
[27] If salt is added, sodium is 218 mg.
[28] If salt is added, sodium is 179 mg.
[29] If salt is added, sodium is 187 mg.
[30] If salt is added, sodium is 131 mg.

	CALORIES	FAT (g)	CHOLESTEROL (mg)	SODIUM (mg)
Peanuts, dry-roasted, salted	164	13.9	0	228[31]
1 oz.				
Pecans, dried	190	19.2	0	0
1 oz. (31 large nuts)				
Pistachios, dry-roasted	172	15	0	2[32]
1 oz.				
Walnuts, black, dried	172	16.1	0	0
1 oz.				

POULTRY

CHICKEN

Broilers or fryers, light meat

	CALORIES	FAT	CHOLESTEROL	SODIUM
With skin, roasted	222	10.9	84	75
3½ oz.				
Without skin, roasted	173	4.5	85	77
3½ oz.				
Without skin, stewed	159	4	77	65
3½ oz.				

Broilers or fryers, dark meat

With skin, roasted	253	15.8	91	87
3½ oz.				
Without skin, roasted	205	9.7	93	93
3½ oz.				
Without skin, stewed	192	9	88	74
3½ oz.				

Broilers or fryers, breast

Without skin, stewed	144	2.9	73	59
½ breast				

[31]If unsalted, sodium is 2 mg.
[32]If salt is added, sodium is 218 mg.

	CALORIES	FAT (g)	CHOLESTEROL (mg)	SODIUM (mg)
Broilers or fryers, drumstick				
Without skin, stewed	76	2.5	41	42
1 drumstick				
Broilers or fryers, thigh				
Without skin, roasted	109	5.7	49	46
1 thigh				
Roasters				
Light meat without skin, roasted	153	4.1	75	51
3½ oz.				
Stewers				
Light meat without skin, stewed	213	8	70	58
3½ oz.				
TURKEY				
Ground, cooked, Louis Rich	61	3.5	24	30
1 oz.				
Light meat with skin, roasted	197	8.3	76	63
3½ oz.				
Light meat without skin, roasted	157	3.2	69	64
3½ oz.				
Sausage, breakfast, cooked, Louis Rich	60	3.9	23	200
1 oz.				

SALAD DRESSINGS[33]

REGULAR
Blue cheese	77	8		
1 tbsp.				

[33] Only oil-free dressings are recommended.

	CALORIES	FAT (g)	CHOLESTEROL (mg)	SODIUM (mg)
French	67	6.4		214
1 tbsp.				
Italian	69	7.1		116
1 tbsp.				
Oil and vinegar, homemade	72	8		0
1 tbsp.				
Russian	76	7.8		133
1 tbsp.				
Thousand Island	59	5.6		109
1 tbsp.				

LOW-CALORIE

	CALORIES	FAT (g)	CHOLESTEROL (mg)	SODIUM (mg)
French	22	0.9	1	128
1 tbsp.				
Italian	16	1.5	1	118
1 tbsp.				
Russian	23	0.7	1	141
1 tbsp.				
Thousand Island	24	1.6	2	153
1 tbsp.				

SAUCES

	CALORIES	FAT (g)	CHOLESTEROL (mg)	SODIUM (mg)
Soy sauce (tamari)	35	0.1	0	3,240
¼ cup				
Spaghetti sauce, canned	272	11.9	0	1,236
1 cup				
Tartar sauce, Hellmann's	70	8.1	5	220
1 tbsp.				
Worcestershire sauce, Heinz	11			234
1 tbsp.				

	CALORIES	FAT (g)	CHOLESTEROL (mg)	SODIUM (mg)
SOUPS				
CANNED				
Beef broth or bouillon	16	0.5	0	782
1 cup				
Black-bean, made with water	116	1.5	0	1,198
1 cup				
Chicken noodle, made with water	75	2.5	7	1,107
1 cup				
Clam chowder, New England, made with water	95	2.9	5	914
1 cup				
Gazpacho, Campbell's	41	0.2		585
1 cup				
Minestrone, made with water	83	2.5		911
1 cup				
Onion, made with water	57	1.7	0	1,053
1 cup				
Tomato, made with water	86	1.9	0	872
1 cup				
Turkey noodle, made with water	69	2	5	815
1 cup				
Vegetable, vegetarian, made with water	72	1.9	0	823
1 cup				
DEHYDRATED, RECONSTITUTED				
Beef broth or bouillon	19	0.7	1	1,358
1 cup				
Chicken broth or bouillon	21	1.1	1	1,484
1 cup				

	CALORIES	FAT (g)	CHOLESTEROL (mg)	SODIUM (mg)
Chicken noodle	53	1.2	3	1,284
1 cup				
Clam chowder, New England	95	3.7	1	745
1 cup				
Minestrone	79	1.7	3	1,026
1 cup				
Mushroom	96	4.9	1	1,019
1 cup				
Onion	28	.6	0	848
1 cup				
Tomato	102	2.4	1	943
1 cup				

SPREADS: BUTTER, MARGARINE, MAYONNAISE [34]

Butter	108	12.2	33	123
1 tbsp.				
Margarine, stick, corn	34	3.8		44[35]
1 tsp.				
Mayonnaise, safflower and soybean	99	11		78
1 tbsp.				

SUGARS, SYRUPS, JAMS, JELLIES, AND OTHER SWEET FOODS

Honey	64	0		1
1 tbsp.				
Jam, all varieties	54	0		2
1 tbsp.				

[34] Not recommended. Information included for comparison.
[35] Unsalted stick margarine contains 1 mg sodium.

	CALORIES	FAT (g)	CHOLESTEROL (mg)	SODIUM (mg)
Jelly, all varieties	49	0		3
1 tbsp.				

SUGAR

	CALORIES	FAT (g)	CHOLESTEROL (mg)	SODIUM (mg)
Brown	541	0		44
1 cup not packed				
White, granulated	770	0		2
1 cup				
Maple syrup	50	0		0
1 tbsp.				

VEGETABLES AND LEGUMES

ALFALFA SEEDS

	CALORIES	FAT (g)	CHOLESTEROL (mg)	SODIUM (mg)
Sprouted, raw	10	0.2	0	2
1 cup				

ARTICHOKE

	CALORIES	FAT (g)	CHOLESTEROL (mg)	SODIUM (mg)
Boiled	53	0.2	0	79
1 medium				

ASPARAGUS

	CALORIES	FAT (g)	CHOLESTEROL (mg)	SODIUM (mg)
Boiled	22	0.3	0	4
½ cup (6 spears)				

AVOCADO

	CALORIES	FAT (g)	CHOLESTEROL (mg)	SODIUM (mg)
Raw (CA)	306	30	0	21
1 medium				

BEANS

	CALORIES	FAT (g)	CHOLESTEROL (mg)	SODIUM (mg)
Baked, canned, Campbell's	248	4		1,037
7.9 oz				

	CALORIES	FAT (g)	CHOLESTEROL (mg)	SODIUM (mg)
Black, boiled	227	0.9	0	1
1 cup				
Kidney, red, boiled	225	0.9	0	4
1 cup				
Kidney, red, canned	216	0.9	0	873
1 cup				
Lima, green, boiled	217	0.7	0	4
1 cup				
Refried, canned	270	2.7		1,071
1 cup				

BEETS

Boiled	26	0	0	42
½ cup slices				

BROCCOLI

Boiled	23	0.2	0	8
½ cup				
Raw, chopped	12	0.2	0	12
½ cup				

BRUSSELS SPROUTS

Boiled	30	0.4	0	17
½ cup (4 sprouts)				

CABBAGE

Green, raw, shredded	8	0.1	0	6
½ cup				
Red, raw, shredded	10	0.1	0	4
½ cup				

	CALORIES	FAT (g)	CHOLESTEROL (mg)	SODIUM (mg)
CARROTS				
Boiled	35	0.1	0	52
½ cup slices				
Raw	31	0.1	0	25
1 medium				
CAULIFLOWER				
Boiled	15	0.1	0	4
½ cup pieces				
Raw	12	0.1	0	7
½ cup pieces				
CELERY				
Raw	6	0.1	0	35
1 stalk (7.5 inches long)				
CHICK-PEAS (GARBANZO BEANS)				
Canned	285	2.7	0	718
1 cup				
CORN, YELLOW				
Canned	66	0.8	0	
½ cup				
Frozen, boiled	67	0.1	0	4
½ cup				
CUCUMBER				
Raw	7	0.1		1
½ cup slices				

	CALORIES	FAT (g)	CHOLESTEROL (mg)	SODIUM (mg)
EGGPLANT				
Boiled	13	0.1	0	2
½ cup				
Raw	11	0	0	1
½ cup pieces				
GREEN BEANS, FRENCH-STYLE				
Boiled	22	.2	0	2
½ cup				
Canned, Heinz, no salt added	16	0.1		1
3½ oz.				
Frozen	18	0.1	0	9
½ cup				
LENTILS				
Boiled	231	0.7	0	4
1 cup				
LETTUCE, RAW				
Iceberg	3	0	0	2
1 leaf				
Romaine (cos), shredded	4	0.1	0	2
½ cup				
MUSHROOMS				
Raw	9	0.2	0	1
½ cup pieces				
ONIONS				
Boiled, chopped	29	0.2		8
½ cup				
Raw, chopped	27	0.2	0	2
½ cup				

	CALORIES	FAT (g)	CHOLESTEROL (mg)	SODIUM (mg)
PARSLEY				
Raw, chopped	10	0.1	0	12
½ cup				
PARSNIPS				
Boiled	63	0.2	0	8
½ cup slices				
PEAS				
Boiled	67	0.2	0	2
½ cup				
Raw	63	0.3	0	4
½ cup				
PEPPERS, GREEN AND RED, SWEET				
Raw	12	0.2	0	2
½ cup chopped				
POTATOES, WHITE				
Baked with skin	220	0.2	0	16
1 med. potato				
Boiled without skin	116	0.1	0	7
1 med. potato				
French fried, frozen, heated[36]	111	4.4	0	15
10 pieces				
Hash brown, homemade[37]	163	10.9		19
10 pieces				

[36] Not recommended due to high fat content, but information included for comparison.
[37] Not recommended due to high fat content, but information included for comparison.

	CALORIES	FAT (g)	CHOLESTEROL (mg)	SODIUM (mg)
RADISHES				
Raw	7	0.2	0	11
10 radishes				
RICE				
Brown, cooked	232	1.2	0	0[38]
1 cup				
White, enriched, cooked	223	0.2		0[39]
1 cup				
SPINACH				
Boiled, chopped	21	0.2	0	63
½ cup				
Raw, chopped	6	0.1	0	22
½ cup				
SQUASH				
Summer, all varieties, boiled	18	0.3	0	1
½ cup slices				
Winter, all varieties, baked	39	0.6	0	1
½ cup cubes				
SWEET POTATOES				
Baked	118	0.1	0	12
1 med. sweet potato				
TOFU				
Raw, firm	183	11	0	17
½ cup				
TOMATOES, RED				
Canned, whole, peeled	24	0.3	0	195
½ cup				

[38]If salt is added as specified on package, sodium is 550 mg.
[39]If salt is added as specified on package, sodium is 767 mg.

	CALORIES	FAT (g)	CHOLESTEROL (mg)	SODIUM (mg)
Raw	24	0.3	0	10
1 tomato				
Tomato paste, canned	110	1.2	0	86[40]
½ cup				
Tomato puree	102	0.3	0	49[41]
1 cup				

TURNIPS

Boiled	14	0.1	0	39
½ cup cubes				

VEGETABLE OILS [42]

Coconut oil	120	13.6		
1 tbsp.				
Corn oil	120	13.6		
1 tbsp.				
Olive oil	119	13.5		0
1 tbsp.				
Palm-kernel oil	120	13.6		
1 tbsp.				
Peanut oil	119	13.5		0
1 tbsp.				
Safflower oil	120	13.6		
1 tbsp.				
Soybean oil	120	13.6		0
1 tbsp.				

[40]If salt is added, sodium is 1,035 mg.
[41]If salt is added, sodium is 998 mg.
[42] Not recommended (although olive oil may be used in limited quantities). Information included for comparison.

APPENDIX 3

Charts for the Kurzweil Challenge

The Kurzweil Challenge is a ten-step program that enables you to try out the principles of the 10% solution on a trial basis, to determine for yourself the impact it can have on your immediate health, cholesterol levels, weight, and sense of well-being. It also allows you to test the assertion that your tastes and attitudes toward food can change. The Kurzweil Challenge is described in chapter 9.

These charts are intended to be used in this program. The Baseline Chart is to be used at the beginning of the program to establish your initial state. This is essentially the "before" picture of your health. After a one-month period of gradual change and then a two-month period of full compliance with the guidelines of the 10% solution you should fill out a copy of the Progress Chart to evaluate the impact that this three-month period has had. Assuming that you subsequently make a long-term commitment to this life-style, I suggest that you fill out another Progress Chart after another nine months (which is twelve months from the beginning of the program). The Weekly Chart should be filled out each week for at least the first three months to track basic eating patterns and exercise. You should copy these charts onto separate pieces of paper rather than write in the book, so that multiple copies of these blank forms can be made.

It is strongly suggested that you read the full contents of this book, and in particular the chapter on the Kurzweil Challenge, before beginning this program. I also want to emphasize step 2 of the Kurzweil Challenge, which is to consult with your physician before attempting any program of dietary change or exercise to make sure that your individual health concerns and issues will be appropriately monitored if necessary. This is particularly important if you have such health conditions as heart disease, advanced atherosclerosis or angina pain, diabetes, hypertension, or any other serious disease or condition.

BASELINE CHART
(FOR STEP 3)

I. GENERAL DATA

1. Name: _____

2. Sex: _____

3. Age: _____

4. Date: _____

5. Physician: _____

6. Date on which physician was consulted on this dietary and exercise program:

_____

II. LIPID (BLOOD) LEVELS

7. Total cholesterol: _____

8. HDL cholesterol: _____

9. Ratio of total cholesterol divided by HDL cholesterol: _____

10. LDL cholesterol: _____

11. Triglycerides: _____

12. Fasting glucose: _____

13. Any abnormal levels from kidney, liver, and thyroid tests: _____

_____

_____

_____

III. OTHER HEALTH DATA

14. Blood pressure: _____

15. Weight: _____

16. Percentage body fat: _____

17. Chest measurement: _____

18. Waist measurement:_____

19. Hips measurement:_____

IV. MAJOR HEALTH PROBLEMS

20. Any indication or history of heart disease: _____

_____

_____

21. Family history of heart disease:_____

_____

_____

22. Angina pain:_____

23. Type I diabetes:_____

24. Type II diabetes: _____

25. Diabetes medication (if any):_____

26. Hypertension: _____

27. Hypertension medication (if any):_____

28. History of cancer: _____

_____

_____

29. Other major health disease, condition, or issue: _____

_____

_____

V. OTHER HEALTH ISSUES

30. Gastrointestinal discomforts or problems: _____

_____

31. Regularity: _____

_____

_____

32. Aches or pains: _____

_____

33. Complexion problems: _____

_____

34. Other (minor) health issues: _____

_____

VI. SUBJECTIVE EVALUATION

35. How do you feel? _____

_____

_____

_____

36. How well do you sleep?_____

_____

_____

37. Characterize your mood: _____

_____

_____

38. Characterize your general outlook:_____

_____

_____

PROGRESS CHART
(FOR STEP 7, AFTER TWO MONTHS OF CAREFUL COMPLIANCE, AND FOR STEP 9, AFTER ONE YEAR)

I. GENERAL DATA

1. Name: _____

2. Date: _____

3. Date of follow-up examination: _____

II. LIPID (BLOOD) LEVELS

4. Total cholesterol:_____

5. HDL cholesterol:_____

6. Ratio of total cholesterol divided by HDL cholesterol: _____

7. LDL cholesterol: _____

8. Triglycerides:_____

9. Fasting glucose: _____

10. Any abnormal levels from kidney, liver, and thyroid tests:_____

_____

_____

III. OTHER HEALTH DATA

11. Blood pressure: _____

12. Weight:_____

13. Percentage body fat: _____

14. Chest measurement:_____

15. Waist measurement:_____

16. Hips measurement:_____

IV. MAJOR HEALTH PROBLEMS

17. Any improvement in angina pain? _____

_____

18. Any improvement in diabetic condition?_____

_____

19. Any changes in diabetes medication (if any)? _____

_____

20. Any improvement in hypertension? _____

_____

21. Any changes in hypertension medication (if any)? _____

_____

22. Any changes or improvement in other major health disease, condition, issue?___

_____

_____

_____

V. OTHER HEALTH ISSUES

23. Any changes in gastrointestinal functioning? _____

_____

24. Any changes in regularity?_____

_____

25. Any changes in aches or pains? _____

_____

26. Any changes in complexion? _____

_____

27. Other (minor) health issues: _____

_____

VI. SUBJECTIVE EVALUATION

28. How do you feel? _____

_____

_____

29. Changes in alertness and/or energy level:_____

_____

30. How well do you sleep?_____

_____

31. Characterize your mood: _____

_____

32. Characterize your outlook:_____

_____

33. Any other changes or improvements from the Baseline Chart or the last

Progress Chart?_____

_____

_____

VII. ENJOYMENT OF DIET

34. Describe how you like/dislike the diet: _____

_____

_____

35. Do you miss foods you used to eat? _____

_____

_____

36. How well have you adapted to the guidelines of the 10% solution? _____

_____

_____

37. Have you noted changes in your tastes?_____

_____

_____

_____

38. Do you find the diet satisfying? _____

_____

_____

39. Are you ever hungry? _____

_____

_____

WEEKLY CHART

Name:_____

Date (for Monday):_____

DAY	CALORIES	FAT GRAMS	CALORIES EXPENDED IN EXERCISE
Monday	_____	_____	_____
Tuesday	_____	_____	_____
Wednesday	_____	_____	_____
Thursday	_____	_____	_____
Friday	_____	_____	_____
Saturday	_____	_____	_____
Sunday	_____	_____	_____
Total	_____	_____	_____
Average	_____	_____	_____

(divide total by 7)

Percentage of calories from fat (multiply fat grams by 9 and divide by calories):

_____

APPENDIX 4

Body Fat Charts

DETERMINING PERCENTAGE BODY FAT FOR WOMEN

1. Determine constants *A, B,* and *C* from the tables below.
2. Your percentage of body fat = $A + B - C$.

HIPS (AT WIDEST POINT)		ABDOMEN (AT LEVEL OF NAVEL)		HEIGHT	
INCHES	CONSTANT A	INCHES	CONSTANT B	INCHES	CONSTANT C
30	33.48	20	14.22	55	33.52
31	34.87	21	14.93	56	34.13
32	36.27	22	15.64	57	34.74
33	37.67	23	16.35	58	35.35
34	39.06	24	17.06	59	35.96
35	40.46	25	17.78	60	36.57
36	41.86	26	18.49	61	37.18
37	43.25	27	19.20	62	37.79
38	44.65	28	19.91	63	38.40
39	46.05	29	20.62	64	39.01
40	47.44	30	21.33	65	39.62
41	48.84	31	22.04	66	40.23
42	50.24	32	22.75	67	40.84
43	51.64	33	23.46	68	41.45
44	53.03	34	24.18	69	42.06
45	54.43	35	24.89	70	42.67
46	55.83	36	25.60	71	43.28
47	57.22	37	26.31	72	43.89
48	58.62	38	27.02	73	44.50
49	60.02	39	27.73	74	45.11
50	61.42	40	28.44	75	45.72
51	62.81	41	29.15	76	46.32
52	64.21	42	29.87	77	46.93
53	65.61	43	30.58	78	47.54
54	67.00	44	31.29	79	48.15
55	68.40	45	32.00	80	48.76
56	69.80	46	32.71	81	49.37
57	71.19	47	33.42	82	49.98
58	72.59	48	34.13	83	50.59
59	73.99	49	34.84	84	51.20
60	75.39	50	35.56	85	51.81

From D. Remington, G. Fisher, and E. Parent, How to Lower Your Fat Thermostat, © Copyright 1983 by Vitality House International, Inc. All Rights Reserved. Used by Permission.

DETERMINING PERCENTAGE OF BODY FAT FOR MEN

1. Determine your abdominal circumference at the level of your navel.
2. Measure your wrist circumference in front of the wrist bones where the wrist bends.
3. Subtract wrist circumference from abdominal circumference.
4. Determine your weight.
5. Look up your percentage of body fat in the table below.

ABDOMINAL CIRCUMFERENCE MINUS WRIST CIRCUMFERENCE (INCHES)

WEIGHT	22	22.5	23	23.5	24	24.5	25	25.5	26	26.5	27	27.5	28	28.5
120	4	6	8	10	12	14	16	18	20	21	23	25	27	29
125	4	6	7	9	11	13	15	17	19	20	22	24	26	28
130	3	5	7	9	11	12	14	16	18	20	21	23	25	27
135	3	5	7	8	10	12	13	15	17	19	20	22	24	26
140	3	5	6	8	10	11	13	15	16	18	19	21	23	24
145	3	4	6	7	9	11	12	14	15	17	19	20	22	23
150	2	4	6	7	9	10	12	13	15	16	18	19	21	23
155	2	4	5	7	8	10	11	13	14	16	17	19	20	22
160	2	4	5	6	8	9	11	12	14	15	17	18	19	21
165	2	3	5	6	8	9	10	12	13	15	16	17	19	20
170	2	3	4	6	7	9	10	11	13	14	15	17	18	19
175	2	3	4	6	7	8	10	11	12	13	15	16	17	19
180	1	3	4	5	7	8	9	10	12	13	14	16	17	18
185	1	3	4	5	6	8	9	10	11	13	14	15	16	18
190	1	2	4	5	6	7	8	10	11	12	13	15	16	17
195	1	2	3	5	6	7	8	9	11	12	13	14	15	16
200	1	2	3	4	6	7	8	9	10	11	12	14	15	16
205	1	2	3	4	5	6	8	9	10	11	12	13	14	15
210	1	2	3	4	5	6	7	8	9	11	12	13	14	15
215	1	2	3	4	5	6	7	8	9	10	11	12	13	15
220	0	2	3	4	5	6	7	8	9	10	11	12	13	14
225	0	1	2	3	4	6	7	8	9	10	11	12	13	14
230	0	1	2	3	4	5	6	7	8	9	10	11	12	13
235	0	1	2	3	4	5	6	7	8	9	10	11	12	13
240	0	1	2	3	4	5	6	7	8	9	10	11	12	13
245	0	1	2	3	4	5	6	7	8	9	9	10	11	12
250	0	1	2	3	4	5	6	6	7	8	9	10	11	12
255	0	1	2	3	3	4	5	6	7	8	9	10	11	12
260	0	1	2	2	3	4	5	6	7	8	9	10	10	11
265	0	1	1	2	3	4	5	6	7	8	8	9	10	11
270	0	1	1	2	3	4	5	6	7	7	8	9	10	11
275	0	0	1	2	3	4	5	5	6	7	8	9	10	11
280	0	0	1	2	3	4	4	5	6	7	8	9	9	10
285	0	0	1	2	3	4	4	5	6	7	8	8	9	10
290	0	0	1	2	3	3	4	5	6	7	7	8	9	10
295	0	0	1	2	2	3	4	5	6	6	7	8	9	10
300	0	0	1	2	2	3	4	5	5	6	7	8	9	9

From D. Remington, G. Fisher, and E. Parent, <u>How to Lower Your Fat Thermostat</u>, © Copyright 1983 by Vitality House International, Inc. All Rights Reserved. Used by Permission.

DETERMINING PERCENTAGE OF BODY FAT FOR MEN

ABDOMINAL CIRCUMFERENCE MINUS WRIST CIRCUMFERENCE (INCHES)

WEIGHT	29	29.5	30	30.5	31	31.5	32	32.5	33	33.5	34	34.5	35	35.5	36
120	31	33	35	37	39	41	43	45	47	49	50	52	54	56	58
125	30	32	33	35	37	39	41	43	45	46	48	50	52	54	56
130	28	30	32	34	36	37	39	41	43	44	46	48	50	52	53
135	27	29	31	32	34	36	38	39	41	43	44	46	48	50	51
140	26	28	29	31	33	34	36	38	39	41	43	44	46	48	49
145	25	27	28	30	31	33	35	36	38	39	41	43	44	46	47
150	24	26	27	29	30	32	33	35	36	38	40	41	43	44	46
155	23	25	26	28	29	31	32	34	35	37	38	40	41	43	44
160	22	24	25	27	28	30	31	33	34	35	37	38	40	41	43
165	22	23	24	26	27	29	30	31	33	34	36	37	38	40	41
170	21	22	24	25	26	28	29	30	32	33	34	36	37	39	40
175	20	21	23	24	25	27	28	29	31	32	33	35	36	37	39
180	19	21	22	23	25	26	27	28	30	31	32	34	35	36	37
185	19	20	21	23	24	25	26	28	29	30	31	33	34	35	36
190	18	19	21	22	23	24	26	27	28	29	30	32	33	34	35
195	18	19	20	21	22	24	25	26	27	28	30	31	32	33	34
200	17	18	19	21	22	23	24	25	26	28	29	30	31	32	33
205	17	18	19	20	21	22	23	25	26	27	28	29	30	31	32
210	16	17	18	19	21	22	23	24	25	26	27	28	29	30	32
215	16	17	18	19	20	21	22	23	24	25	26	28	29	30	31
220	15	16	17	18	19	20	22	23	24	25	26	27	28	29	30
225	15	16	17	18	19	20	21	22	23	24	25	26	27	28	29
230	14	15	16	17	18	19	20	21	22	23	24	25	26	27	28
235	14	15	16	17	18	19	20	21	22	23	24	25	26	27	28
240	14	15	16	17	17	18	19	20	21	22	23	24	25	26	27
245	13	14	15	16	17	18	19	20	21	22	23	24	25	26	27
250	13	14	15	16	17	18	18	19	20	21	22	23	24	25	26
255	13	14	14	15	16	17	18	19	20	21	22	23	24	24	25
260	12	13	14	15	16	17	18	19	19	20	21	22	23	24	25
265	12	13	14	15	15	16	17	18	19	20	21	22	22	23	24
270	12	13	13	14	15	16	17	18	19	19	20	21	22	23	24
275	11	12	13	14	15	16	16	17	18	19	20	21	22	22	23
280	11	12	13	14	14	15	16	17	18	19	19	20	21	22	23
285	11	12	12	13	14	15	16	17	17	18	19	20	21	21	22
290	11	11	12	13	14	15	15	16	17	18	19	19	20	21	22
295	10	11	12	13	14	14	15	16	17	17	18	19	20	21	21
300	10	11	12	12	13	14	15	16	16	17	18	19	19	20	21

DETERMINING PERCENTAGE OF BODY FAT FOR MEN

ABDOMINAL CIRCUMFERENCE MINUS WRIST CIRCUMFERENCE (INCHES)

WEIGHT	36.5	37	37.5	38	38.5	39	39.5	40	40.5	41	41.5	42	42.5	43
120	60	62	64	66	68	70	72	74	76	77	79	81	83	85
125	58	59	61	63	65	67	69	71	72	74	76	78	80	82
130	55	57	59	61	62	64	66	68	69	71	73	75	77	78
135	53	55	56	58	60	62	63	65	67	68	70	72	74	75
140	51	53	54	56	58	59	61	63	64	66	68	69	71	72
145	49	51	52	54	55	57	59	60	62	63	65	67	68	70
150	47	49	50	52	53	55	57	58	60	61	63	64	66	67
155	46	47	49	50	52	53	55	56	58	59	61	62	64	65
160	44	46	47	48	50	51	53	54	56	57	59	60	61	63
165	43	44	45	47	48	50	51	52	54	55	57	58	60	61
170	41	43	44	45	47	48	49	51	52	54	55	56	58	59
175	40	41	43	44	45	47	48	49	51	52	53	55	56	57
180	39	40	41	43	44	45	47	48	49	50	52	53	54	56
185	38	39	40	41	43	44	45	46	48	49	50	51	53	54
190	37	38	39	40	41	43	44	45	46	48	49	50	51	52
195	35	37	38	39	40	41	43	44	45	46	47	49	50	51
200	35	36	37	38	39	40	41	43	44	45	46	47	48	50
205	34	35	36	37	38	39	40	41	43	44	45	46	47	48
210	33	34	35	36	37	38	39	40	42	43	44	45	46	47
215	32	33	34	35	36	37	38	39	40	42	43	44	45	46
220	31	32	33	34	35	36	37	38	39	41	42	43	44	45
225	30	31	32	33	34	35	36	37	38	40	41	42	43	44
230	30	31	32	33	34	35	36	37	38	39	40	41	42	43
235	29	30	31	32	33	34	35	36	37	38	39	40	41	42
240	28	29	30	31	32	33	34	35	36	37	38	39	40	41
245	27	28	29	30	31	32	33	34	35	36	37	38	39	40
250	27	28	29	30	31	31	32	33	34	35	36	37	38	39
255	26	27	28	29	30	31	32	33	34	34	35	36	37	38
260	26	27	27	28	29	30	31	32	33	34	35	35	36	37
265	25	26	27	28	29	29	30	31	32	33	34	35	36	36
270	25	25	26	27	28	29	30	31	31	32	33	34	35	36
275	24	25	26	27	27	28	29	30	31	32	32	33	34	35
280	24	24	25	26	27	28	29	29	30	31	32	33	33	34
285	23	24	25	26	26	27	28	29	30	30	31	32	33	34
290	23	23	24	25	26	27	27	28	29	30	31	31	32	33
295	22	23	24	25	25	26	27	28	28	29	30	31	32	32
300	22	22	23	24	25	26	26	27	28	29	29	30	31	32

DETERMINING PERCENTAGE OF BODY FAT FOR MEN

ABDOMINAL CIRCUMFERENCE MINUS WRIST CIRCUMFERENCE (INCHES)

WEIGHT	43.5	44	44.5	45	45.5	46	46.5	47	47.5	48	48.5	49	49.5	50
120	87	89	91	93	95	97	99	99	99	99	99	99	99	99
125	84	85	87	89	91	93	95	96	98	99	99	99	99	99
130	80	82	84	86	87	89	91	93	94	96	98	99	99	99
135	77	79	80	82	84	86	87	89	91	92	94	96	98	99
140	74	76	77	79	81	82	84	86	87	89	91	92	94	96
145	71	73	75	76	78	79	81	83	84	86	87	89	91	92
150	69	70	72	74	75	77	78	80	81	83	84	86	87	89
155	67	68	70	71	73	74	76	77	79	80	82	83	85	86
160	64	66	67	69	70	72	73	75	76	77	79	80	82	83
165	62	64	65	67	68	69	71	72	74	75	76	78	79	81
170	60	62	63	64	66	67	69	70	71	73	74	75	77	78
175	59	60	61	63	64	65	66	68	69	70	72	73	74	76
180	57	58	59	61	62	63	65	66	67	68	70	71	72	74
185	55	56	58	59	60	61	63	64	65	66	68	69	70	71
190	54	55	56	57	58	60	61	62	63	65	66	67	68	69
195	52	53	55	56	57	58	59	60	62	63	64	65	66	68
200	51	52	53	54	55	57	58	59	60	61	62	63	65	66
205	49	51	52	53	54	55	56	57	58	60	61	62	63	64
210	48	49	50	51	53	54	55	56	57	58	59	60	61	62
215	47	48	49	50	51	52	53	54	56	57	58	59	60	61
220	46	47	48	49	50	51	52	53	54	55	56	57	58	59
225	45	46	47	48	49	50	51	52	53	54	55	56	57	58
230	44	45	46	47	48	49	50	51	52	53	54	55	56	57
235	43	44	45	46	47	48	49	50	51	51	52	53	54	55
240	42	43	44	45	46	46	47	48	49	50	51	52	53	54
245	41	42	43	44	44	45	46	47	48	49	50	51	52	53
250	40	41	42	43	44	44	45	46	47	48	49	50	51	52
255	39	40	41	42	43	44	44	45	46	47	48	49	50	51
260	38	39	40	41	42	43	43	44	45	46	47	48	49	50
265	37	38	39	40	41	42	43	43	44	45	46	47	48	49
270	37	37	38	39	40	41	42	43	43	44	45	46	47	48
275	36	37	38	38	39	40	41	42	43	43	44	45	46	47
280	35	36	37	38	38	39	40	41	42	43	43	44	45	46
285	34	35	36	37	38	39	39	40	41	42	43	43	44	45
290	34	35	35	36	37	38	39	39	40	41	42	43	43	44
295	33	34	35	36	36	37	38	39	39	40	41	42	43	43
300	33	33	34	35	36	36	37	38	39	39	40	41	42	43

GLOSSARY

Adrenaline: also known as epinephrine. A hormone secreted by the adrenal gland during stressful situations. Adrenaline stimulates the heart and nervous system, preparing the body for action. Muscles contract, **blood pressure** and heartbeat increase, and the immune and digestive systems shut down.

Adult-onset diabetes: see Type II diabetes mellitus.

Aerobic exercise: exercise that lasts more than ninety seconds, works large muscle groups, and provides oxygen to the muscles. Examples: brisk walking, running, swimming.

Aflatoxin: a **carcinogen** produced by a mold that grows on potatoes, corn, and peanuts.

Anaerobic exercise: high-intensity exercise that does not supply oxygen to the muscles or lasts for less than ninety seconds. Examples: weight training, sprinting, calisthenics.

Aneurysm: a bulging area of a weakened blood vessel, usually an **artery**. An aneurysm often develops as a result of **atherosclerosis**.

Angina: a condition marked by chest pains or pressure due to decreased blood supply to the heart. Angina is often a symptom of advanced **atherosclerosis**.

Aorta: the main and largest **artery** in the human body. The aorta supplies all other arteries with oxygen-rich blood.

Arrhythmia: irregularity or loss of rhythm in the heartbeat.

Artery: a vessel that carries blood from the heart to tissues throughout the body.

Arthritis: inflammation of the joints and other connective tissues.

Atherosclerosis: a progressive disease in which **plaque** forms in the inner lining of arteries, causing narrowing or blockage of **artery** walls.

Balloon angioplasty: a treatment to widen a blood vessel severely narrowed by **plaque**. An inflatable device is inserted past the narrowed part of the blood vessel and is inflated, forcing the narrowed vessel open.

Barbiturate: a group of drugs, used as sedatives and tranquilizers, that depress the central nervous system and respiration, decrease **blood pressure**, and affect heart rate.

Benzodiazepine: a group of tranquilizers and sleeping pills that temporarily reduce anxiety but can produce long-term dependency and depression. Examples of tranquilizers: Valium (diazepam), Librium (chlordiazepoxide), and Tranxene (clorazepate). Examples of sleeping pills: Dalmane (flurazepam) and Halcion (triazolam).

Beta blockers: an agent capable of blocking nerve impulses to special sites in the brain. Beta blockers, which reduce heartbeat rate and the force of the heart's contractions, are prescribed to treat **high blood pressure**.

Bile acid: a fluid produced by the liver and used for fat digestion.

Biofeedback: a technique that teaches control of breathing, heartbeat, and **blood pressure**. Biofeedback is used to combat anxiety disorders and chronic **stress**.

Blood cell aggregation: also known as sludging or sludged blood. A condition in which red blood cells cluster together, often clogging smaller blood vessels.

Blood pressure: the force of blood against **artery** walls. Systolic blood pressure measures the force of blood as the heart contracts and pushes blood through the circulatory system. Diastolic blood pressure measures the force of blood in arteries as the heart relaxes.

Caffeine: a stimulant found in coffee, tea, chocolate, and cola drinks.

Calcium: the body's most abundant **mineral**, most of which is stored in the bones. Calcium aids in nerve and muscle function, building of bones and teeth, and blood clotting. Dietary calcium is found in milk; cheese; sardines; dark-green, leafy vegetables; citrus fruits; and dried beans and peas.

Caloric restriction: a nutritional guideline that limits calorie intake to less than 100 percent (but no less than 95 percent is recommended) of the calories needed to maintain one's **ideal body weight**. When following this guideline, one should also obtain adequate **nutrition** by eating a variety of vegetables, fruits, grains, legumes, and certain low-fat meat and dairy products.

Calorie: a unit of heat that is burned by the body. The term *calorie* may refer to a measurement of energy expenditure (exercise, daily living) or energy intake (food eaten).

Cancer: abnormal, uncontrollable growth of cells that spreads to other parts of the body. The three most common kinds of cancer are lung, breast, and colon.

Capillaries: minute vessels that connect arterioles and venules (small branches of arteries and veins).

Carbohydrate: one of six **nutrients** needed to sustain human life. Carbohydrates are the basic source of energy for **metabolism** and for muscle use. Cabohydrates are classified as simple (sugars) or complex (starches). Carbohydrates are found in grains, cereals, pasta, breads, vegetables, and dairy products.

Carcinogen: a cancer-causing substance. Examples: **aflatoxins** and **tar**.

Cardiovascular disease: a disease of the heart and blood vessels.

Carnivore: an animal that eats meat.

Cataract: a clouding of the eye lens, causing partial or total blindness.

Cerebral hemorrhage: a type of **stroke** due to bleeding from a ruptured blood vessel in the brain. A cerebral hemorrhage is typically the result of **high blood pressure**.

Chinese County Study: called the Grand Prix of epidemiology, a massive study of 6,500 Chinese individuals conducted by a team of Chinese and American researchers that compared patterns of diet and disease in 65 Chinese counties. Among other dramatic results, the study found that the rate of heart disease in the rural counties of China is 155 times lower than in the United States. In those Chinese counties in which people eat higher levels of fat and cholesterol, rates of heart disease, cancer, and other diseases are substantially higher (as compared to the low-fat counties). The study also found links between salt consumption and hypertension.

Cholesterol: (1) serum or blood cholesterol: a fat-soluble waxy substance (specifically the crystalline steroid alcohol $C_{27}H_{45}OH$) in the blood that is often deposited in **artery** walls. Cholesterol is used to produce **bile acids** and certain hormones and to construct cell membranes. Excess blood cholesterol is a result of a high-fat, high-cholesterol diet, or of genetic factors. **(2) dietary cholesterol:** a naturally occurring waxy substance ($C_{27}H_{45}OH$, see above) found in animal fats and oils.

Cirrhosis: extensive scarring and destruction of the cells in the liver, often due to excessive alcohol intake.

"Civilized" diet: in Western societies, a diet high in **fat, cholesterol**, and **protein**. A lifelong intake of this diet often results in one or more of the "diseases of affluence": **stroke, high blood pressure, atherosclerosis** (which leads to **coronary heart disease, claudication, impotence** in men, and other conditions), **type II diabetes,** and **cancer**.

Claudication: attacks of limping, lameness, or pain in the legs, often due to diseased arteries caused by **atherosclerosis**.

Cocaine: a stimulant produced from the leaves of the coca bush. An illegal, addictive drug, cocaine produces feelings of euphoria and high energy by altering the regulation of **neurotransmitters** in the brain.

Collateral circulation: small side capillaries that carry blood around a site of blockage in an **artery**.

Complex carbohydrate: also known as starch. The type of carbohydrate used for energy. Complex carbohydrates are in cereals, grains, fruits, and vegetables. A diet high in complex carbohydrates is a key nutritional guideline of the 10% solution.

Coronary artery disease: narrowing of arteries that encircle the heart, resulting in inadequate blood supply to the heart muscle.

Coronary flow reserve: the measure of blood flow to the heart.

Coronary heart disease: a disease of the heart and its surrounding arteries.

Coronary insufficiency: see coronary artery disease.

Coronary thrombosis: a blockage of one or more of the coronary arteries due to a blood clot in the presence of advanced **atherosclerosis**.

Deoxyribonucleic acid (DNA): a complex molecule in cells that contains genetic information necessary for cell replication.

Diabetes mellitus: a chronic disease in which the body is unable to convert **carbohydrates, fats,** and **proteins** into energy due to inadequate use or production of **insulin.** The two types of diabetes are **Type I diabetes mellitus** and **Type II diabetes mellitus.**

Dietary fiber: the indigestible part of plant cells. Fiber helps to regulate digestion and cleanse waste products from the intestines.

Diuretic: an agent that increases secretion of urine.

Embolic stroke: a type of stroke caused by a circulating blood clot getting stuck in the plaque of a coronary artery (which is the result of advanced atherosclerosis), causing blockage of that artery.

Emphysema: a lung disease characterized by rapid, shallow breathing and deterioration of the lungs. Emphysema is usually caused by long-term smoking.

Endorphins: natural, morphinelike tranquilizers released in the brain during **aerobic exercise.** Endorphins block **stress** and pain sensations and may produce a positive mood.

Enzyme: a **protein** capable of generating or accelerating change in another substance. Enzymes aid in digesting food.

Epidemiology: the study of the frequency and control of diseases in populations.

Essential fatty acid: a fatty acid that cannot be produced by the body and therefore is required in the diet. Linoleic acid, an essential fatty acid, may be found in a variety of vegetables.

Estrogen: a female sex hormone that regulates menstrual cycles.

Excretion: the removal of waste products from the body.

Exercise stress test: a test that evaluates the heart's response to exercise. During the test, a person's heartbeat is monitored while he or she exercises on a treadmill, stair climber, or stationary bicycle until the training heart rate is reached.

Fat: (1) body fat: a tissue that provides insulation and a reserve supply of energy. Body fat also aids in the construction of cell membranes and the regulation of menstrual cycles. **(2) dietary fat:** one of six **nutrients** needed to sustain human life. Dietary fats help transport certain **vitamins** through the digestive system. Dietary fat is found in meats, certain vegetables, and dairy products. An excessive level of dietary fat is regarded as a primary factor in the development of coronary heart and artery disease, **cancer,** and other illnesses.

Fight-or-flight response: in certain animals, a reaction necessary for survival. When confronted with danger, the animal prepares to either fight or flee. As a result of this evolutionary heritage, the fight-or-flight response in humans today is a physiological reaction to stressful situations.

Food craving: an urge to eat certain foods, especially foods with high salt, sugar, or fat content. Often, cravings for sugar are a result of a diet high in both fat and sugar.

Framingham Study: A renowned study that has spawned many journal articles over the years. The Framingham Study has been tracing approximately five thousand individuals (in Framingham, Massachusetts) since 1948 to determine the risk factors for coronary heart disease and has yielded landmark evidence establishing the link between dietary fat consumption, lipid cholesterol levels, high blood pressure, smoking, obesity, and diabetes and the risk of coronary heart disease.

Gallstones: a stonelike mass that forms in the gallbladder and is composed mainly of **cholesterol** crystals.

Glaucoma: an eye disease characterized by built-up pressure of fluid in the eyeball.

Glucose: (1) **blood glucose:** the amount of sugar in one's blood. Glucose is the main energy source for the body. (2) a simple sugar in certain **carbohydrates** such as fruit.

Glucose intolerance: the inability of the body to efficiently convert **carbohydrates** into energy. An elevated blood **glucose** level indicates glucose intolerance.

Glycogen: the form of **glucose** that is stored in the liver and muscles and used for energy.

Gout: a painful condition in which **uric acid** deposits buildup in and around the joints; also characterized at times by an excessive amount of uric acid in the blood.

High blood pressure: an excessively high level of pressure of blood against **artery** walls.

High-density lipoprotein (HDL): also known as the "good" **cholesterol**. High-density lipoproteins are **lipoproteins** that carry cholesterol back to the liver. HDLs also aid the liver in disposing of excess cholesterol. **Aerobic exercise** increases HDL levels.

Hydrogenation: a chemical process that converts liquid fats to solid fats.

Hypercholesterolemia: an excessively high level of **cholesterol** in the blood.

Hypertension: see high blood pressure.

Hypoglycemia: an excessively low level of **glucose** in the blood.

Ideal body weight: the optimal weight for one's height, age, sex, and body build.

Impotence: inability of the male to have an erection. Impotence may have a physiological or psychological basis. A common cause of impotence is a high level of **atherosclerosis** in the arteries feeding the penis.

Insulin: a hormone, secreted by the pancreas, that controls the level of **glucose** in the blood. **Diabetes** occurs when the pancreas is unable to produce insulin, or the body is unable to effectively utilize the insulin produced.

Intracerebral hemorrhage: see cerebral hemorrhage.

Iron: (1) one of the main components of red blood cells. (2) a **mineral** found in red meats; egg yolk; green, leafy vegetables; dried beans and peas; and potatoes.

Juvenile-onset diabetes: see Type I diabetes mellitus.

Ketosis: incomplete **metabolism** of fatty acids. Ketosis occurs in diabetic patients or when not enough **carbohydrates** are eaten.

Kidney stone: stones in kidneys. Kidneys stones often occur because of a metabolic disorder or from too much **calcium** in the blood.

Lesion: a sore or wound in human tissue, usually from disease or injury.

Linoleic acid: an **essential fatty acid** needed to produce fat in the body.

Lipids: forms of fats and waxes in the blood. Lipids include various forms of **cholesterol** and **triglycerides**.

Lipoprotein: a fatty protein. Lipoproteins transport **lipids** (specifically **fats** and **cholesterol**) through the bloodstream.

Low-density lipoproteins (LDL): also known as the "bad" cholesterol. Low-density lipoproteins are **lipoproteins** that circulate **cholesterol** throughout the blood and promote the deposit of cholesterol on **artery** walls. A diet high in fat, particularly **saturated fat**, will often result in a high level of LDLs.

Meditation: a technique in which a relaxed state of mind and body is induced by focused breathing or the repetition of a mantra (a phrase or word selected by the person meditating).

Meprobamate: a white powder used in sedatives and antianxiety medications.

Metabolism: the sum of chemical changes in the body, involving energy-consuming and energy-producing processes.

Mineral: one of six types of **nutrients** needed to sustain life. Among other roles, minerals help keep the nervous and cardiorespiratory systems functioning. The two types of minerals are macrominerals (such as **sodium** and **potassium**), needed in large amounts, and trace minerals (such as zinc), needed in small amounts. Minerals are found in meat and dairy products, vegetables, fruits, grains, seeds, seafood, and salt.

Monounsaturated fat: a form of fat found in olive and peanut oil, peanuts, almonds, and avocados. Monounsaturated fat does not raise **LDL** ("bad" cholesterol) levels as much as **saturated fat** and does not depress **HDL** ("good" cholesterol) levels as much as **polyunsaturated fat**.

MR FIT Study: the Multiple Risk Factor Intervention Trial study followed 15,000 men at high risk for heart disease for 7 years. The study showed that the conventional medical recommendations (i.e., reducing fat to 30 percent of calories, reducing cholesterol intake to 300 mg per day) reduced the number of coronary deaths and events by more than 30 percent.

Myocardial infarction: also known as a heart attack. The death of cells in an area of the heart due to blockage of coronary arteries.

Neurotransmitter: released by nerves. Substances that transmit impulses throughout the central nervous system.

Nicotine: an addictive substance found in all forms of tobacco, including cigarettes.

Nitrates and **nitrites:** chemicals used as curing agents, coloring, and flavoring in meats. Nitrates and nitrites are also present in human saliva and in drinking water contaminated by farmland fertilizers. Although the nitrates and nitrites in saliva are not harmful, those in drinking water and meats have been linked to stomach cancer.

Nutrient: a nourishing substance. The six types of nutrients are water, **minerals**, **vitamins**, **carbohydrates**, **fats**, and **proteins**.

Nutrition: the study of dietary requirements for people.

Obesity: excessive body weight. A person is obese when he or she is 20 percent over his or her **ideal body weight.**

Occlusion: any blockage in blood flow from an organ or tissue.

Omega-3 fatty acids: a type of fatty acid, commonly found in fish and fish oils. Omega-3 fatty acids consumed in moderate quantities are thought to reduce the risk of **coronary artery disease** in some individuals.

Osteoporosis: a condition in which bones become brittle and fracture easily, commonly as a result of **calcium** loss associated with aging.

Overweight: excessive body weight. A person is overweight when he or she is over his or her **ideal body weight.**

Pathogens: a microorganism that produces disease.

Placebo: an inert substance given to patients or subjects in place of medication. Placebos are usually administered in research studies as a control in order to compare and evaluate the effect of the real medication or treatment under study.

Plaque: a deposit of hard organic material in the lining of blood vessels, typically composed of **cholesterol** and fibrous matter. A buildup of plaque in the coronary arteries is a primary symptom of **coronary artery disease.**

Polyunsaturated fat: a form of fat in food, usually a major constituent of oils from certain vegetables and seeds. While polyunsaturated fats appear to raise **LDL** ("bad" cholesterol) levels less than **saturated fat**, they appear to depress **HDL** ("good" cholesterol) levels more than saturated fat and have been implicated as a promoter of **cancer** growth.

Potassium: a mineral essential for muscle function, balance of body fluids, and transmission of nerve impulses. Potassium is found in cereals, dried peas and beans, fresh vegetables and fruits, certain seeds, fresh fish, and certain meats.

Protein: one of six types of nutrients needed to sustain human life. Protein is used to build muscles, connective tissues, and cell walls. It is found in meat and dairy products; legumes such as kidney and lima beans; rice; and certain seeds, nuts, and vegetables.

Quantitative coronary angiography: a procedure that determines the degree of blockage in arteries. Radioactive dye is injected into the heart, and X rays are taken to locate blocked arteries.

Relaxation response: a physical state that is the opposite of the **fight-or-flight response**. The relaxation response results in reduced **blood pressure** and blood **glucose** levels, and lower breathing and heart rates.

Risk factor: any medical condition (such as **high blood pressure**) or life-style behavior (such as smoking) that indicates the increased risk of the development of a medical problem.

Saturated fat: a form of fat in meat, coconut and palm oils, and animal sources such as whole-milk dairy products. These fats raise blood **cholesterol** levels, particularly **LDL** ("bad" cholesterol) levels.

Secretion: the formation and release of a substance in the body.

Set-point theory: the theory that each person has an individual thermostat governing how much food they want to eat and how much fat they will store from food intake. According to this theory, obese individuals may have difficulty losing weight because their set-point increases their hunger for food and stores more fat from food eaten.

Seven Countries Study: a study by Ancel Keys of sixteen population groups in seven countries over a span of ten years. It was the first study to compare the epidemiology of heart disease in different countries and provided rich evidence that fat in the diet was the primary cause of heart disease.

Simple carbohydrates: also known as sugars. Simple carbohydrates are found in "natural" foods, such as fruits and vegetables, and "refined" or "processed" foods, such as cookies, candy, and cakes. Simple carbohydrates provide calories but no other nutritional value.

Sodium: a **mineral** that helps regulate the balance of water around cells in the body. Table salt is a form of sodium.

Stress: the body's response to any demand or challenge. Among other effects, stress results in the **fight-or-flight response** and the secretion of **adrenaline**.

Stroke: brain damage due to a rupture or blockage of a blood vessel, depriving the brain of blood supply. See **cerebral hemorrhage**, **embolic stroke**, and **thrombotic stroke**.

Sugar: a **simple carbohydrate** found in animal and vegetable products.

Tar: a carcinogen in tobacco.

10% solution: a **nutrition**, exercise, and life-style program designed to improve quality and length of life. 10% refers to a guideline of this program that recommends limiting **fat** consumption to no more than 10 percent of daily caloric intake.

Thrombosis: the formation or presence of a blood clot in a blood vessel.

Thrombotic stroke: a type of stroke due to loss of blood flow to a portion of the brain that results when a coronary artery is blocked by a blood clot that forms on the plaque in that artery (the result of advanced atherosclerosis).

Training heart rate: also known as target heart rate. The heart rate at which the body reaches 65 to 85 percent of its maximum capacity during strenuous exercise.

Triglyceride: a type of **lipid** carried in the bloodstream that may subsequently be used for energy.

Tumor: a growth of tissue that is progressive and often uncontrolled.

Type A personality: a hardworking, ambitious, and aggressive personality traditionally thought to be at greater risk for heart disease than other personality types. Contemporary studies show that having a Type A personality is only a risk factor for heart disease in regard to certain Type A characteristics, including frequent anger, chronic hostility, or inherent cynicism.

Type B personality: an easygoing, accepting, and complacent personality.

Type I diabetes mellitus: formerly known as juvenile-onset diabetes; also called insulin-dependent diabetes mellitus. This form of diabetes usually develops in people under age 25. It is characterized by the inability of the pancreas to produce sufficient **insulin**.

Type II diabetes mellitus: formerly known as adult-onset diabetes; also known as non–insulin-dependent diabetes mellitus. This is the most common form of diabetes, in which the pancreas is able to produce **insulin** but the body is unable to use it effectively. This form of diabetes occurs most often in adults over age 40 and may be controlled by diet, exercise, and attainment of optimal weight.

Uric acid: a waste product in urine.

Very low density lipoprotein (VLDL): a **lipoprotein**, related to **triglycerides**, that is linked to **atherosclerosis**.

Vitamin: one of the six types of nutrients needed to sustain human life. Vitamins help form blood cells, hormones, and genetic material. Vitamins are found in meat and dairy products, vegetables, fruits, cereals, and grains.

Weight plateau: during weight loss, a period of time in which weight stabilizes. Often temporary, weight plateaus are usually the result of one or more factors, including increased exercise, increased intake of **complex carbohydrates**, water retention, menstruation, or constipation.

Index

■

activity level, 90
additives, food, 77, 175
adrenal glands, 120, 176
adrenaline, 58, 120, 125, 128, 176, 334
advertising, food, 72, 163, 164
aflatoxins, 259, 334
Africa, 12, 260
aging, 72, 80, 248–250
   blood pressure increase in, 52
   maximum life expectancy and, 155
   premature, 49, 60
   retardation of, *see* caloric
      restriction
airline travel, 100–101, 181, 210
Alaska, 252
alcohol, 44, 46, 72, 131, 132, 143,
     169–170, 177–178, 180, 253
   cancer and, 174
   daily allowance of, 179
   heart disease and, 71, 126–127,
     174, 255
   stress and, 126–128, 177
   wine, 71, 127, 177, 180, 255
ambition, 120, 121
American Heart Association, xiv, 8, 9,
     17
   dietary recommendations of, xvii,
     xviii, xix, 16, 22, 28–29
   phase 3, guideline of, 22
aneurysms, aortic, 7, 10, 38–39, 170,
     334
anger, 121–122, 176
angina, 8, 10, 17, 23, 58, 161, 251, 334
angiography, quantitative coronary,
     17, 341
animals, xvii, 11, 14
   in caloric restriction studies, 151,
     152–153, 154, 155, 172, 173
   wild, fat content of, 34

appetizers, 204, 232–234
apples, 4, 26, 298
arm swinging, 110
arthritis, xvii, 35, 57, 72, 170, 334
Aspergillus flavus, 259
Athapaskans, 252
atherosclerosis, xv, 3–25, 35–36,
     45, 46, 51, 54, 71, 74, 92,
     117, 161, 162, 247, 250, 253,
     256–257
   in ancient times, 251
   collateral circulation vs., 36, 336
   conditions caused by, 7, 10, 38–39,
     52, 170, 336, 338
   definition of, 6–7
   genetic factors in, 11, 13, 18, 24
   incidence of, 6, 80
   medical procedures for, 8
   "normality" of, 9–10
   plaque in, 6–8, 9, 12, 16–17, 29–30,
     36, 52, 58, 334, 337, 340
   rate of, 10, 25
   reversal of, 11, 14, 16–17, 21, 23,
     28, 36
   risk factors for, 10
   stress in, 13–16, 57–58
   symptoms absent in, 8, 23, 59
   in women, 23–25, 30, 57, 80
   see also fat, dietary
Atlantic, The, 21
avocados, 27, 50, 97, 178, 179, 204,
     313

backsliding, 147, 182
bacteria, 43
bagels, 27, 184, 186, 300
baguettes, 184
baked goods, to avoid, 203
baking, 201

Defatted Chicken Stock, 221
deli meats, 179
deoxycholic acid, 43
deoxyribonucleic acid (DNA), 153,
    173, 337
depression, 129, 130, 334
desserts, 189, 192, 203
    nutritional content of, 291–294
    recipes for, 243–246
dextrose, 97, 179
diabetes, 10, 14, 19, 57, 60, 72, 87,
    152, 178, 248, 252, 253, 255, 256,
    260
    dietary approach to, 53–54, 55–56,
        162
    glucose intolerance in, xiv,
        xvi, xxi, 53, 338
    insulin and, 32, 53, 54–55, 56, 62,
        338
    medications for, 53, 54–55, 144, 170
    type I (juvenile-onset), 53, 55, 337,
        342
    type II (adult-onset), xiv, xxi, 25,
        32, 35, 53–56, 89, 161, 162, 170,
        251, 257, 334, 337, 342
diazepam (Valium), 129, 334
diet:
    "civilized," xviii, 33, 252–253
    in evolution, 4, 33, 65, 170
    meanings of term, 61
    misconceptions about, 79–82
    moderation in, 33, 73, 79
    nutritional counseling and, 55, 162
    see also diets, societal; fat, dietary;
        sodium, dietary; 10% solution
diets, societal, xvii, 11–16, 248–260
    high-sodium, 19, 44, 46, 51, 52, 96,
        99, 172, 250, 251, 257, 259, 336
    low-fat, xvii, 10, 11–12, 13, 14,
        18–19, 32, 39, 44, 45, 52, 56, 60,
        75, 248–251, 256–257, 259, 260
    low-sodium, 12, 16, 32, 46, 52, 251,
        159, 260
    typical American, 4, 5, 11, 13,
        33–34, 45, 54, 56, 62, 171, 251,
        252–254, 259, 336
    see also China; Europe; Japan

dining out, 204–210
    at parties, 100–101, 181
    tips on, 204–205
    see also restaurants
dinners, 27
    frozen, 190–191
    recommended foods for, 188–189
Dip, Lazy Bean, 232
Dip Mexicano, Bean, 232–234
diuretics, 51–52, 337
DNA (deoxyribonucleic acid), 153,
    173, 337
doctors, xiii–xiv, xv–xvi, xix, xxi–xxiv,
    19, 55, 121, 160–162, 166
    exercise and, 104–105, 144, 175
    food sensitivities and, 212
    guidance needed from, 160–161
    nutritional training needed by, 78,
        144, 161–162
    recommended consultation with,
        77–78, 107, 144–145, 320
dopamine, 130
Dosti, Rose, 214
Dressing, Carrot-Raisin Salad with,
    231
Dried Beans, 220
drug abuse, 124, 125–131, 132, 143,
    170, 175, 177
Drunken Scallops, 239
Duke University, 122

eating disorders, 124, 125, 155, 177
Egg Omelette, Fat-Free, 223–224
eggs, 5, 29, 97, 204, 257
    nutritional content of, 294–295
    substitutes for, 27, 98, 184, 295
    whites, 27, 98, 179, 184, 294
    yolks, 95, 180, 294
Egypt, ancient, 251
electrocardiogram (ECG), 105, 175
embolic stroke, 7, 38, 52, 170, 248,
    250, 257, 337
empathy, 136, 177
emphysema, 44, 126, 253, 255, 256,
    337
endometrial (uterine) cancer, 39, 57,
    89, 170, 257